Approaches to Teaching Momaday's

The Way to Rainy Mountain

Edited by

Kenneth M. Roemer

The Modern Language Association of America
New York   1988

© 1988 by The Modern Language Association of America
All rights reserved
Printed in the United States of America
Fourth printing 1998

For information about obtaining permission to reprint material from
MLA book publications, send your request by mail (see address below),
e-mail (permissions@mla.org), or fax (212 477-9863).

Library of Congress Cataloging-in-Publication Data
Bibliography: p.   Includes index.
1. Momaday, N. Scott, 1934–   . Way to rainy mountain. 2. Kiowa Indians–Legends.
3. Indians of North America–Great Plains–Legends.
I. Roemer, Kenneth M., 1945–   . II. Series.
E99.K5M6432   1988   398.2'08997   88-8959
ISBN 0-87352-509-4
ISBN 0-87352-510-8 (pbk.)
ISSN 1059-1133

Cover illustration of the paperback edition: N. Scott Momaday, *Mammedaty*, graphite and wash
drawing on paper, 1976. Courtesy of the artist.

Published by The Modern Language Association of America
10 Astor Place, New York, New York 10003-6981

Approaches to Teaching Momaday's *The Way to Rainy Mountain*

Approaches to Teaching
World Literature
Joseph Gibaldi, series editor

For a complete listing of titles,
see the last pages of this book.

CONTENTS

Epilogue

PREFACE TO THE SERIES

In *The Art of Teaching* Gilbert Highet wrote, "Bad teaching wastes a great deal of effort, and spoils many lives which might have been full of energy and happiness." All too many teachers have failed in their work, Highet argued, simply "because they have not thought about it." We hope that the Approaches to Teaching World Literature series, sponsored by the Modern Language Association's Committee on Teaching and Related Professional Activities, will not only improve the craft—as well as the art—of teaching but also encourage serious and continuing discussion of the aims and methods of teaching literature.

The principal objective of the series is to collect within each volume different points of view on teaching a specific literary work, a literary tradition, or a writer widely taught at the undergraduate level. The preparation of each volume begins with a wide-ranging survey of instructors, thus enabling us to include in the volume the philosophies and approaches, thoughts and methods of scores of experienced teachers. The result is a sourcebook of material, information, and ideas on teaching the subject of the volume to undergraduates.

The series is intended to serve nonspecialists as well as specialists, inexperienced as well as experienced teachers, graduate students who wish to learn effective ways of teaching as well as senior professors who wish to compare their own approaches with the approaches of colleagues in other schools. Of course, no volume in the series can ever substitute for erudition, intelligence, creativity, and sensitivity in teaching. We hope merely that each book will point readers in useful directions; at most each will offer only a first step in the long journey to successful teaching.

Joseph Gibaldi
Series Editor

PREFACE TO THE VOLUME

Pre-preface might be a better title for these introductory remarks. In a series like this one, the editor can often assume that most readers are familiar with the book under discussion and that many have even taught it. I cannot make such assumptions. In his preface in this Approaches series, Steven G. Kellman notes that "the jury is still out" on whether Albert Camus's *Plague* will obtain "a permanent niche in the Western pantheon" (ix). The verdict on N. Scott Momaday's *Way to Rainy Mountain* is still more uncertain. Many college instructors have never had the opportunity to examine the advantages of teaching this unique and exciting work. Hence I have the delightful task of rectifying that situation. I also hope that the materials and approaches described in this volume will help instructors who are familiar with *Rainy Mountain* to discover new ways to enjoy and teach the book.

One obvious advantage of introducing *The Way to Rainy Mountain* to undergraduates is that its unfamiliarity and its intriguing combination of forms can lead students to consider whether traditional critical and evaluative approaches are appropriate for works that are not yet regarded as classics of the Western pantheon and that do not fit neatly into generic categories. The varieties of visual, poetic, and prose forms (which include Kiowa and family oral narratives) created and assembled by Momaday; by his artist-father, Al Momaday; and by the book's designer, Bruce Gentry, should also encourage students to question standard definitions of *authorship, literature,* and *text.*

The Way to Rainy Mountain is a highly personal, selective, and imaginative work written by only one of the one and a half million American Indians and dealing with only one of the more than three hundred Indian cultural groups (representing about 200 languages) that have inhabited North America for almost thirty thousand years (Ruoff, "American Indian Literatures" 2). Still, Momaday successfully implies networks of representative Native American values and aesthetics that non-Indians should consider as valuable alternative perspectives to dominant Western attitudes and as provocative opportunities for the expansion of literary canons. These perspectives include seeing the land as a crucial aspect of personal identity formation and human ecology; discovering concepts of personal relations — especially with elders — that can provide models for resolving twentieth-century identity and social problems; acknowledging the power of Native American concepts of sacredness, beauty, and harmony; and revering a sense of oral narration and performance that encompasses economy, delight, wonder, and intrinsic power. By presenting these perspectives in the work of a challenging contemporary author, instructors can help students overcome the notion that Indian values, though laudable, are the heritage of a group of "vanished" Americans. Momaday's portrayal of his responses to Kiowa traditions and the responses of instructors and students described in this volume demonstrate that Native American viewpoints can continue to be relevant for Indians and non-Indians.

Rainy Mountain is a small knoll, near a small road, in a sparsely populated area in southwestern Oklahoma—hardly a high point on the world traveler's itinerary. Nevertheless, Momaday's varied background and the complex mixtures of literary forms in *Rainy Mountain* can invite discussions as far-ranging and diversified as can classes about authors and works categorized as "worldly" and "cosmopolitan." As a child Momaday experienced close contacts with several southwestern tribes; he has attended and taught in a variety of schools, from small reservation schools to elite American and European universities; he has written for regional publications as well as for international publishers and the *Columbia Literary History of the United States*; he is a member of the Kiowa Gourd Clan and a winner of Guggenheim and Pulitzer awards. No wonder he has developed a catholic reading taste that ranges from Native American oral narratives to Melville, Faulkner, Dickinson, Joyce, Stevens, and, especially, Isak Dinesen. No wonder *The Way to Rainy Mountain* combines many different types of literature, and no wonder non-Indian students often find the example of Momaday's life a fascinating touchstone for discussions of racial, cultural, and professional identities and frequently compare aspects of his book to family stories, Greek mythology, the Bible, American autobiographies, and British and European modernist works.

Of course, the works of several other talented modern authors with Indian heritages also offer instructors the advantages described above, as anyone knows who is familiar with the poetry and fiction of Leslie Marmon Silko, Louise Erdrich, Michael Dorris, James Welch, Gerald Vizenor, Paula Gunn Allen, or Simon Ortiz, to name only a few. And several of these authors are being taught along with Momaday in survey and specialized literature courses. (See Wiget, "Identity and Direction," and the many course designs in Allen, *Studies*.) But Momaday is typically regarded as the leading inspiration for, and dean of, contemporary Indian authors—the author whose works, especially the Pulitzer Prize–winning *House Made of Dawn* and *Rainy Mountain*, initiated what is sometimes referred to as the renaissance of Indian writing (Momaday, "Interview by J. Bruchac" 18).

The Way to Rainy Mountain, which Momaday has on several occasions identified as his favorite work, is, moreover, a practical and appealing introduction to both contemporary written and traditional oral Indian literatures. It is accessible to students and adaptable for instructors. The historical and personal voices that correspond to each of the written versions of oral narratives help to make distant and unfamiliar material less remote to non-Kiowa students. The book is inexpensive and short enough to be assigned for a single class meeting and to offer a reading experience with the intensity of a brief story or a narrative poem.

Yet, the multiple-journey motif combined with the rich mixtures of narrative voices and genres adds to the reading experience a complexity that is usually associated with much longer works. *Rainy Mountain* contains excellent examples of contemporary Indian prose and poetry, varieties of tribal history and personal autobiography, lyric versions of tribal narratives, and a few songs. This diversity ensures that instructors can use the book in a wide range of courses. The respondents to the survey distributed in preparation for writing part 1 of this volume described approximately one hundred different courses. About one-third of these were intermediate or upper-level Native American literature classes. Another third were divided among lower- and upper-level American literature survey, period, and regional courses, comparative literature, thematic, or special-topic courses, and history, sociology, and anthropology courses. The remaining third (actually the largest percentage) were writing courses, especially freshman composition — a trend reflected by the selection of a passage from *The Way to Rainy Mountain* for discussion on the 1986 Advanced Placement Examination in English Language and Composition, prepared by the Educational Testing Service. Few literary texts can serve so many classroom audiences so well.

This volume, like the others in the series, has two main parts: part 1 surveys materials useful to classroom instruction; part 2 offers a variety of approaches to teaching *The Way to Rainy Mountain*. I am indebted to many who helped me complete both parts. I would first like to thank N. Scott Momaday for reading and commenting on the manuscript and for encouraging me at every stage of the project. Larry Evers initially urged me to submit a prospectus for the book; he and Paula Gunn Allen, Gary Kodaseet, and A. LaVonne Brown Ruoff made helpful suggestions for revising the preface and part 1. The contributors to part 2 also read drafts of the material and offered constructive advice. Of course, without the help of the instructors who responded to the questionnaire on teaching *Rainy Mountain*, it would have been very difficult to write part 1, practically every paragraph of which could be prefaced with "according to the respondents." I thank Gary Kodaseet for his willingness to give and help edit the interview and for introducing me to several other Kiowa tribal members, especially Roland N. Whitehorse and Sherman Chaddlesone, who suggested areas of discussion for the interview, and Billy Evans Horse, who told me his family versions of many of the Kiowa stories included in *Rainy Mountain*. Gary Kodaseet and George Younkin encouraged and helped me to attend the Kiowa Black Leggings and Gourd Clan ceremonials and to visit the tribal museum in Carnegie, Oklahoma. These experiences greatly expanded my understanding of and appreciation for the tribal roots of *Rainy Mountain*. The contributions of Joseph Gibaldi, his staff, the MLA Committee on Teaching and Related Professional Activities, Elizabeth Holland, and the outside readers ranged from specific advice about copyediting to general recommendations about structure and content. A special sense of vitality was added to the volume by the students who gave permission to publish excerpts from their writing: Darren Baumgarten, Gloria Gaspar (Ponca), Fay Chaudier, Dale Hunt, Eileen Le Beau (Lakhota), Susan LaFreniere (Ojibwa), and Lucille Wolfe St. Germaine (Winnebago). Jenny and Cecil Tsatoke (Kiowa) told family stories summarized in Norma C. Wilson's essay. Finally, I would like to thank my family, who encouraged me and accompanied me on my first trip to Rainy Mountain in a disabled car on a particularly windy and dismal day.

I am grateful to the Japan Society for Promotion of Science for support during the final stages of manuscript editing.

The following publisher and journals granted permission to include revised versions of published material as sections of three of the essays in part 2: University of Oklahoma Press, *English Notes: A Newsletter of the South Dakota Council of Teachers of English,* and *Perspectives on Contemporary Literature.* For the specific acknowledgments, see the essays by Matthias Schubnell, Norma C. Wilson, and J. Frank Papovich.

KMR

Part One

MATERIALS

Kenneth M. Roemer

Editions

The best edition for classroom use—and the one used for all page references in this volume—is the reasonably priced University of New Mexico Press paperback reprint (first printing, 1976) of the first edition (1969), also published by New Mexico. With the notable exception of the impressive cover of the first edition (brown buffalo skull, circle, and crescent designs on a background blend of orange and tan), the reprint preserves the striking physical qualities of the 1969 edition: the large-page format, the varied typefaces for the different voices, the hand-set titles, the placement of the written versions of Kiowa and family oral narratives on the verso pages and the "answering" historical and personal voices on the recto pages, and Momaday's father's eleven full-page illustrations. Momaday maintains that he "had nothing to do with" the physical appearance of the book but that Bruce Gentry, the designer, did a "wonderful job" because the reader can "open it [practically] anyplace and . . . have three voices on facing pages . . . " (*N. Scott Momaday: Interview with Kay Bonetti*). (For further comment on the physical design, see the discussion of Mick McAllister's essay in the section "Critical Studies" and the essays by William Oandasan and Helen Jaskoski in pt. 2.) A few respondents to the survey preferred the only other edition—a small, inexpensive Ballantine paperback (1970; now out of print) that did not reproduce the format of the first edition.

The respondents strongly opposed using excerpts from *The Way to Rainy Mountain* in literature courses because of its brevity and, to quote one of them, because "much of the impact of the book comes from experiencing the whole." Nevertheless, literature instructors can find excerpts in anthologies such as *America in Literature*, volume 2, edited by Alan Trachtenberg and Benjamin DeMott; *American Indian Authors*, edited by Natachee Scott Momaday (Momaday's mother); *The Harper American Literature*, volume 2, and the Compact Edition, edited by Donald McQuade et al. (they contain the *House Made of Dawn* version of part of *Rainy Mountain*'s introduction); and the forthcoming *Heath Anthology of American Literature*, edited by Paul Lauter et al. Writing instructors searching for excellent brief prose models can find Momaday's introduction to *Rainy Mountain* in composition readers; the following sampling was compiled by David Hoehner, a contributor to part 2: *The Riverside Reader* (Trimmer and Hairston, 1981), *The Heath Reader* (Litzinger, 1983), *Outlooks and Insights* (Eschholz and Rosa, 1983), *The Borzoi College Reader*, 5th edition (Muscatine and Griffith, 1984), *Fields of Writing* (Comley et al., 1984), *The Harvest Reader* (Hefferman, 1984), and the *The McGraw-Hill Reader*, 2nd edition (Muller, 1985).

Other Works by Momaday

Placing a literary work within the context of the author's other writings usually helps students to gain more complex understandings of the single text. This general rule is especially applicable to *The Way to Rainy Mountain*. Momaday does not perceive his individual writings as separate entities. In a recent interview with Kay Bonetti, he talked about his tendency to repeat certain subjects, characters, themes, and even entire sections, saying, "I think I'm telling one story. It's long, and I can't do it all at once. . . . But it's all one story" (*N. Scott Momaday: Interview*). It is not, however, a static story, as Momaday made clear in another interview, with Joseph Bruchac: "I'm concerned to keep the story going. I mean to keep the same subject, to carry it farther with each telling" ("Interview" 17). The best analogy for this process appears in the often-quoted "remembered earth" voice of section 24, which urges us to give ourselves up at least once in our lives "to a particular landscape in [our] experience, to look at it from as many angles as [we] can, to wonder about it, to dwell upon it" (83). Momaday's "remembered earth" is also his remembered word. He dwells on his stories, not to fossilize or enshrine them, but to renew them endlessly. Instructors can introduce students to this renewing process by assigning "The Man Made of Words" or all, or parts, of *House Made of Dawn*, by far the two supplementary readings most frequently recommended by the survey respondents.

"The Man Made of Words" first appeared in 1970 in *Indian Voices: The First Convocation of American Indian Scholars*. (This text is difficult to obtain; therefore the page references in this volume will be to a readily available reprint of the entire essay without the follow-up discussions: Geary Hobson's *The Remembered Earth* [162–73].) The essay by Momaday deals with one of his central themes: "our most essential being consists in language" (162). He describes how words allow us to imagine and to bring into existence ourselves, others, and the land. He draws his primary examples from *The Way to Rainy Mountain*, especially sections 13, 24, and the epilogue. Writing the epilogue enabled him to imagine the old Kiowa woman Ko-sahn so well that for a miraculous moment she appeared before his writing desk, "whole" and as real, or more real, than he was.

"The Man Made of Words" is also essential reading because in it Momaday describes the composition process and the nature of *Rainy Mountain* (169–70). He retraced the Kiowa migration route from Montana to Oklahoma and collected a "remarkable body of history and learning, fact and fiction—all of it in the oral tradition" from Kiowa elders. He compiled a "small number of translations" from this material and presented the stories in a privately printed volume, *The Journey of Tai-me*. To this collection he added his father's illustrations and the "commentary" voices so that each "of the translations is followed by two kinds of commentary; the first is the documentary and the second is the privately reminiscent." The commentary voices "provide a context" that enables the oral tradition to "transcend the categorical limits of prehistory, anonymity, and archaeology in the narrow sense" and allow readers to perceive the stories as existing "within the framework of a literary continuance." The multiple voices also transform the journey motif from a one-dimensional migration into a journey "made with the whole memory, that experience of the mind which is legendary as well as historical, personal as well as cultural."

The most obvious link between *The Way to Rainy Mountain* and Momaday's first book, *House Made of Dawn*, is that *Rainy Mountain*'s introduction appeared as Tosamah's second sermon (117–25), a section of the novel that first appeared in 1967 in the *Reporter* as an essay entitled "The Way to Rainy Mountain" (41–43). (The Perennial Library–Harper reprint of *House Made of Dawn* [1977] is the only paperback edition available.) Comparing the three versions and their contexts is an excellent way to introduce students to Momaday's retelling process, particularly since there are significant differences between the introduction and the sermon, differences that only a few critics have briefly noted (e.g., Zachrau 64; Wiget, *Native American* 83–84; see also William Oandasan's and Vernon Lattin's essays in part 2). Another point of conversion is the landscape "story." The Jemez Pueblo, Los Angeles, and World War II environments of Abel, the protagonist in *House Made of Dawn*, and the southwestern landscape of Aho, Momaday's grandmother, are very different, but the various places of both works are consistently presented from multiple narrative and historical viewpoints. One of the many other possible classroom comparisons can be made between the ideas in *Rainy Mountain* and the first sermon of Tosamah. He attacks the Anglo tendency to inflate, clutter, and desanctify language. This sermon is a manifesto for *The Way to Rainy Mountain*. The economical style, the artistic visual placement of the words, and the sacred and wonderful tones of the Kiowa voices are antidotes for the verbal diseases Tosamah dissects.

Instructors might also wish to discuss or assign several other supplemental readings. In his memoir *The Names* (available in paper from the U of Arizona P), Momaday uses a complex mixed-genre narrative to tell his life story through his adolescence at Jemez Pueblo. In part 1 (1–57; Harper, 1976) he reinforces images offered in *Rainy Mountain* by providing more information about his Kiowa relatives. He also reveals new perspectives on his family by describing relatives not introduced before (e.g., his uncle James) and by delineating previously unmentioned facets of relatives' personalities (e.g., Aho's uncompromising antagonism toward his mother). In "The Morality of Indian Hating," a mixed-genre essay published five years before *Rainy Mountain*, several passages that eventually appeared in that book are contrasted to passages concerning non-Indian intolerance and pity for Indians (sec. 10, first voice; 13, third voice; 19, first voice; 22, third voice; and portions of the introd. and epilogue); and in another mixed-genre piece, "A First American Views His Land," we find a discussion of the family story that opens the final section (24). In "I Am Alive," an article published after *Rainy Mountain*, Momaday includes a version of section 10, third voice, that combines poetry, exposition, and prose narrative. The opening paragraph expands our knowledge of Mammedaty, Momaday's paternal grandfather, who died before his birth and who is a central focus of the latter sections of *Rainy Mountain*. The vivid dramatization of the meeting of the Gourd Dance Clan and of the presentation of a horse to his grandfather is one of Momaday's finest renderings of a "blood recollection" made "whole and irrevocable" in words and through an act of the imagination (sec. 14).

For intensive classroom studies of *Rainy Mountain* four other titles are relevant. In "The Native Voice" Momaday defines traditional Indian concepts of language and illuminates his theories with a discussion of section 13 (11–14). *The Gourd Dancer*, Momaday's second book of poetry, continues the imaginative recreation of Mammedaty, especially in the series of poems entitled "The Gourd Dancer." Other parts of *Rainy Mountain* are found in the collection, including an expanded version of voice one, section 20. As Kenneth Fields has convincingly argued, one of Momaday's early poems in the collection, "Angle of Geese," can be read as a moving introduction to the concepts of language implied by *The Way to Rainy Mountain* (197–98). Although *The Journey of Tai-me* exists only in a hundred hand-printed copies, students can read in *Sun Tracks* the six stories from *Journey* that were not incorporated into *Rainy Mountain* ("Kiowa Legends"). If "Angle of Geese" and *The Journey of Tai-me* hint at the past of *Rainy Mountain*, "Tsoai and the Shieldmaker" hints at its future. This brief mixture of legend, fiction, and history expands the Devil's Tower (Tsoai) story in *Rainy Mountain*'s introduction and is part of a work in progress tentatively entitled *Set* (Kiowa for *bear*) that will focus on a man who is the reincarnation of the boy-turned-to-bear of the legend. (See also the excerpt in Mary Dougherty Bartlett's *New Native American Novel*. This *Approaches* volume uses Momaday's spellings of Kiowa words; for an alternative spelling system, see Boyd's *Kiowa Voices* volumes.)

The foregoing discussion hardly touches on the numerous opportunities to encourage students to discover Momaday's concept of "telling one story" as it relates to *The Way to Rainy Mountain*. Instructors seeking other titles by Momaday should consult the "Works by N. Scott Momaday" section of Matthias Schubnell's *N. Scott Momaday* (299–307).

Reference Works

Schubnell's book is one of three published since 1982 that contain extremely useful bibliographies relevant to teaching *The Way to Rainy Mountain* and Momaday's other works. The most comprehensive bibliography, Schubnell's listing, is divided into three sections. The first, "Works by N. Scott Momaday" (299–307), opens with a valuable subsection, "Unpublished Materials," that includes *Rainy Mountain* "Notes and fragments," part of the Momaday collection at the University of California, Berkeley. The remainder of the section lists published works: books, recordings, short prose, anthologies containing Momaday's works (composition readers are omitted), interviews, and weekly columns for *Viva*. Schubnell divides "Works about" Momaday (307–15) into unpublished materials and published studies (critical works, dissertations and theses, newspaper articles and reviews). The "Selected List of Background Material" (315–23) is an eclectic bibliography covering Kiowa and other tribal scholarship, as well as more general studies of Indian literatures, Indians, mythology, and literary theory and criticism. Students of *Rainy Mountain* will find a few minor errors (e.g., the Ballantine edition appeared in 1970, not 1969) and two significant omissions (Kay Bonetti's recorded interview and Maurice Boyd's two volumes of *Kiowa Voices*).

The two other bibliographies mentioned by respondents, while not as extensive as Schubnell's, may be as, or more, accessible and meaningful to undergraduates because one is in essay form and the other is annotated. Building on her 1973 pamphlet, *N. Scott Momaday*, Martha Scott Trimble contributed the Momaday chapter to Fred Erisman and Richard W. Etulain's *Fifty Western Writers: A Bio-Bibliographical Sourcebook*. Although limited in its coverage of *The Way to Rainy Mountain* (she focuses on three studies: Berner, Nicholas, and Strelke), Trimble's essay can be highly recommended to students. She begins with possibly the best short biographical sketch available and follows up with a "Major Themes" section that examines three concerns relevant to *Rainy Mountain*: (1) a complex view of landscape that encompasses an awareness of the physical world and of the power of the imagination to create meaning and being in a landscape and to extend a sense of place into a sense of morality; (2) the importance and sacredness of oral and written language; and (3) the critical need for self-knowledge. The "Survey of Criticism" concentrates on these three themes and emphasizes analyses of *House Made of Dawn*. The essay concludes with a selected listing of primary and secondary sources. For students of *Rainy Mountain* the obvious value of the Momaday chapter of Tom Colonnese and Louis Owens's *American Indian Novelists: An Annotated Critical Bibliography* is that reading the annotations of the selected studies of *House Made of Dawn* will help them to understand the strong stylistic and thematic relationships between Momaday's first two books. (For general reference works relating to American Indian literatures, see "American Indian Literary Genres" in this volume.)

Background Studies

Practically all the survey respondents recommended that instructors read other works by Momaday, glance at a reference work, possibly assign parts or all of "Man Made of Words" or *House Made of Dawn*, and use a few relevant illustrations (see "Teaching Guides and Audiovisual Aids."). There was much less agreement about how much "background" instructors and students need to know in order to appreciate *The Way to Rainy Mountain*. This disagreement reflects a larger controversy about the use of background materials in the teaching of American Indian literatures (e.g., see Ballinger 1–3; Beidler 471). With particular reference to teaching *Rainy Mountain*, two survey respondents commented that too much background discussion can "transform the book into a 'sourcebook'" and that *Rainy Mountain* "is largely self-contained and self-annotating." This latter view is at least indirectly supported by Momaday's definition of the historical and personal voices as "commentaries" that provide contexts in which oral narratives can "transcend" narrow ethnographic meanings ("Man Made of Words" 170).

Nevertheless, the addition by Momaday of commentary voices suggests the need for some contextual knowledge, a viewpoint that has been supported convincingly by Jarold Ramsey ("Teacher"), Larry Evers ("Native American Oral Literatures"), Michael Dorris, and many of the contributors to Paula Gunn Allen's *Studies in American Indian Literature*. Instructors need some background knowledge or at least the ability to point out to classes that, as Momaday says, "there is a difference in viewpoints" between Indian and non-Indian worldviews ("Interview," with Bataille, 1979, 29) and to direct inquiring students to writings about Momaday's life, the Kiowas, and various types of Indian literatures; otherwise, instructors run the risk of perpetuating misleading stereotypes. Furthermore, a few brief classroom exercises that compare Momaday's text and related biographical, cultural, or literary materials can raise fascinating questions about how life experiences, oral traditions, and historical facts became *The Way to Rainy Mountain* and about how stories originally spoken to family or tribal members were transformed into readings for a much wider audience.

Biography

Three types of biographical information are especially useful to instructors: short sketches that can be assigned to students, longer autobiographical writings, and scholarly essays from which instructors can benefit. Colonnese and Owens list twenty-six short sketches (60–61), though one of the best is omitted: the previously mentioned biography by Trimble ("Momaday" 313–15). Clearly the best long autobiographical source relating to *Rainy Mountain* is part 1 of *The Names* (1–57). Students who enjoy interviews might also like to listen to Momaday's comments about himself on tape (*N. Scott Momaday:*

Interview) and to browse through the long interviews listed by Schubnell (303–04). Forthcoming at this writing is a new collection of interviews with Momaday, tentatively titled *Tsoai-talee: Interviews with N. Scott Momaday.* Until 1985 Trimble's pamphlet *N. Scott Momaday* was the most complete scholarly biography. Schubnell's *N. Scott Momaday*, notably chapter 1 (13–39), has super-seded Trimble's work. *The Names* contains a fuller portrait of Momaday's Ki-owa and other tribal heritages, but, unlike the earlier portraits, Schubnell's biography extends Momaday's life story through the mid-eighties, and it also offers the most complete account we have of the non-Indian experiences that helped to shape Momaday's writings. For the study of *The Way to Rainy Mountain* the most relevant biographical discussions appear in chapter 5 (140–66, esp. 140–46). Schubnell describes Momaday's growing interest in his Kiowa heritage during his early thirties, as well as important specific events and in-fluences, notably Momaday's visits to the keeper of the Tai-me and to Aho's grave, the collecting of the stories for *The Journey of Tai-me*, and the crucial influence of Yvor Winters, his Stanford mentor and friend, who encouraged Momaday to write about his Kiowa heritage and to mix genres. (See Schub-nell's essay in part 2 of this volume; see also the description of Kenneth Lin-coln's "Tai-me to Rainy Mountain," in the "Critical Studies" section, and appendix B.)

Culture

Trying to identify cultural and historical sources for and parallels to *The Way to Rainy Mountain* can be a tricky business. Take for example the account of the Leonid meteor shower of 1833, which Momaday depicts as marking the beginnings of the end of the Kiowa golden era (85). Was his description based on James Mooney's *Calendar History of the Kiowa Indians* (260–61), Mildred Mayhall's *Kiowas* (169), a *New York Times* article ("Meteor Shower Is Due Tonight") by Walter Sullivan that Schubnell found among the *Rainy Mountain* "Notes and fragments" (Schubnell, interview), Faulkner's brief al-lusion to the falling stars of 1833 in section 4 of "The Bear" (269), the first entry in old Pohd-lohk's ledger book (Momaday, *Names* 48), or the type of family storytelling experiences that constitute Momaday's earliest memories ("Story of the Arrowmaker" 2)? Tracking down Momaday's specific sources can be a frustrating and even wrongheaded endeavor for instructors and stu-dents. Nevertheless, some of the written sources available to Momaday as he composed *Rainy Mountain* reveal why, as Jarold Ramsey puts it, Momaday "is a kind of paradigm" of the "artistic mediator" role played by the best con-temporary Indian authors ("Teacher" 167). Examining works about the Ki-owas that appeared after the publication of *Rainy Mountain*, especially Maurice Boyd's *Kiowa Voices* volumes, can also help students to place Momaday's ar-tistic, imaginative transformations within ancient and modern tribal contexts.

Correspondence and interviews indicate that Momaday consulted several well-known books about the Kiowas (e.g., Schubnell, *N. Scott Momaday* 145, 281n19, 284n69; Momaday *"MELUS* Interview" 83). In *The Way to Rainy Mountain* he specifically acknowledges his debt to Mooney's *Calendar History*, a late nineteenth-century publication available to students in a 1979 paperback reprint. Mooney drew on his extensive contacts with the Kiowas, written sources, and several Kiowa pictorial calendars. He presents detailed Kiowa background material (141–253, 381–444) and a chronological survey of important tribal events from 1832 to 1892 (254–379; see also app. B of this volume). Before the publication of *Rainy Mountain*, Mayhall's *Kiowas* was the most complete modern account of the tribe. The content of chapters 1 and 4 (3–21, 168–210) parallel episodes in *Rainy Mountain*, and the moving tone of the foreword (ix–xiii) approaches the tone Momaday achieves in his introduction. Alice Marriott's *Ten Grandmothers* is an intriguing background source because it combines oral narratives and history with fictional techniques and emphasizes Kiowa women's perspectives. (There is little evidence that Momaday used Marriott's *Saynday's People.*) Though Wilbur Sturtevant Nye's *Bad Medicine and Good* and *Carbine and Lance* emphasize Kiowa raiding and fighting more than Momaday does, Nye's books clearly establish the importance of the Rainy Mountain area to the Kiowas. Schubnell and I have not found any strong evidence that Momaday used Elsie Clews Parsons's *Kiowa Tales*, though there are obvious parallels between her translations and the stories Momaday collected from family and tribal members.

Boyd's *Kiowa Voices* volumes, especially *Myths, Legends and Folktales* (vol. 2), are the most important sources of tribal background material to appear since the publication of *Rainy Mountain*. (A third volume is forthcoming.) These are the first studies of the Kiowas to make extensive use of the Susan Peters Collection (see Boyd, 1: 148–49; 2: xxviii) and to exhibit a close collaboration with Kiowa elders, especially Linn Pauahty and the other members of the Kiowa Historical and Research Society. (Momaday collected some of his stories from these elders.) Volume 2 contains the most complete collection of ancient and contemporary Kiowa narratives ever compiled and enables instructors and students to locate Momaday's short versions of stories within the broad context of Kiowa oral traditions.

In *The American Indian: Language and Literature* Jack Marken lists other background studies of the Kiowa published since *Rainy Mountain* appeared. Floyd C. Watkins includes a few paragraphs on Momaday's book in his examination of place in *House Made of Dawn* (161–62), though the best introduction to Native American concepts of place, as they appear in Momaday's work, is found in Larry Evers's "Words and Place: A Reading of *House Made of Dawn.*"

As appendix A, "Selected Comparative Possibilities," suggests, there are numerous opportunities for instructors to compare Momaday's text and passages in the aforementioned and other works. Momaday's omissions—of, for example, central mythic figures like Saynday—are as intriguing as his inclusions in defining his role as artistic mediator between cultures. The listing in appendix A of approximately two hundred comparisons, while not exhaustive, should help students begin examining the cultural and literary implications of the similarities and differences between Momaday's text and works that appeared before and after its publication.

American Indian Literary Genres

In fewer than ten small-sized pamphlet pages, Trimble uses the following terms to describe *The Way to Rainy Mountain: autobiography, epic, poem, nonfiction, tragedy, verse, drama, sonnet, prose, vision,* and *creation hymn* (*Momaday* 27–35). Momaday has used terms such as *lyrical prose* and *quintessential novels* ("Interview by J. Bruchac" 14, 15). To be prepared for Momaday's mixed genres and juxtaposed voices, undergraduates should have some notion of the characteristics of different genres and some knowledge of literature with a discontinuous narrative structure. Schubnell's discussions of Momaday's favorite non-Indian authors, especially Faulkner (e.g., 68), and Yvor Winters's encouraging words about mixing genres and "controlled association" (*Forms of Discovery* 143–44) might help instructors to build on their students' understanding of genres and structure.

Instructors cannot, however, assume that students will have a familiarity with Native American oral and written genres. Fortunately, there are several short and good introductions that can acquaint instructors and students with the basic outlines of Indian literatures. The first section (2–23) of A. LaVonne Brown Ruoff's excellent bibliographic essay "American Indian Literatures" will quickly introduce instructors to the primary oral and written genres while highlighting texts particularly suitable for classroom use. Two other praiseworthy starting points are Andrew Wiget's bibliographic survey "Native American Literature" and a special section in the Summer 1983 issue of the *ADE Bulletin*, which contains valuable, brief surveys (Ramsey's "Overview" and Ruoff's two-page annotated bibliography) and concise descriptions of particular genres (Ruoff on prose and Evers on oral literature). A few other types of brief introductions include bibliographies arranged by genre (e.g., Larry Evers's discussion of primary and secondary sources ["Native American Literature"]), Arnold Krupat's provocative essay "Native American Literature and the Canon," Kenneth Lincoln's brief overview of scholarship (*Native American* 10–13), Carol Hunter's examination of oral literature and modern fiction, and Simon Ortiz's survey of contemporary fiction and poetry, which emphasizes the theme of political oppression ("Literature").

Instructors and students seeking more thorough introductions should consider reading three very different valuable book-length works. Andrew Wiget's *Native American Literature* is the best overview available; it offers concise, often chapter-length discussions of the genres found in *Rainy Mountain*. (Wiget is currently preparing a dictionary of Native American literature to be published by Greenwood Press.) Abraham Chapman's out-of-print *Literature of the American Indians* is a diversified gathering of oral narratives and essays by Indian and non-Indian authors, including Momaday's "Man Made of Words" and Paula Gunn Allen's "Sacred Hoop," which are particularly relevant to the study of *The Way to Rainy Mountain*. Allen's *Studies in American Indian Literature* includes three sections ("Oral Literature," "Personal Narrative," and "Modern and Contemporary") that provide important literary background material for Momaday's use of Kiowa stories, private and family memories, and poetry. Appended to *Studies*, Ruoff's "Guide" (281–309) directs readers to numerous works, such as H. David Brumble's *Annotated Bibliography of American Indian and Eskimo Autobiographies*, that will help students who want to do specialized background studies of *Rainy Mountain*. (Chapter 8 of Brumble's forthcoming *American Indian Autobiography* places *Rainy Mountain* in the context of the history of Native American autobiographies.)

As a supplement or alternative to scholarly introductions, instructors should consider assigning a well-known Indian autobiography, such as John G. Neihardt's *Black Elk Speaks*; selections from poetry anthologies, such as Duane Niatum's *Carriers of the Dream Wheel* and *Harper's Anthology of Twentieth Century Native American Poetry*; or a contemporary work characterized by mixed genres, multiple voices, or a discontinuous narrative: for example, Leslie Marmon Silko's *Ceremony* and *Storyteller*, Paula Gunn Allen's *Woman Who Owned the Shadows*, Gerald Vizenor's *Darkness in Saint Louis Bearheart*, James Welch's *Winter in the Blood*, Louise Erdrich's *Love Medicine* and *The Beet Queen*, or even Hyemeyohsts Storm's controversial *Seven Arrows*. Instructors who assign the autobiography should read the provocative comparative studies of *Black Elk Speaks* and *Rainy Mountain* by William Bloodworth and Lincoln (*Native American* 82–116) and pay particular attention to Robert L. Berner's essay in part 2 of this volume. Those who use contemporary fiction may want to consult Charles R. Larson's *American Indian Fiction* and Alan R. Velie's *Four American Indian Literary Masters*.

Critical Studies

Most of the critical studies about Momaday focus on *House Made of Dawn.* There are, however, several analyses of *The Way to Rainy Mountain* that can help instructors to define classroom approaches to interpretation. These studies tend to emphasize the circumstances of composition and publication, the form of the book, themes relating to identity formation, sense of place, the power of language and imagination, and important specific motifs such as horse and grandmother images.

Kenneth Lincoln's "Tai-me to Rainy Mountain" is probably the first critical-biographical essay that instructors should read. Using letters and manuscripts in the Bancroft Library at Berkeley, Lincoln reconstructs the general development of *Rainy Mountain* from 17 October 1967, when Momaday wrote to Gus Blaisdell about a copy of *The Journey of Tai-me* that Momaday's parents had left for Blaisdell at the University of New Mexico Press, until 3 March 1969, when Momaday declared that the design of *Rainy Mountain* was "SMASHING" (115). Lincoln offers numerous hints about how the "commentary" voices evolved and about how Momaday, his father, and Blaisdell integrated the illustrations into the book's verbal and visual design. The quotations from both negative and positive readers' reports and from Momaday's responses are fascinating indexes to non-Indian and Indian, "literary" and "social science" attitudes about defining and communicating contemporary literature by and about Indians.

Kenneth Fields, one of Blaisdell's readers, was one of the first and is still one of the best interpreters of the functions of *Rainy Mountain*'s structure. He sees the intensity of the one-paragraph voices and the mixtures and juxtapositions of genres as vehicles that allow readers to approach understandings of paradoxical feelings that "are beyond exact formulations" (201): for instance, feelings about the muted presence of a dead past that still lives. According to Fields, "In form [*Rainy Mountain*] resembles those ancient texts with subsequent commentaries which, taken altogether, present strange complexes of intelligence: not only the author's, but with it that of the man in whose mind the author was able to live again" (200).

Four other structural studies were mentioned by survey respondents. In "Racial Memory and Individual Imagination" Barbara Strelke relates the three parts of the body of the book ("Setting Out," "Going On," and "Closing In") to the ways individual perceptions can "lend credence" to group experiences (348). Robert L. Berner also concentrates on the impact of the three parts, placing special emphasis on the oral narrative voices. He delineates a general, three-part process that traces the origins, power, and collapse of a language tradition. This broad decline is counterpointed against the artist-writer's ability to imagine an ordering of past and present, tribal and personal that leads to discoveries of vitality and shared perspectives. Kenneth Lincoln and Mick McAllister concentrate on the complexities and implications of smaller structural units. Pointing to examples such as the description of Aho's house, Lincoln argues that the juxtapositions of four "modes" (he adds "pictorial" to oral, historical, and personal) create instances in which the apparently small and fragmentary become infinite and whole and thus gain a significance far beyond their isolated realities (*Native American* 102–09). In "The Topology of Remembrance" McAllister offers the most intricate and detailed analysis of *Rainy Mountain*'s structure that has been published to date. He examines verbal, numerical, and pictorial patterns. His analyses of illustrations demonstrate the stengths and weaknesses of his approach. For example, he identifies important networks of rise and fall patterns that are central to the journey motif, but he also reduces the buffalo drawings to an iconographic representation of the rise and decline of the buffalo and Kiowas.

In one of the best critical studies ("Hard Journey Back") Charles A. Nicholas uses Joseph Campbell's concept of the "collapse of traditional mythology and its displacement by creative mythology" to examine how Momaday's personal voice establishes an identity with Kiowa traditions. Nicholas claims that the structure of the book and the intensity of the family and private memories of Kiowa history and ancestors allow Momaday to go "one step further" than Campbell to posit "the essential continuity between these two kinds of mythology, insisting that both are acts of the imagination and both are capable of generating the same kind of belief" (150). Another analysis of identity formation, Thekla Zachrau's "Towards Indian Identity," concludes with some misleading comments about the "noble savage" but does outline several interesting comparisons between *Rainy Mountain* and *House Made of Dawn* and *The Names*. Matthias Schubnell and J. Frank Papovich analyze the relations between identity and place. Schubnell's overview of the body of *Rainy Mountain* sometimes tends toward summary; but his previously mentioned background material is very good, and he makes excellent use of J. K. Wright and Yi-Fu Tuan's concept of "geopiety" to interpret the process of identity formation implied in Momaday's introduction (149–57, 282n31). In "Landscape, Tradition, and Identity" Papovich effectively contrasts the well-known nineteenth-century Anglo-American wilderness story of retreat, exploration, and return to the integrating concepts found in the landscapes of *Rainy Mountain* — concepts of animal and human life and the individual and society. (He further develops these contrasts in his essay in pt. 2.)

The power of language in five Kiowa stories in *Rainy Mountain* (secs. 1, 13, 14, 16, 17) is the focus of Roland Garrett's "Notions of Language," which would have been much more convincing had he placed his examples within the context of Kiowa storytelling traditions. Lincoln's brief analysis of naming also reflects the theme of the power of language by indicating how names of the people, mountain, rivers, and plants in *Rainy Mountain* embody the "ability to deal with the world on reciprocal terms" and to "encode and transmit culture" (111, 114).

In chapter 2 of *Four American Indian Literary Masters* (11–31) Alan R. Velie emphasizes the importance of the book's structure and the themes of identity and word power. He goes on to establish the significance of the horse images, which demonstrate Momaday's ability to express the glories and harsh realities of the past and the regenerative personal memories of the present (29–30). Discussion of the structural and thematic functions of another specific and important image — the grandmother figure — can be found at the conclusion of Berner's essay (66–67).

Teaching Guides and Audiovisual Aids

Teachers of *The Way to Rainy Mountain* can certainly benefit from the guides to teaching Indian literatures that have appeared since 1975. These include the previously noted bibliographies and the articles that address the issue of tribal background material (Ballinger; Dorris; Evers, "Native American Oral Literatures"; and Ramsey, "Teacher"). Mention of *Rainy Mountain* appears only in the sample syllabi appended to R. D. Thiesz's *Perspectives on Teaching American Indian Literature* and only briefly in Agnes Grant's *Native Literature in the Curriculum* (68–69). Nevertheless, Thiesz's observations about ethical and ideological issues can be readily applied to the teaching of Momaday's book, and Grant's claims about the psychological effects of teaching Indian literature (e.g., 29–31) and about Canadian Native American writers (60–62, 69–73) offer provocative contexts for discussing *Rainy Mountain*. The most important general aid is, of course, Paula Gunn Allen's *Studies in American Indian Literature*. The essays, bibliographies, and course designs (many of which include *Rainy Mountain*) make Allen's collection indispensable.

At least seven articles focus specifically on teaching *The Way to Rainy Mountain*: four on literature courses, three on writing courses. In "Survey Courses" I argue that *Rainy Mountain* is a good Native American selection for American or world literature surveys because it includes different types of oral and written Indian literatures, the historical and personal voices provide important contexts for approaching the tribal stories, and the complex structure raises interesting literary questions and undercuts stereotypes about storytelling and Indians. Norma C. Wilson contends that often the best response to reading imaginative literature is writing imaginative literature. Her students respond to their readings in oral literatures by adopting Momaday's three-voice structure. (See her essay in pt. 2 for examples of student writing.) In 1971 Richard F. Fleck began experimenting with classroom oral readings of *Rainy Mountain*, an approach used by several contributors to part 2. His experiments culminated in group readings at an ancient medicine wheel in Wyoming and in a tipi—experiences that convinced him that oral readings in outdoor settings greatly enhanced students' intellectual and emotional responses to the book ("Outdoor Teaching"). High school students' dissatisfaction with a literature anthology motivated Marie Smith to try a different type of experiment with *Rainy Mountain*. She required the students to write parallel and invented legends; their writing improved and their stereotypes about legends were undercut ("Legends and Students"). Andrew Wiget's students were quite different from Smith's teenagers. They were New Mexico inmate college students who used *The Way to Rainy Mountain* as a model for autobiographical sketches, several of which appear in the "Where I'm From" section of *A World of Hope* (2–13). During the past ten years, I have encouraged Indian and non-Indian students in America and Japan to use Momaday's book as a model for autobiographical writing that focuses on a particular landscape. Theoretical justifications for this approach to writing and samples of student work can be found in my "Inventive Modeling" and "Japanese Ways to Rainy Mountain." (Clyde Moneyhun and Jeff Huffman have used my approach to produce a ninety-page book of Japanese student writing called *The Rains of the Dragon*.)

A clear majority of the survey respondents thought that using illustrations to teach *The Way to Rainy Mountain* was as crucial to teaching success as was reading "Man Made of Words," *House Made of Dawn*, a reference work, and Allen's *Studies*. Four books provide easy access to photographs and illustrations. Momaday's *Names* includes photographs of Rainy Mountain (27), the family arbor (7), Aho (31, 44), Mammedaty (95; this is the photo described in sec. 20, second voice), and Ko-sahn (162); it also includes his own sketch of Devil's Tower (69) and photographs of members of his family tree: Huantoa, or Alfred (father); Aho and Mammedaty (grandmother and grandfather); Keahdinekeah and Pohd-lohk (great-grandmother and great-grand-stepfather); and Kau-au-ointy (great-great-grandmother) ([vii]). In the paperback reprint of Mooney's *Calendar History* students can locate the migration map that guided Momaday's retracing of his Kiowa ancestors' journey (facing 249), the George Catlin drawing of Kotsatoah described in section 15, third voice (facing 268; see also Boyd 1: 12), the heraldic tipi mentioned in section 12, second voice (inset between 336 and 337; see also Mayhall 282), and a replica of the Tai-me (facing 242; see also Boyd 1: 30; Mayhall 157). Maurice Boyd's two volumes of *Kiowa Voices* are visual treasure houses. Many of the stories Momaday uses and ceremonies he describes are illustrated by contemporary Kiowa artists. Students can even discover a painting by Al Momaday (1: facing 125) and old and new images similar to several of his drawings in *The Way to Rainy Mountain*: for example, nineteenth-century paintings of storm horses on doe skin (1: 3) and modern versions of peyote birds (1: ix, 108, 109, facing 112). *A Chronicle of the Kiowa Indians*, a reprint of the Dohasan calendar, offers students visual impressions of many of the events of tribal history described in *Rainy Mountain*. (See the essays by Lawana Trout and Gretchen Bataille in pt. 2 for other suggestions about illustrations.)

The best way for students to experience the visual impact of the landscape and culture that informs *Rainy Mountain* is to see Rainy Mountain, which is northwest of Lawton, Oklahoma; to observe important Kiowa ceremonials in Anadarko (Black Leggings in October and May) and Carnegie (Gourd Dance Clan in July); and to visit the tribal museum in Carnegie. Since such journeys are impractical for most classes, another option for instructors is to assign Joan Frederick Denton's "Kiowa Murals" in the July 1987 issue of *Southwest Art*. Denton relates *Rainy Mountain* to the styles and themes of Kiowa art in general and specifically to the ten stunning murals housed in the museum and reproduced in her article (70). The murals, painted by three contemporary Kiowa artists (Parker Boyiddle, Mirac Creepingbear, and Sherman Chaddlesone), can easily be related to many sections of Momaday's book; Rainy Mountain itself is featured in two of the murals (68–69, 74).

As Trimble observes, Momaday "leaves a trail of [private] video/audio tapes across the United States" ("Momaday" 313). Nevertheless, commercially produced tapes are a bit more difficult than illustrations to obtain. Fortunately, important sections of "The Man Made of Words" (excerpts from 167–70 and all of 171–73) are included on a National Public Radio cassette entitled *Land as Symbol: The American Indian* (the tape also includes a lecture by Peter Nabokov). Kay Bonetti taped an excellent interview with Momaday in 1983 (*N. Scott Momaday*). She and Momaday discuss broad issues (e.g., Indian identity and the sacredness of oral traditions), as well as specific aspects of *Rainy Mountain* (e.g., physical design). Recordings of Momaday reading from his works include a cassette tape entitled *N. Scott Momaday Reads* . . . (excerpts from *House Made of Dawn* and *The Names*, "Gourd Dancer," and "Tsoai") and a record, *Remember My Horse* (excerpts from *House Made of Dawn* and poetry). One other possibility is my audiotape survey of oral narratives that includes a discussion of and reading from *Rainy Mountain* (*American Indian Folklore*).

Of the numerous films about Indians, possibly the most appropriate for the teacher of *Rainy Mountain* is *House Made of Dawn*, which uses a Native American film crew and features many Indian actors. Some of Momaday's responses to the film are recorded in Gretchen Bataille's interview, which appeared in a special film issue of the newsletter *Studies in American Indian Literatures* ("Interview"). Filmstrip 2 of *American Indian Literature* concludes with comments on Momaday's work. *More Than Bows and Arrows* should help instructors to undercut their students' Indian stereotypes; narrated by Momaday, it surveys the contributions of many different tribes. Two slide-audio-cassette programs that will also help dispel stereotypes are *Inside the Cigar Store: Images of the American Indian* (Bataille) and *The Make-Believe Indian: Native Americans in the Movies* (Bataille and Silet). Instructors who emphasize the Kiowa narratives and the sense of place in *Rainy Mountain* might want to use one or more of the excellent videotapes in the *Words and Place: Native Literature from the American Southwest* series. The series provides fine study guides and includes traditional storytelling (e.g., Hopi coyote tales) and interviews with and readings by contemporary authors (e.g., Leslie Marmon Silko).

I hope that the foregoing sampling of numerous possibilities for introducing various background, critical, and pedagogical perspectives to students does not obscure one crucial point. Whether an instructor decides to use a minimal amount of material—a few passages from "Man Made of Words" and *House Made of Dawn*, a couple relevant illustratons, and a reference to one or two good introductions to Momaday and Indian literature—or chooses to use a great deal of supplemental material, the primary classroom goal should be to present *The Way to Rainy Mountain* as an exciting reading experience that can enlarge students' concepts of literature, their environment, and themselves. The contributors to part 2 recognize the work's potential, and I thank them for their willingness to help other instructors to achieve this awareness.

Part Two

APPROACHES

INTRODUCTION

Part 2 suggests the variety of settings suitable for teaching *The Way to Rainy Mountain*. The contributors have taught Momaday's book successfully in many different parts of the United States and other countries, at open-admissions two-year colleges and competitive research-oriented universities, at small and large private liberal arts colleges, at small and large public universities, in classes without any Indian students and in all-Indian classes taught in off-campus Indian community programs. (See "Participants in the Survey.") The courses described range from introductory freshman composition to lower-level interdisciplinary courses and required literature surveys to upper-level electives. The contributors represent all professional teaching levels — graduate teaching assistant to full professor.

The essays, which were selected from proposals submitted with the survey responses, reflect the common denominators and the diversities of the responses and parallel the organization of part 1. Most of the contributors recommend that instructors be familiar with a few of Momaday's other works. Beyond that, they take a variety of approaches; some focus on biographical, cultural, and generic backgrounds; others emphasize critical analyses of structure and theme; still others adapt their approaches to particular teaching situations.

The contributors to the first section of part 2 introduce background contexts that help their students answer important questions about *Rainy Mountain*. Starting with a biographical orientation, Matthias Schubnell stresses how the book "grew out of a personal and historical need for self-definition" — an approach he finds useful in answering questions about the criteria that define "Indian" identity. After finding that students had difficulty appreciating the meanings of and relations between secular and sacred Kiowa history, Lawana Trout developed a series of introductions to Kiowa history and culture that culminated in students' attempts to write their own personal histories. H. David Brumble handles his students' questions about the generic characteristics of *Rainy Mountain* by placing the book within the context of autobiography, especially the discontinuous, oral narrative form of the Plains Indian war tales called coup stories.

Four different types of structural approaches open the second section. Joan Henley's interpretation of the voices of *Rainy Mountain* as representing various though interrelated forms of "epistemological exploration" is particularly appropriate for general humanities and interdisciplinary courses. Robert L. Berner and William Oandasan respond to their students' questions about the organization of *Rainy Mountain* by offering textual and contextual interpretations. Berner takes a synthetic approach—he convincingly integrates the traditional American Indian emphasis on four perspectives with *Rainy Mountain's* apparent three-part structure. Oandasan takes a polysemous approach—he demonstrates how *Rainy Mountain* can be seen as having dual, tripartite, and quadripartite structure and attempts to place it within the structure of some of Momaday's other publications, while suggesting possible cross-disciplinary contexts for *Rainy Mountain*. Helen Jaskoski perceives *Rainy Mountain* as a lyric and meditative work. She encourages students to appreciate the importance of the visual impact of the book and to cultivate silence and stillness as necessary responses to Momaday's text.

The second section concludes with examinations of three themes or motifs mentioned frequently in Momaday scholarship and in the survey responses: the significance of identity formation, oral traditions, and a sense of sacred place. In an interdisciplinary course, Gretchen M. Bataille examines visual images, legal testimony, contemporary Indian literature, biographical information, and characteristics of Native American worldviews to help her students understand how Momaday imagined his identity. Norma C. Wilson encourages her students, especially her Indian students, to value their family and community stories by having them read traditional oral literature and *Rainy Mountain* and then write about their own stories and landscapes. Susan Scarberry-García claims that the primary obstacle to teaching *Rainy Mountain* is that students are immersed in a secular culture that inhibits their understanding of the sacredness of particular places and events described by Momaday. By presenting these scenes and acts as "life-giving religious stories," rather than as fictional fables, she hopes to expand students' concepts of the functions of *Rainy Mountain* and oral traditions.

The last section of part 2 focuses on *Rainy Mountain* within the contexts of particular composition and literature courses. Each contributor suggests how the approach in his or her course could benefit teachers of similar courses. As Lauri Anderson explains, at Suomi College—a two-year institution that attracts Finnish, Croatian, Italian, Cornish, and Native American residents of Upper Michigan—all the freshmen study *Rainy Mountain* as a model for gathering, integrating, and writing family history. A small, select group of freshmen at the University of Utah encounter *Rainy Mountain* in the context of a team-taught humanities and writing sequence entitled "The Utah Plan." According to David Hoehner, more than any other text studied in this sequence, *Rainy Mountain* helps the students to gain a cross-cultural aware-ness. Suzanne Evertsen Lundquist uses *Rainy Mountain* to help her compo-sition students at Brigham Young University achieve literacy—defined as the ability to connect "with one's history, society, and culture through language." Including *Rainy Mountain* in a thematic introduction to nineteenth- and twentieth-century American literature at the University of Virginia allows J. Frank Papovich to contrast Momaday's concept of place, which integrates in-dividual, social, and environmental identities, to concepts of the land in "clas-sic" American literature that pit the individual against the land and society. At the University of Wisconsin, Madison, Vernon E. Lattin uses pastoral im-ages to place *Rainy Mountain* within another type of American literary con-text: familiar modern American novels and ethnic—especially Chicano—fiction. Kathryn S. Vangen reminds us that one of the serious draw-backs to teaching *Rainy Mountain* is that non-Indian students often respond to it by indulging in nostalgia or in guilt feelings about sins committed in the distant past. In her Indian literature courses at the University of Michi-gan and the University of Washington, she introduces her students to con-cepts and cross-cultural comparisons that undermine simplistic responses and emphasizes parts of *Rainy Mountain* involving integrations of loss, change, and continuity. In an off-campus program sponsored by Brandon University in Canada, Agnes Grant teaches an oral-narrative course to classes quite differ-ent from Vangen's; hers consist of Cree and Ojibway students preparing to be teachers. Momaday's book helps them to understand that family and tribal stories can inspire profound written literature and to see the value of their own community stories, which they tell with skill and imagination. As a mem-ber of the MLA Committee on Teaching and Related Professional Activities commented, "If every class that used Momaday's [*Rainy Mountain*] could bor-row a few students from Grant, the [reading] experience would be much richer."

The epilogue is a significant, perhaps essential complement to part 2. Al-though the contributors include American Indian scholars and although most of the students whose writing is excerpted have Indian heritages, I wanted to conclude the book with the observations of a respected Kiowa who could offer important insights about contemporary Kiowa responses to *The Way to Rainy Mountain* and provide advice to instructors and students. Gary Kodaseet, whose background is described in the headnote to his interview, had both the qualifications and enthusiasm to fulfill this role.

BIOGRAPHICAL, CULTURAL, AND GENERIC CONTEXTS

Tribal Identity and the Imagination

Matthias Schubnell

My approach to *The Way to Rainy Mountain* is essentially biographical and historical and suggests that the work be read as Momaday's imaginative and artistic creation of his Kiowa identity. Anthropologists such as Murray L. Wax tell us that "identity for a traditional Indian band was given and irrevocable" but that contemporary Native Americans living in a mass society must maintain the status of Indian by a "forceful act of will in the face of pressure and hostility, both from within and without the Indian world" (173). For Momaday, this act of will is realized in an act of the imagination. The material presented here illuminates the personal and historical situation that compelled Momaday to explore his racial heritage and determine his place in it. Besides applying Momaday's concept of the imagination to his search for a tribal identity in *The Way to Rainy Mountain*, I highlight the role of Momaday's Stanford teacher and friend Yvor Winters in the work's conception and artistic development and trace the evolution of the privately printed *The Journey of Tai-me*, a collection of Kiowa folktales, to the sophisticated multigenre work in its published form. This evolution reflects Momaday's growing sense of identity as a Kiowa Indian in the course of the work's composition.

Much of the information used in this approach is based on a scholarly examination of Momaday's personal circumstances when he began work on the *Way to Rainy Mountain* project. While Momaday's correspondence with Yvor Winters may be of greater interest to students in advanced undergraduate courses or in graduate seminars, even freshmen and sophomores benefit from an awareness that *The Way to Rainy Mountain* grew out of a personal and historical need for self-definition. Instructors using the work in writing courses and in courses on biography and autobiography can emphasize the role of the imagination in identity formation. In classes that deal with other works by contemporary American Indian writers, the proposed approach may prove valuable in introducing the recurrent theme of cultural identity and related issues such as alienation and cultural relativity, which are central to many of these works. For similar reasons, the approach may be useful when *The Way to Rainy Mountain* is taught in a survey course together with other works by ethnic as well as Anglo-American writers.

My main purpose, however, is to help answer the difficult question often posed by students regarding the criteria that define an Indian identity and to dispel common stereotypes and misconceptions. Two preparatory steps may prove pedagogically fruitful. First, students should be encouraged to share their ideas on what constitutes an Indian identity. Second, students should be introduced to Momaday's concept of identity as a function of an imaginative, emotional, and intellectual interaction with a tribal heritage. This can best be achieved by assigning Momaday's essay "The Man Made of Words," which sums up his concept of the imagination and its role in the creation of identity: "We are what we imagine. Our very existence consists in our imagination of ourselves" (167).

A class discussion about Indian identity will almost always reveal misunderstandings in the students' minds resulting from stereotypes in movies or in literature. Students may have difficulties in reconciling stereotypical images of the Indian with the contemporary reality of Indian life, whether on the reservation or in an urban setting. What is it then, they may ask, that makes an Indian an Indian? Such criteria as degree of Indian blood, tribal enrollment, recognition by tribal communities, competence in an Indian language, and active participation in religious ceremonials should be examined and put into perspective. The instructor may want to introduce as perhaps the most significant denominator of an Indian identity the intellectual, emotional, and imaginative interaction of American Indians with their tribal heritages. Momaday stresses the importance of this interaction in the prologue to *Rainy Mountain* when he states that "the imaginative experience and the historical express equally the tradition of man's reality" (4). Another Indian author, T. E. Sawyer, affirms that a people's historical experience constitutes the basis of their sense of self and belonging and thus precludes cultural assimilation:

> It is the same historical experience which gives rise to the identity of a people. And it is a common misunderstanding to think that group identity is the sum of cultural traits. Identity is a conception of and feeling about the events which a people have lived. It is the meaning of events in which one's ancestors took part, in ways that make one proud, which differentiate people into ethnic groups. (203)

This definition captures precisely Momaday's endeavor in *The Way to Rainy Mountain*.

Once students recognize imagination as a crucial force in the determination of a personal identity, the assignment and discussion of "The Man Made of Words" will prepare them for a keener understanding of *The Way to Rainy Mountain*. This key essay clarifies the connection in Momaday's art between Kiowa oral tradition and his sense of self. Two quotations from the beginning of the piece suffice to establish the proper context for examining *The Way to Rainy Mountain*. With regard to the significance of language, Momaday notes: "It seems to me that in a certain sense we are all made of words; that our most essential being consists in language. It is the element in which we think and dream and act, in which we live our daily lives. There is no way in which we can exist apart from the morality of a verbal dimension" (162). To the extent, then, that Momaday explores the body of oral literature handed down to him by his Kiowa ancestors, he can conceive of himself as a Kiowa. His definition of an American Indian now becomes more readily intelligible: "an Indian is an idea a given man has of himself. And it is a moral idea, for it accounts for the way in which he reacts to other men and the world in general. And that idea, in order to be realized completely, has to be expressed" (162). This last sentence indicates clearly that most of Momaday's writings must be read as self-conscious realizations of his Kiowa identity, that, indeed, they constitute a survival technique for Kiowa culture as a whole.

It is apparent from Momaday's biographical background that not until relatively late in life did Momaday become fully conscious of his place in Kiowa tradition: "At a certain point in my life . . . when I was in my early thirties, I began to wonder about my heritage which I had always taken for granted. I got fascinated in that business and made a point of looking at it and finding out as much as I could about it, which turned out to be a great intellectual exercise for me and a very fascinating thing" (interview, with students, Las Cruces). In another context he elaborated on the significance of this event:

> I think of myself as an Indian because at one time in my life I suddenly realized that my father had grown up speaking a language that I didn't grow up speaking, that my forebears on his side had made a migration from Canada along with . . . Athapaskan peoples I knew nothing about, and so I determined to find out something about these things, and in the process I acquired an identity: it is an Indian identity, as far as I am concerned.   ("American Indian")

Momaday's interest in exploring Kiowa tradition may have been sharpened by the views of Yvor Winters, Momaday's mentor at Stanford. Winters suggests that "unless we understand the history which produced us, we are determined by that history; we may be determined in any event, but the understanding gives us a chance" (*Forms of Discovery* xix). Elsewhere he comments: "[M]an lives and changes; but man has a memory, personal, historical, and racial, so that his changing is not absolute and should not be irresponsible. His changing may be growth, diminution, or disintegration, and the choice among these possibilities is his own" ("Forms of Discovery" 4). Momaday's inquiry into his racial past has shaped him and the degree to which he has become detached from the mythical worldview of his ancestors. As Momaday describes the purpose of this deeply personal journey, "In *The Way to Rainy Mountain* I was more concerned to reveal something to myself than to anyone else" (Nabokov). In a different context he says: "If I don't understand my Kiowa background, I foresake a lot of my human potential. By understanding it as far as I can I fulfill my capacity for being alive as a human being" (personal interview, with Schubnell).

In the course of his successful integration into mainstream American society, Momaday realized that the link to his aboriginal background had become tenuous and that the continuity of tribal cultures is threatened. This recognition may be considered the starting point of *The Way to Rainy Mountain*. Two specific events helped to develop in Momaday a sense of responsibility for the preservation of Kiowa culture.

Momaday's encounter with the Tai-me bundle, the sacred Sun Dance fetish of the Kiowa tribe, was one of these events. Tai-me, the Kiowas' most powerful medicine, was worshiped as the bringer of good luck and exhibited for viewing only during the Sun Dance. After the last performance of this ceremony by the Kiowas in 1887, the Sun Dance doll remained with the Tai-me keeper, a Kiowa man responsible for the storing and opening of the medicine bundle. With the demise of the Sun Dance the bundle remain closed, and after the death of the keeper it was passed on to his daughter.

In 1963, Momaday's grandmother Aho told him that the Tai-me bundle was extant and could be seen on request. Momaday traveled to Oklahoma with her and his father, Al, and visited this Kiowa woman, who, in a storytelling session, told him about Tai-me and instructed him in the formalities of viewing the medicine bundle. After making the traditional offering of cloth, Momaday was admitted into the presence of Tai-me, which was hanging from a small forked tree in a closetlike recess of a room. Momaday experienced "one of the most intense religious feelings" he had ever known, the certainty of being in the presence of a sacred object ("Interview," with Abbott, 22). In a manuscript fragment written some years after the journey, Momaday described the lasting effect of this visit:

> From the time I stood before the Tai-me issikia I knew a certain restlessness. I felt that I had come to know something about myself I had never known before. I became more keenly aware of myself as someone who walked through time and in whose blood there is something inestimably old and undying. It was as if I had remembered something that happened two hundred years ago. I meant then to seek after the source of my memory and myself. But there were not many who could help me. Aho was dead; Mammedaty had died before I was born. Theirs

was the last generation, I believe, that could claim to be of the living culture of [the Kiowas].   ("Notes")

The second significant event followed naturally from the first. Momaday went to Rainy Mountain cemetery to mourn Aho, who had died shortly after their visit to the Tai-me bundle. His grandfather Mammedaty, his great-grandmother Kau-au-ointy, his aunt, and many great Kiowa warriors and chiefs are also buried there. It appears that his physical presence in the realm of his dead ancestors reinforced Momaday's urgency to understand the connection between him and them:

When I go and walk among the stones of Rainy Mountain cemetery where my grandmother, in an unmarked grave, and my aunt, dead in infancy, are buried, I am conscious of something terribly important to my being. I could sense in that situation the vitality in myself; I could sense it but could not take possession of it until I translated it into language. But that is only half the truth, I think. Language is not an aid at all, but an essence. My poem, "Rainy Mountain Cemetery," is an act of understanding. Beyond that there is no other way. . . . It was important that I stood before my grandfather's grave at Rainy Mountain cemetery, and I had to put it into words.   (qtd. in Nabokov)

Immediately after confronting his ancestors' graves, Momaday felt a separation; the past seemed obliterated. Yet at the same time Momaday became determined to establish a bond with Mammedaty, Aho, and their common Kiowa culture. The obvious vehicle was the Kiowas' extant oral tradition, which became for Momaday a personal and academic preoccupation.

The Way to Rainy Mountain gradually took shape over a period of six years following Momaday's revelatory encounter with the Tai-me bundle and his experience at Rainy Mountain cemetery. The earliest evidence of Momaday's research into Kiowa oral literature is his essay, "The Morality of Indian Hating," in which he relates and interprets two Kiowa stories (33, 34, 36). Within the framework of the essay, which combines narrative passages with an expository presentation of the development of Indian-white relations, the tales illustrate tribal evolution. In a letter to Momaday, Yvor Winters, who took a keen interest in the work's progress, commented on the article's structure and its potential:

The form is flexible. It could be applied to primarily expository matter, to matter calling for exposition plus a narrative (fiction, historical, or conceivably legendary, although the task of giving adequate body to the legendary might be difficult and call for a good deal of research or imagination). But I think that you ought to pursue the possibilities for a time at least. It might result in a great book: a collection of such pieces, perhaps.   (Letter, 23 July 1968)

These remarks, of course, anticipate the final structure of *The Way to Rainy Mountain*.

As Momaday focused his attention on retrieving the remnants of Kiowa oral tradition, he realized how much American Indian oral poetry and mythology had already deteriorated and that speedy research was imperative to salvage what was still within reach. Deprived of his grandparents as living sources of Kiowa tradition, Momaday collected stories from tribal elders. His inability to speak the Kiowa language greatly hampered this fieldwork. The crucial role of interviewing informers and translating the recorded material fell to Momaday's father, Al, who passed on to his son his own recollection of traditional Kiowa life and the stories he used to hear as a boy. The correspondence between him and Momaday shows that he had forgotten many details, a telling reminder of the fragility of an oral tradition.

Like many contemporary American Indians, Momaday had to take recourse in written materials compiled by anthropologists, folklorists, and translators of Kiowa oral tradition. Some may consider that Momaday's inability to speak Kiowa and his dependence on translations of Kiowa stories prevented him from capturing the true spirit of his oral heritage. Momaday, however, believes that his writing preserves the spirit of the Kiowa language, if not the language itself. He contends that "there is no danger of the spirit of the language being lost . . . because the spirit proceeds out of the people themselves" (qtd. in Rodebaugh). The works of James Mooney, Mildred Mayhall, Alice Marriott, and Wilbur S. Nye are a significant part of the raw material from which Momaday wrought *The Way to Rainy Mountain*.

In the early stages of the project, Momaday was interested only in a collection of stories, at one point considering the tentative title "The Tai-me Keeper: A Migration Literature of the Kiowas" (Letter to Blake). The first, privately published version, entitled *The Journey of Tai-me*, appeared in 1967. It contained all the traditional material subsequently published in *The Way to Rainy Mountain* and an additional six stories that were later collected separately as "Kiowa Legends from *The Journey of Tai-me*." The introduction, prologue, and epilogue, as well as the two poems that frame the final edition are later additions.

The casting of the traditional material and the historical and personal commentaries in three distinct but complementary voices followed Winters's initial proposal to apply the structure of "The Morality of Indian Hating" to a more complex body of material. In a letter to Momaday, Winters reiterated this suggestion and his conviction that the combination of personal comment and historical material would be very effective:

> I wonder what would happen if you set yourself an exercise on a philosophical subject or a historical subject, to be done in a stanza somewhat like the crucifixion piece [Momaday's poem "Before an Old Painting of the Crucifixion"]. Fort Sill, for example: not the historical, per se, but its various aspects as you look back. You are a long way from there,

and yet you must be very close. Your father must have eyewitness stories from his grandparents. That sort of thing as seen personally and in the long view of history might be very moving. (21 Apr. 1965)

Although Winters was thinking of a poetic cycle, his ideas anticipated the changes Momaday made in transforming *The Journey of Tai-me* into *The Way to Rainy Mountain*.

On 26 January 1967, before the completion of *The Journey of Tai-me*, Momaday published his essay entitled "The Way to Rainy Mountain" in the *Reporter*. Invited by the magazine's editors to write an appreciation of the piece, Winters commented on the emerging structure, which would find its fullest manifestation in the final, book-length version:

> I think Momaday's essay is one of the greatest pieces of short prose I have ever read. I should have trouble naming another; it is very short, yet it contains: the history of a people (the Kiowas) and the pathos of their combined grandeur and triviality; the biography of a Kiowa (Aho), in which the history is summed up; a commentary on both the grandson and author. N. Scott Momaday can hardly drop a short phrase which does not haunt one. Nothing is wasted in this essay. Few poems stay in my mind as this prose stays.

The development of *Rainy Mountain* from a collection of Kiowa tales to the blending of these stories with anthropological material and personal reminiscences reflects a growing crystallization of Momaday's Kiowa identity. The associations between the three voices in each triad—the legendary-mythical, the historical-anthropological, and the personal-autobiographical—result in a fusion of these different views of reality in the author's imagination into a unified whole, which manifests the core of Momaday's understanding of himself. As he puts it in the prologue:

> The journey herein recalled continues to be made anew each time the miracle comes to mind, for that is peculiarly the right and responsibility of the imagination. It is a whole journey, intricate with motion and meaning; and it is made with the whole memory, that experience of the mind which is legendary as well as historical, personal as well as cultural. (4)

In a seminar discussion with students at Bucknell University, Momaday recently reiterated his conviction that tribal identity and survival for contemporary American Indians depend increasingly on their imaginative preservation of tribal heritages. As the number of native speakers of aboriginal languages diminishes and oral traditions become fragile, whatever remains of racial, tribal, familial, and personal memories must be kept alive in the imagination of their modern heirs. *The Way to Rainy Mountain* constitutes one attempt by a modern American Indian to preserve the soul of his culture and to reaffirm his identity as a Kiowa.

The way in which Momaday has appropriated his past to his existence in a modern world not only represents a cultural survival technique for American Indians but—as is suggested by several essays in this volume—may serve as a model for students who want to overcome their sense of alienation and rootlessness by exploring their familial and cultural backgrounds. The proposed approach to teaching *The Way to Rainy Mountain*, then, may help students better understand Indian people and motivate them to determine their own identities through the power of the imagination.[1]

NOTE

[1]Several passages in this article have previously been published in my book *N. Scott Momaday: The Cultural and Literary Background* and are reprinted here with the permission of the University of Oklahoma Press.

The Way to Rainy Mountain:
Arrow of History, Spiral of Myth
Lawana Trout

At Rainy Mountain, or, as the Kiowas call it, *Se-pya-dalda*, many histories meet: secular, sacred, and private. Here in this physical and metaphysical mountain, oral stories and written literature also converge. To the outsider, Rainy Mountain may lack sacred stature—"a large lumpy hill," as one Oklahoma student described it—but for the Kiowas, *Se-pya-dalda* remains the sacred center of their tribal history. For Momaday, it is the metaphorical mountain: eternal guardian of his grandmother's grave, beginning and ending of his private quest. Sometimes, this literary and historical nexus blocks my students' understanding of the book.

In teaching *The Way to Rainy Mountain* for fifteen years to undergraduates and to teachers of English and history, I have learned to listen to their questions when they are initially puzzled by Momaday's form and purpose. First, they cannot "read" the interplay among secular, sacred, and private histories; they do not "hear" the three voices talking across the pages. Students do not know secular Kiowa history; nor can they relate it to sacred history. Concepts of *the sacred* confuse some students who live linear lives in linear time on a secular landscape. America is not their holy land, and they see no sacred metaphors arising from the American earth.[1] For them, Momaday's lyrical personal history appears to be marginal family tales rather than one part of a unique literary structure. Because most students have not heard Kiowa oral stories, they cannot trace Momaday's written literature to its oral home.

With these literary and historical skeins in mind, I begin to unravel the meanings and techniques of *The Way to Rainy Mountain* with students in a spiraling process: (1) reviewing relevant points of Kiowa secular history; (2) examining Kiowa calendars; (3) discussing and performing sections of the text; (4) telling and writing personal narratives; and (5) returning to the text as we look back on our *way* to Rainy Mountain. By this time, students recognize that their way coincides with many journeys in one: the actual Kiowa migration; the memory journey that lives in Kiowas today who still tell stories in Rainy Mountain country; the real and imaginary journey of Momaday; and the vicarious journey that his words enable American Indians and other readers to take. Three themes permeate our study: the continuity of Kiowa spirit, the persistence of Kiowa images, and the survival of Kiowa stories.

My students first meet Momaday in his stories. They have a right to experience the book without interference from biographical background, historical notes, or literary analysis. After their initial reading, we discuss sacred and secular Kiowa history. Momaday explains, "I'm not concerned to write the history of a people except as that history bears upon me directly" (Schubnell 148). He shares tribal consciousness with his kindred who told him "the tribal history and literature which informs this book" (*Rainy Mountain*, acknowledgments). Students profit from vicarious access to that informing heritage as they examine his motifs of the remembered earth, the sacred word, and the creative imagination.

This background is critical for some Native Americans as well as for other students. Once, at the beginning of the semester, I held the book up before my American Indian literature class, and a young Kiowa exclaimed, "That book is not true. He was never around our people that much." Stunned, I swallowed my defense and invited the young man to continue. His attack made personal and tribal demands on the book in defiance of Momaday's statement in his essay "Man Made of Words": "Myth, legend, and lore, according to our definitions of these terms, impart a separate and distinct order of reality. We are concerned here not so much with an accurate representation of actuality, but with the realization of the imaginative experience" (168). In our subsequent discussions, that student's comments became the catalyst for our defining terms such as *literature, history, myth, sacred,* and *secular.* At appropriate junctures, we reexamined our definitions according to students' expectations and experiences. In one class, I may have students from ten to fifteen different tribes as well as nontribal students, and they generate lively debates.

Our definition of terms appears in conjunction with my background lecture, organized around a brief chronology of Kiowa secular history, a reprint of the Dohasan calendar, and a presentation of relevant slides.[2] (App. B offers a basic Kiowa chronology.) The slides of Kiowa photographs, tribal art, and calendars present the Kiowas as real people in contrast to the transparent stereotypes my students see on television and in the movies. Students have copies of the chronology and the Dohasan calendar before them as we review passages from Mooney, Mayhall, and Boyd. Drawing on ethnographic reports written by somewhat ethnocentric observers who visited Kiowa country, my classes and I imagine that we witness dramatic scenes from Kiowa history. Students share their visions as we picture the migration that Momaday placed at the center of his prologue. We watch the people leave their northern homeland by the Yellowstone and Missouri rivers circa 1680–1700 and enter their golden age on the Plains. When did the Kiowas first see horses? How did these strange, beautiful beings transform Kiowa warriors into centaurs of the Plains? What happened when the Kiowas first met their mentors, the Crows, who shared great gifts of the Sun Dance, Tai-me, and buffalo medicine? We imagine the Kiowas garnering wealth in horses from trade fairs with the Arikara and Mandan and from raids on Spanish frontiers. Following their friendship with the Crows, we see the Kiowas take hold of their new homes in the Black Hills until the invading Dakotas and Cheyennes drive them southward sometime before 1775. The Kiowas could not keep the Black Hills, but they created stories of the seven sisters, their brother, and the origin of Devil's Tower. (My students and I find delight in knowing what the Kiowas could not have imagined as they left Devil's Tower—that two centuries later one of their descendants who was named for Tsoai would immortalize their journey in his written masterpiece.) The stories lived after they reached the Wichita Mountains, for in 1923, Big Tree, keeper of a calendar, said of the old ones: "They carried dreams in their voices / . . . They told us old stories / and they sang the spirit song" (Boyd 1: 6).

Continuing our journey, we follow reports of early contacts between the Native Americans and Euramericans. In 1821 Jacob Fowler, who was on a trading trip to the Rocky Mountains, recorded that his expedition encountered the Kiowas in what is now Pueblo County, Colorado. The Indians fed the visitors meat, beans, and boiled corn; carried the white men across the frozen river behind them on their horses; and shared lodges as refuge from ten inches of snow. Fowler describes one encampment of Kiowas, Comanches, Arapahoes, and other nations as encompassing seven hundred lodges and twenty thousand horses (Mayhall 63–64). My students are amazed that the Southern Plains Confederacy marshalled such numbers. From the center of Rainy Mountain country, we imagine the Kiowas earning Momaday's title of "a lordly society of warriors" ("Man Made of Words" 170).

Then in 1833 a miracle happened. The Kiowas created calendars for storing their history. Their painted annals are outlines of visual images that evoke memorized and systematized history for oral historians. What can we learn from these pictographic records? Why and how does Momaday use them? These literary and historical chronicles enable us to hear voices from inside the Kiowa world. Here, sacred and secular histories become one history. Students may see what events the Kiowas chose to symbolize on a small space. As we study handsome reprints of the Dohasan chronicle, students are intrigued by the miniature figures and labyrinthian design that enfold sixty years on a single page. Dohasan, Kiowa head chief for more than thirty years, probably kept the first calendar that may have been an inspiration for the Sett'an calendar. In 1892 Mooney obtained the Sett'an calendar that is frequently the source for Momaday's historical voice in *The Way to Rainy Mountain*. Mooney and Captain Scott compared notes on information they collected from the Kiowas about the similar records.

The calendar keeper arranged his pictographs in a continuous spiral: winter events appear above an upright black bar indicating dead vegetation, and summer events appear above a picture of the medicine lodge, sacred center of the annual religious ceremony. During the long nights of winter camp Kiowas brought out the calendars for telling oral history in the circle about the tipi fire. My students and I imagine what might have been said on such a night. What did the Kiowas say, for example, about *D'a-p'egya-de Sai* 'Winter that the stars fell'? Dohasan drew three stars above the winter bar to note the memorable meteor shower that happened shortly before daylight on 13 November 1833. The Kiowas told Mooney that the entire camp was asleep when sudden light woke them. Running from their tipis, they found the "night as bright as day," with meteors darting through the sky. Parents roused their children, saying, "Get up, get up, there is something awful going on!" (Mooney 261).

As they study the calendar, students are always drawn to the radiant images of the Sun Dance lodge that signal each summer in spiraling years. This important event brought together all members of the tribe, who lived in small, independent bands the rest of the year. The ritual sealed spiritual and physical unity as the people engaged in renewing friendships, arranging marriages, trading property, and reciting heroic stories. The ceremony, held when the bison were fat, was always preceded by a hunt in order to feed the people and to provide the bison skin and head to be honored on the center pole in the Sun Dance lodge. Each Sun Dance site and perishable lodge lives in Kiowa sacred history as a specific place, albeit temporarily occupied, where imminent supernatural power met with humankind. After the four-day dance, the bands departed, leaving the lodge intact and giving the Sun Dance name to that special summer. These Sun Dance names reflect the pulse of tribal life. Some express exuberant energy: War Bonnet Sun Dance, Sun Flowers Growing Sun Dance, and Love-Making Spring Sun Dance. Others bear death names. In 1849 the tribe was ravaged by a disease so dreadful that people who woke up in perfect health were dead a few hours later; whole families perished and camps were exterminated, leaving their tipis standing empty. The Kiowas called it *Mayiagya K'ado* 'Cholera Sun Dance.'

Calendric winters speak of the relentless invasion of outsiders into the southern plains world. Twin tipis above the winter bar of 1864 mark Kit Carson's attack on a Kiowa camp. In 1867 the Kiowas, Comanches, and Kiowa-Apaches were forced to move onto a reservation. In 1874 the tribes made their last concentrated military effort against the invaders. Big-Meet was killed by the soldiers. In the winter of 1875 came the final irony, when the government confiscated ten thousand horses from the three tribes, sold them, and brought domestic animals to replace the bison. Killing a single bison became a rare event. At last, the Kiowas had to kill and eat their ponies to keep from starving during the summer named *Tsen-pia K'ado* 'Horse-Eating Sun Dance.'

By the summer of 1882, Dohasan, whose hereditary duty it was to secure the buffalo for the Sun Dance, was unable to find even one, and there was no dance. In the final decade of the calendar years, a somber echo resounds: 1884 No Sun Dance; 1886 No Sun Dance; 1889 No Sun Dance. Everyone stayed at home. In 1890 "Sun Dance When the Forked Poles Were Left Standing" tells of the Indian agent calling United States troops to disband the Kiowas as they were preparing for their sacred ritual, which the government considered barbaric and disruptive. Thus was Kiowa culture brought to its knees. Momaday argues, however, that despite the destruction and defeat, the Kiowas fulfilled their destiny as they had imagined it: "It was there. It was there for all of us" (interview, with Mueller). One hundred years later, my students and I affirm, "It is here. It is here for all of us." It is our shared American literary heritage preserved in the stories of a living Kiowa author.

Since many of my undergraduates have a modest literary background, I frequently open the discussion by asking, "What did you like or dislike about the book?" Aho always impresses them deeply. As we move from the tribal history in the prologue to a single life history in the introduction, students identify with this wonderful old woman in an almost mythical way. Perhaps their need for such an elder to love and respect in their own lives transcends the tribal, historical, and geographical boundaries. Students speak of Aho as if she lives for them long after they have left my class. I refrain from imposing too much analysis on their private pleasure with her. They select passages for class consideration, and by our final discussion we have identified at least three major themes: Aho's unity with the land, her function in the book as journey maker and storyteller, and her role as bearer of tribal motifs and images — especially the stars, the mountain, Tai-me, and the sun–Sun Dance. Students relate Aho's reverence for the sun to the supernatural sun motifs in the subsequent triads, such as the child bride who bore the Sun's child and brought divine power to the Kiowa world. Momaday tells us that Aho held the landscape of the continent in her racial memory, but scenes from her life near Rainy Mountain make her real for students. They are drawn to the small girl who saw the last Sun Dance, and they enjoy the mature Aho who welcomed the "old council of warlords" and their women to her summer home. After her death, the "funeral silence" juxtaposed to "final word" causes students to speak of the vacancy left by the death of their own family members. Aho dramatically linked Momaday to his sacred heritage and to the Kiowa golden age of history. As her grandson, Momaday also becomes real for students. As we discuss the personal stories in the triads, Aho may be the anchor for students' comments on family history involving her, Momaday, and Mammedaty. In addition to considering Aho's story, we focus our second lecture-discussion on other sections of *The Way to Rainy Mountain* and on Momaday's comments about his creative process.

Momaday is a great teacher as well as a great writer, and his essay "The Man Made of Words" is ideal for teaching students about the supremacy of language in imagining, ordering, and expressing experience. Storytellers and stories form the cultural matrix of his essay and our discussion. Momaday has talked of his first questions about Kiowa stories: "What are they? How is it that I have possession of these rare things?" (interview, with Mueller). This curiosity caused him to consider the oral tradition and Indian motifs. In "The Man Made of Words" he writes, "I began to wonder about the way in which myths, legends, and lore evolve into that mature condition of expression which we call 'literature'" (169).

If literature is the final product of an evolutionary process, then surely oral storytellers lay the foundation, and literary storytellers shape the ultimate end of that process. How is this process revealed in *The Way to Rainy Mountain*? We break this overarching question into parts: Who are the storytellers? What tribal images, metaphors, and icons permeate their tales? How is Momaday similar to, yet always different from, the other storytellers? Finally, how does he use the myriad storytellers and the layers of stories to create "literature"? Obviously, the old storytellers are Aho, Ko-sahn, Mammedaty, and the nameless Kiowas, epitomized in the arrow maker. They control tribal images, exemplify the book's structure, and demonstrate Momaday's theory of oral tradition evolving toward literature.

One prime example is the arrow maker. How does a man making arrows become, for Momaday, a man made of words? First, the man turns himself into a story that moves through generations of voices to Momaday as a child. The child loves the story and grows to an adult who still treasures it: "I have no memory that is older than that of hearing it. . . . The more I think of that story, the more I tell it, the more I see" (address). In the Kiowa golden age, the story celebrated tribal ideals: speaking quietly and facing danger calmly, acting cautiously yet decisively, making good arrows. In the age of "The Man Made of Words," Momaday writes for a linguistically sophisticated audience and explains that language must be "the means by which words proceed to the formulation of meaning and emotional effect" (168). My students discuss Momaday's other theoretical statements about the power, risk, and responsibility of language. When we relate his theoretical concepts to the arrow-maker story, it becomes an extended metaphor for human beings' survival through language. For the arrow maker, language is also his definition and destiny because he becomes his own story. Momaday has given a useful explanation for helping students understand his concept of metamorphosis for storyteller and story. In "To Save a Great Vision," Momaday writes explicitly of Black Elk and implicitly of all mythic storytellers. The mythic storyteller speaks in a formal manner and is careful not to intrude on the narrative. He creates himself and his listeners, through the power of "his imagination, his expression, his devotion to important details. . . . He is a holy man; his function is sacred." The storyteller will survive as long as his words survive: "The storyteller and the story told are one" (32–36).

Next, we turn to the arrow-maker triad in *The Way to Rainy Mountain* (sec. 13) to apply Momaday's requirements for a mythic narrator. We discover "literature." Momaday does not intrude on the story, and he moves it beyond the limits of time and space: "Once there was a man and his wife." The imagery is specific; for example, the words *aim, string,* and *straight* carry the zing of the arrow to the enemy's heart and to our eyes and ears (46).

In the reminiscence about the arrow maker Cheney, the personal voice also uses detailed imagery as it describes the lean old man in braids who paints his wrinkled face. The two arrow makers share the power of silence and speech. Cheney makes his prayers from sacred words. The *word* controls the fate of the arrow maker as he waits for *a Kiowa name* from the ominous figure staring into his tipi. Silence is deadly significant here, and silence is a significant space in Cheney's chanting. Finally, the mythic and personal voices complete a circular structure as the final line of the personal story, "It takes hold of you and will not let you go," seems to turn us to the arrow maker's mythic story that will not let us go (46–47).

Ko-sahn, another storyteller, is a woman made of words. Again, my students and I begin with Momaday's thoughts on his creative process. In "The Man Made of Words," Momaday introduces Ko-sahn by saying, "Let me tell you a story," and then allows us to listen to his imaginary conversation with her.

He evokes Ko-sahn by calling her name, and she tells him she remembers the first Sun Dance and even the Kiowas emerging from the hollow log. Later, she disappears into the language he has made after assuring him, "You see, I have existence, whole being, in your imagination" (163–64). Through Ko-sahn, ancient purveyor of the sacred earth, Momaday teaches us lessons about language, survival, and the land. If we are to survive, we must remember our moral obligation to the sacred earth. She demonstrates that we may survive through making ourselves out of language: we are what we imagine. We tell our stories to explain our experiences, and in a sacred sense we may reach for immortality by imagining ourselves through language.

Turning from Momaday's thoughts on his creative process, we again discover "literature" in the epilogue. Through Ko-sahn, Momaday demonstrates an evolving pattern from historical event to oral story to written literature. For example, we recognize that the Kiowa chronicle recorded the historic 1833 meteor shower. We see that Momaday imposes a prophetic voice on the chronicled Kiowa fear that the shower was dangerous and ominous. We note that he makes images more vivid: "With the speed and intensity of a driving rain, stars were falling in the universe" (85). According to Momaday, Kiowa oral history was so vivid that Ko-sahn imagined seeing the meteor shower. Then we discuss how Momaday achieves closure with a circular question: "And in her mind, did she see the falling stars?" (88).

Ko-sahn carries a second major tribal image—the Sun Dance. In Momaday's treatment of this motif, the living memory is transcended by the verbal tradition that he transforms into literature. Ko-sahn personifies the transcendence. His own living memory calls forth his visionary meeting with her, and she imagines the first Sun Dance. In the polished, literary epilogue, Ko-sahn chants in oral-tradition pattern as she tells how the people wore "beautiful buckskin and beads" and closes with " . . . oh, it was beautiful! That was the beginning of the Sun Dance. It was all for Tai-me you know, and it was a long time ago" (88). This repetitive cadence from oral storytelling ties the epilogue to the repetition of the final lines of the prologue. In considering the sun motif and other tribal images carried by Ko-sahn and Aho, students recognize that the two women lend a feminine symmetry to *The Way to Rainy Mountain*.

In our next stage of study, the class transforms the triads into a readers' theater performance. A trio of voices prepare a triad to present to the class audience. The lines come alive as students become the storytellers.[3] They also prepare literary and historical commentary, drawing ideas from our previous discussions of Momaday's theories, the storyteller's function in tribal culture, and sacred and secular history. Sometimes, they write their analysis and read it as a fourth voice.

Reading *The Way to Rainy Mountain*, discussing the history and the calendars, and performing the text enable students to observe Momaday's seeking, discovering, and expressing his private history. We discuss how he shaped secular and sacred histories in the book and how, in a sense, he created a new personal history as the various histories impacted on his search and discovery. Experiencing Momaday's process frequently stimulates students to search and discover, to invent, imagine, and write their family histories.

Sometimes a line from Momaday reaches out to a student. "Now that I can have her only in my memory . . . " (10) evoked this scene from a freshman student:

> Most of the family was home. My brother came running in the house, crying. He asked for his gun, and my dad said he didn't know where it was. Then my brother remembered where my dad kept it, so he took everything out of his pockets and put them in his hat. He told my mom he was going to kill himself, but she didn't believe him. Then he went outside, and right in the backyard beside the tree, he put the gun to his head and pulled the trigger. He spun around, fell face down, and died.

The style is not lyrical like Momaday's, but his loss of Aho brought forth thoughts of this student's loss.

Sometimes Momaday's family history evokes memories one or more generations back. The following passages from Lucille Wolfe St. Germaine's family history recount her father's and grandparents' encounter with school officials of the Bureau of Indian affairs:

> My father, George T. Wolfe, was one of eight children born to Abel and Sarah Wolfe. They lived on the small Winnebago reservation in Nebraska. "Little Georgie T.," as he was called by the white farmers, picked up the English language from his brothers and sisters, who had been sent to the BIA school located at the Indian agency in Winnebago. One by one, his brothers and sisters passed away, unable to withstand the scourge of tuberculosis. When dad was seven, his mother, Sarah, joined her children, leaving him in the care of his aged grandparents and father, Abel. Shortly after his mother died, Little Georgie T. was busy with his chores when he heard a wagon coming. Quickly he hid in the brush, and was able to see and hear the visitors, without being seen. The visitors from the Winnebago Indian Agency informed the elders that they were taking Little Georgie T. to school. Since they could not find the child, they told the stunned grandparents and father that they would be back the next day for him. All his clothes would be taken and marked at the school. My father was afraid. He thought, "If I go there like my brothers and sisters, I will come back in a wooden box like they did." Later, his father comforted him: "No, my boy, you and I will leave tonight." His grandparents soon had clothes, blankets, and a large supply of food packed in the wagon. Then they picked up their only surviving grandchild and with tears on their faces, kissed the boy and put him in the wagon. They must have known that they would never see their grandson again, and they never did.

Most of my Native American students call English "the enemy." Studying *The Way to Rainy Mountain* unlocks many students' memories, and they can write about their family history in a holistic way. Students create themselves on paper and slowly trust their written words in English. In *The Names*, Momaday explains this link: "I have said it; I have set it down. I trace the words; I touch myself to the words, and they stand for me" (93). As Indian and other students share their compositions, they often find common ground in family memories.

When my approach to *The Way to Rainy Mountain* works for students, they gain new insights about myth, history, and literature in relation to themselves. They realize that myth becomes history becomes personal reminiscence becomes myth in an evolving circle. Students also recognize the evolutionary process that moves from oral tradition to written literature, and they appreciate N. Scott Momaday as a great literary storyteller. Momaday warns that oral stories have been one voice away from extinction. Students believe that their metamorphosis wrought by his stories is one way of storing Kiowa stories for the future. They have become part of the process. After reading Kiowa stories, witnessing Kiowa history, speaking tribal images, and shaping personal scenes, some students turn again to the slim volume to read and to imagine. Momaday was once asked for suggestions on how to read *The Way to Rainy Mountain*. With wry delight he replied, "Someone recently suggested that the way to read *The Way to Rainy Mountain* is again and again and again" (interview, with Mueller). My students and I agree.

NOTES

[1] In his poetic essay "A First American Views His Land," Momaday explains the intricate network of rights and responsibilities that has been evolving between Native Americans and the American landscape for approximately thirty thousand years. Students rate this dramatic essay as a good companion to "Man Made of Words."

[2] Zo-Tom, Silverhorn, Stephen Mopope, and other Kiowa artists painted traditional portraits and scenes that allow students to see the Kiowa as they saw themselves. Two sources of Silverhorn slides are the Newberry Library and the Field Museum of Natural History, both in Chicago. Kiowa ledger artists appear in Karen D. Petersen's two books *Plains Indian Art from Fort Marion* and *1877: Plains Indian Sketch Books of Zo-Tom and Howling Wolf*. The "Kiowa Five" artists appear in Jamake Highwater's *Song from the Earth: American Indian Painting*. Dohasan's nephew gave his calendar to Hugh L. Scott at Fort Sill, Oklahoma, on the Kiowa reservation in 1892. He told Scott that the calendar had been kept in his family since his youth and had been originally painted on hides that were renewed from time to time as they wore out from age and handling. Scott's copy is drawn with colored pencils on heavy manila paper. A reprint of the calendar plus notes and references is available as a pamphlet, *A Chronicle of the Kiowa Indians*, from the R. H. Lowie Museum of Anthropology, University of California, Berkeley 94720, for $1.00.

[3] Students may add Momaday's "Tsoai and the Shieldmaker" to their performance. This story is complemented by Momaday's shield etchings.

The Way to Rainy Mountain and the Traditional Forms of American Indian Autobiography

H. David Brumble III

Momaday began *The Names*, the second installment of his autobiographical project, in this way:

> In general my narrative is an autobiographical account. Specifically, it is an act of the imagination. When I turn my mind to my early life, it is the imaginative part of it that comes first and irresistibly into reach, and of that part I take hold. This is one way to tell a story. In this instance it is my way and it is the way of my people. When Pohd-lohk told a story he began by being quiet. Then he said *Ah-keah-de*, "They were camping," and he said it every time. I have tried to write in the same way, in the same spirit. Imagine: they were camping. (xi)

This passage could as well have appeared in *The Way to Rainy Mountain*. In both books Momaday aims to write autobiography after the fashion of an oral storyteller—in the way of his people.[1] But one might well wonder just what Momaday had in mind here, since there was no autobiography as we know it among the preliterate Indians. This is true in the literal sense, of course: how could there be autobio*graphy* among preliterate Indians? But there was no tradition of extended first-person narrative either, no tradition among the preliterate Indians that could call forth a narrative telling the story of a whole life.[2]

The Indians did, however, tell many different kinds of autobiographical stories, stories of their hunts, their battles, their failings, their quests for powers. Over the years anthropologists and Indian enthusiasts have taken down many of these narratives (see Brumble, *Annotated Bibliography*). Most are brief accounts of individual episodes in the life of the teller. (The published autobiographies of preliterate Indians that seem more extensive were generally narrated as many individual tales and answers to questions, and then sewn together into a longer, consecutive narrative by an Anglo editor—the seams more or less visible according to the editor's predilections.)

Some of these traditional, non-Western autobiographical narratives seem particularly useful as analogies for N. Scott Momaday's *Way to Rainy Mountain*. I have found that these stories can help students to enter into Momaday's narrative assumptions, to appreciate Momaday's discontinuous style. But three qualifications are in order. In the first place, I am not claiming that Momaday had read these narratives; indeed, Momaday has told me that he had read virtually none of the published Indian autobiographies by the time he began work on *The Way to Rainy Mountain* (personal interview). Second, to read these narratives is to miss much that would have been a part of the original oral performances (Hymes, "Discovering," *In Vain*; Tedlock, *Finding*,

"Toward an Oral Poetics," *Spoken Word*). Finally, there were certainly other, non-Indian influences on Momaday's style. Faulkner, for example, must also have influenced Momaday's decision to experiment with discontinuous narrative and multiple points of view.[3]

With these qualifications in mind, I want to examine autobiographical narratives that can enhance students' understanding of what Momaday is about. For Momaday is trying, in *The Way to Rainy Mountain*, to give his literate audience a sense of what it is like to experience stories in an oral culture, a sense of what it might mean to conceive of the self in an ancient way. Let us first turn to the coup tales.

The coup tales were special versions of war stories, the "authorized" versions.[4] In general, a Plains warrior could count as coups only such feats as his tribe recognized and graded as coups. And only such coups was he allowed to recount in public. In the Plains tribes, for example, a warrior's right to recount his war honors was carefully monitored, and precautions were taken to discourage fraudulent claims. On important occasions at least one witness would be on hand to corroborate what was being told. Warriors could—and frequently did—tell the story of their part in this battle or that with all the trappings of the storyteller's art. But warriors were called on to recite their coups—all their coups—in many different situations for many reasons. Often they were required to recount their coups as a condition of their participation in certain rituals. Warriors sometimes recounted their coups to taunt the enemy in the tense moments before the battle was joined (Denig 550). Among the Cheyenne alone there were more than a hundred ritual situations that called for the ceremonial telling of coup tales (Hoebel 75).

Since a warrior usually recounted all his coups, one after another, the individual tales were generally brief. The coup tales may be distinguished, then, from the more elaborate, more detailed versions of the same stories that might be told about the campfire of a winter's eve. Coup tales were formal instruments, recited again and again, usually in formal circumstances, always intended to establish who the teller *was*; they gained and maintained for the warrior the place that was due him in the tribe. Fortunately, a fair number of these coup tales have been preserved. In a monograph on the Sarsi Sun Dance, for example, the anthropologist Pliny Earle Goddard included three tales by Eagle-ribs (born c. 1840). Goddard tells us that he published these tales just as Eagle-ribs dictated them (through an interpreter) "probably in the form in which he was accustomed to recite them in the Sun Dance lodge" (281). Here follow two of the three:

> The two tribes, Blackfoot and Sarsi, went to fight the Cree who had built and were occupying a fort. During the fight a Cree was seen lying [dead]. Then I with a Blackfoot old man caught hold of the body. I tore one side of his scalp and stabbed him in the back many times, while I was stabbing him with a knife the Cree were shooting at me but they did not hit me. On this account I am called a chief.

When I was over there, there were camps in two places. Three of us were going along in advance. I saw them coming toward us. We came back just as they were finishing putting up the lodges. I called to them: "they are coming toward us." Notwithstanding this we hurried with the setting up of a tipi and charged them. A Cree man threw his wife on a horse, but while his horse was running young men came up to her and killed her. My brothers and I killed her husband. I caught the man's scalp just as he fell and tore off one side of it. I stabbed him in the back with a knife only twice. This we did at that time.   (281)

Eagle-ribs provides no story of his childhood to show how he became the sort of warrior who could accomplish such deeds; he provides no summing up, no explanation of what these stories mean in relation to his aspirations, no statement of how these experiences relate to other experiences. Eagle-ribs tells his coup tales and leaves it to his audience to work out for themselves a sense of just who he is, of his standing within the tribe, of his standing as a man and a warrior. In a nearly literal sense he *is* the sum total of the coup tales he has to tell. After the next battle, Eagle-ribs will have another coup to tell—and so his audience, his people, will have to reformulate their sense of just who he is. The coup tales are the formal instrument of his self-actualization. The analogy with Momaday is nearly exact. In "The Man Made of Words"—his own commentary on *Rainy Mountain*—Momaday writes that storytelling is "an act by which man strives to realize his capacity for wonder, meaning and delight" (168). Moreover, we are defined by the stories we tell:

> [Storytelling] is also a process in which man invests and preserves himself in the context of ideas.
> . . . man has consummate being in language, and there only. The state of human *being* is an idea, an idea which man has of himself. Only when he is embodied in an idea, and the idea is realized in language, can man take possession of himself.   (168)

All these assumptions may be seen at work even more clearly in *The Personal Narrative of Chief Joseph White Bull*.[5] White Bull (1849–1947) was a Miniconjou Sioux warrior. He counted his first coup in 1865, at the age when most children today hope to begin their careers at the steering wheel. After surrendering in 1876, he became an important leader on the reservation. He also learned to write, in a syllabary then in use among the Sioux. In 1931 Usher Burdick of Fargo, North Dakota, persuaded White Bull to write a story of his life. White Bull responded with an account that mixed traditional Sioux pictographs with written text in Lakota, in the syllabary. We owe the published version, which combines pictographs and Lakota text with an English translation and astute commentary, to James Howard. Howard provides the following translations to the texts accompanying the pictographs entitled, respectively, "White Bull Recovering a Body" and "White Bull North of Hill-like-a-bear":

> This is White Bull recovering a body. This Cheyenne had been shot down. I went right out in the middle of things again and got him. The Cheyennes were very glad about this. It was very hard, my friends, but I did it just as I have described it. Everything I tell you is the truth, and you have seen that I did it, my friends. This was a battle where I was right in the middle of the action, my friend. It was on Rosebud Creek that this big battle took place. It was a hard fight. I was twenty-six years old at the time, friend. There were soldiers, Shoshonis, and Crows who came charging us, and a lot of men were fighting. The gunfire was heavy. This man was named Sunrise. He was a Cheyenne, my friend. (67)

> This is White Bull. It was north of the Hill-like-a-bear [Bear Butte] where there was an enemy camp. I took it from that camp. There were ten of us Lakotas who went on this raid. They were probably Crow Indians and they really chased us hard. We had a running fight with them and got away. It was a successful raid. I was twenty-three years old at the time. Now I have arrived at the age of eighty-one, August 11, 1931. When we were close to the camp they kept up a heavy fire. (74)

White Bull records his name on almost every page. He also repeats, although not so often, that he is the son of Makes-room, the nephew of Sitting Bull. Again, one is reminded of Momaday—in his insistence on the crucial role that names and family relations play in his conception of self. And there is much else in *The Personal Narrative* that is worthy of attention.[6] But let us consider White Bull's form. *The Personal Narrative* is a collection of brief narratives and images. White Bull tells about more than his coups, but his *Personal Narrative* is essentially like the coup-tale recitations in its lack of connections, transitions, or references from one tale to another. Early in the book White Bull devotes a page to an account of his genealogy:

> I, Chief White Bull, say this. . . . My father was Makes-room. . . . Good-feather-woman is my mother. One Bull is my younger brother. . . .
> Good-feather-woman was the younger sister of Sitting Bull. . . . (5)

He includes a written version of a calendar history.[7] Late in the book he provides a picture and a written account of his tipi; he devotes one page to his work as a reservation police officer and another to the ceremonial camp circle of the Miniconjou. At the center of the book are his coups, one on a page. *The Personal Narrative*, in fine, seems to be just such a collection of brief narratives and verbal and graphic images as *The Way to Rainy Mountain*. It even juxtaposes tribal and personal history, as does *The Way to Rainy Mountain*.

But these two books—and the coup tales—are most strikingly alike in their insistence that the audience must construct a self out of all these narratives and images. And they are alike in assuming that this is how the tellers become who they are essentially. For Eagle-ribs and White Bull it would not have been enough to steal the horses, to kill the enemy, to count coup in dangerous ways. They must also tell about these deeds—not once but many times. Only by telling their tales can they achieve "consummate being."

The coup tales may provide the neatest analogies to Momaday, but there are other published versions of oral autobiographical narratives that may also help to chip away at students' Western narrative expectations—and so prepare them for *The Way to Rainy Mountain*. I would like to conclude by strongly recommending the narratives of Belle Herbert, *Shandaa: In My Lifetime*. Bill Pfisterer, Alice Moses, Katherine Peter, and Jane McGary—a confederation of scholars and Native Alaskans—tape-recorded Herbert and translated her stories. Twenty years ago they would have edited this material into a more-or-less consecutive narrative. Where there were gaps in the narrative, they would have gone back to Herbert to ask questions, to fill in the blanks, to provide transitions. But because of their familiarity with the work of scholars such as Dell Hymes, Dennis Tedlock, and their own colleagues Ronald Scollon and Suzanne Scollon, they aimed instead to find forms that would best translate oral performance. The book, then, preserves the order in which Herbert told her stories. And it preserves Herbert's material as separate, brief narratives. Like Momaday—and like Eagle-ribs and White Bull—Herbert leaves it to her audience to determine who she is out of what must seem at first a welter of tales.

NOTES

[1] In "The Man Made of Words" Momaday talks about how Indian oral literature may enter into a written tradition. For Momaday's relation to oral traditions, see Evers, "Words and Place"; Brumble, "Indian Sacred Materials."

[2] The shamans' lives—the stories told by the shamans of many tribes about how they had come by their special powers—come closest to the modern conception of autobiography. For Aua's shaman's life (Eskimo), see Rasmussen; for Sanimuinak's (Eskimo), see Holm; for a Diegueño narrative, see Toffelmier and Luomola; for Fool's narrative (Kwakiutl), see Boas. For a discussion of the shamans' lives, see Brumble, *American Indian Autobiography*, ch. 1.

[3] Schubnell provides the best and most extended treatment of Momaday's literary sources and influences.

[4] For the best accounts of the coup tales in their relation to Plains Indian warfare, see Marian Smith and Grinnell. For the coup tales in relation to American Indian autobiography, see Brumble, *American Indian Autobiography*.

[5] I take the liberty of referring to this book by its subtitle, because the title proper—*The Warrior Who Killed Custer*—almost certainly perpetuates an error. When James Howard published this remarkable book, he was convinced that White Bull

had, in fact, killed Custer. Raymond DeMallie, however, has recently argued convincingly against this claim *(Warpath* xx-xxii).

[6] For a discussion of White Bull's *Personal Narrative* in relation to the history of American Indian autobiography, see Brumble, *American Indian Autobiography*, ch. 2.

[7] The calendar histories—which the Miniconjou had in common with other Plains tribes—were pictographic tribal records, with one image a year (or, in some calendar histories, one a month). The images served the tribal historians as mnemonics. The best account of the calendars is still Mooney's *Calendar History*.

CRITICAL CONTEXTS: FORMS

Exploring the Ways to Rainy Mountain

Joan Henley

> . . . the way to Rainy Mountain is preeminently the
> history of an idea, man's idea of himself. . . .

With this passage from the prologue to *The Way to Rainy Mountain*, N. Scott
Momaday identifies one dimension of his cultural and personal memoir. It
is an epistemological exploration, an investigation of the ways available to human beings to understand themselves and the world around them. From this
perspective the story is not only about Momaday and the Kiowas, it is about
all of us. In Momaday's words, it probes "the experience of the mind" and
the manner in which "traditions are conceived, developed and interfused"
(4). If Rainy Mountain represents the object of a quest, the destination of
a journey, Momaday's book, through its distinctive form, explores the paths
along which we move to get there.

Approaching the work as a study of the processes by which knowledge is
acquired and transmitted has special value for students who come to it in
settings other than the traditional literature course. When looked at this way,
the book functions effectively in a general humanities, or interdisciplinary,
context, one that emphasizes the work's status as a cultural document. The
narrative raises issues that students can relate to studies in other disciplines
and also to their outside experiences. *The Way to Rainy Mountain*, used as
a mechanism for examining learning itself, encourages readers to think about
the sources of their own self-conceptions.

Such a study begins, of course, with a close reading of the text and a consideration of its unique configuration. The complicated structure of *The Way
to Rainy Mountain* initially baffles students. The central portions of the text

are composed of numbered sections, which are further divided into three parts marked by different typefaces. This unorthodox form—the graphic variation of the individual pages—constitutes an intellectual puzzle. A strategy that responds to this challenge is to work inductively, taking each section and trying to figure out what the parts have in common and what differentiates them. At this point the reading is horizontal, focusing on the numbered sections.

The result of this first reading will be the identification of thematic correspondences between the parts of the sections, correspondences that will most probably be content-centered. All three parts of section 3, for example, contain references to dogs; the parts of section 13 all mention arrows and those who make them. Not all the sections yield their meanings easily, however; a number of sections permit differing interpretations. Section 7 exemplifies these elusive portions of the text. What is the commonality in this section? Is it, as Robert Berner has suggested, division—the boy split into two boys, the horse separated from the rider, the author separate from his reflection in the water (64)? Or is it a variation on the theme of "man's idea of himself": self-reflexiveness, contemplation of one part of the self by another?

It is useful to encourage students to begin looking not only at the content of the sections but at the verbal texture as well. What special locutions and what rhetorical devices are used in each part? Most important for this reading, which is focused on the ways of knowing: By what authority are statements made? In what does their power reside? The reader needs to attend both to the information that Momaday is presenting and to the methods of presentation themselves.

To consider issues like these, students should adopt a different analytical strategy. Instead of reading horizontally through the text, they now need to read vertically through the typefaces, characterizing the materials found in each setting. In this way they discover commonality, not in the individual sections, but in the parts of each section that have the same formal qualities.

This strategy educes categories that may then be defined: one typeface may be designated as myth or legend, another as history or anthropology, the third as personal experience or reminiscence. But the identification of these categories does not exhaust the suggestiveness of Momaday's structure. Further questions can now be taken up. How should these categories be regarded? What is the significance of this taxonomy?

Psychological anthropology offers a way of pursuing answers to these questions. In a classic study, *Personality in Nature, Society and Culture*, Clyde Kluckhohn and Henry A. Murray introduce their discussion of the determinants of personality with the following axioms:

> Every person is in certain respects like all other persons.
> Every person is in certain respects like some other persons.
> Every person is in certain respects like no other person.

(In their original formulation, Kluckhohn and Murray use the generic masculine *man*, but the substitution of *person* avoids the problem of sexist usage.) The value of this scheme is that it calls attention to the different levels of human experience in a way that draws out the implications of Momaday's three-part structure.

The first of these statements reminds us that by virtue of being human we all share certain circumstances. The most important of these for the study of Momaday are not our common biological features but our shared state of being in the world. All human beings must come to some kind of terms with their physical environment. All become aware of movement over time as they progress from birth through the stages of life to death. And finally all develop some sense of the relation between the self and other selves, as they learn from other human beings how to live in the world.

The second statement points out that we obviously resemble some people more than we do others. This cultural clustering is seen most easily in national identifications, but there are many other bases of association, such as class, profession, or skill. The most important of these groupings for Momaday's work is the tribe, the special Kiowa identity that is defined in *The Way to Rainy Mountain.*

Finally, each individual is unique. No one person's experience exactly replicates that of another. Genetic endowment and environment and event come together in a particular conformation that will never be repeated. Access to the special vision of the individual, then, is dependent on the shared media of communication, and language is the most critical of these means of sharing.

Kluckhohn and Murray's schema focuses attention on the different types and qualities of human experience: the panhuman, the cultural, and the personal. When this perspective is taken back to the text of *The Way to Rainy Mountain*, the three-part sections emerge as three ways of experiencing meaning and gaining knowledge.

In the first part of each section Momaday presents traditional Kiowa myths, which function on the panhuman level of meaning. Some of the stories are explanatory, recounting the past, showing how things came to be as they are. The origin myth in the first section explains not only how the Kiowas emerged into the world but also why the tribe is relatively small. Other myths explain the derivation of words (sec. 2) and the importance of treating dogs well (sec. 3), and a sequence of stories explains the source of the Kiowas' special relation to the sun and to the sacred object of their religion, Tai-me (secs. 4–10).

A number of the myths are admonitory. They warn of the dangers of unwise actions, like those of the brother who ate the mysterious meat (sec. 11) and of the people who created an animal they could not control (sec. 14). And they portray the consequences of unbridled emotions—curiosity (sec. 17) and fear (sec. 20). A third type of mythic story is exemplary. These stories illustrate ways of outwitting enemies, through craft and cunning (secs. 12 and 13), and of dealing with threats to the social order, primarily those represented by unfaithful wives (secs. 13, 16). There are also descriptions of heroic feats (sec. 19).

The stories in the mythic mode demonstrate one dimension of the search for meaning. They use narrative to outline the relation of members of the group to one another and to the environment and the forces that are perceived to control the group. This function satisfies the universal human need to make sense out of life in the world. It may seem paradoxical to assert that this portion of the section, seemingly the most remote and exotic, is the universal dimension of the narrative. But the universal application is found not in the content but in the function of these stories.

Students find this idea easier to accept when they consider analogues to the Kiowa stories in their own cultural traditions. Stories of metamorphosis (sec. 11) and of marriage between gods and humans (sec. 4) are familiar from Greek mythology. The monster who is outwitted in the cave (sec. 8) recalls Odysseus's encounter with the Cyclops, and the buffalo with horns of steel and a vulnerable heel (sec. 16) resonates with the fate of Achilles. Woman's disobeying of the god's prohibition (sec. 5) is analogous to the story of Eve in the garden, and the story of the acquisition of Tai-me (sec. 10) echoes the encounter of Moses with the deity and the calling of the chosen people.

The sacred being who converts his substance into nourishment for his followers (sec. 9) recalls the significance of the Eucharist to Christians; the transformation of an archetypal rebel into a water monster (sec. 11) suggests Satan's metamorphosis into a reptile in *Paradise Lost*. The killing of a powerful male progenitor (sec. 9) reverberates with both literary allusions (Oedipus) and psychological correspondences (Freud); the passage on the dangers of curiosity (sec. 18) has analogues in fairy tales; what happens when human beings create something they cannot control (sec. 14) is played out in the numerous variants of the Frankenstein story.

These parallels, many of which will occur to students as they read, support the idea that one way to know Rainy Mountain is through the narratives that have come down from the distant past, narratives that are designed to help humans think about their situation. Looking at the language of these stories adds to an understanding of their significance. "This is how it was," "This is why," "This is what they knew," "That is how you know." These statements establish the authority of the mythic mode: this is the wisdom handed down from previous to succeeding generations. "Once upon a time" is a notification in our tradition of this kind of story, and there are similar cues in the stories Momaday relates: "Long ago," "A long time ago," "Once." Another cue is the interjected expression, "you know" or "you see," which calls attention to the shared status of these narratives.

"Every person is . . . like some other persons." This is the cultural level of inquiry, which centers on the characterization of a group, the description of its practices, and the record of its activities. In *The Way to Rainy Mountain* the historical mode of learning is presented in the second panel of each three-part section. Here, in contrast to the mythic mode, we find dates, names, and references to specific events: "In the winter of 1848–49 . . . in the vicinity of Bent's Fork, Colorado" (19); "In the autumn of 1874 . . . towards the Staked

Plains" (27); "During the Sun Dance of 1843" (59). The information found here is drawn from studies of the customs, social structure, and rituals of the group and constitutes a definition of group identity. Material objects also become important: artifacts are examined; paintings and photographs are studied.

The historical mode, like the mythic mode, has its characteristic locutions. The voice does not speak *for* the group; it speaks *of* the group. The point of view is detached; the rhetorical stance is that of the observer. Statements are authorized in a different way: "It was once a custom" (17); "According to ancient custom" (19); "Tradition has it" (21). In this category of knowledge, the author has recourse to the testimony of authorities: he cites Mooney, the anthropologist, and adduces the paintings of Catlin. The language of scholarship injects itself; such formulations as Mooney's "It is unnecessary to dilate upon" (61) are contrasted, by inference, to the language of myth, and the intellectual relation of the materials in the second mode to those in the first is made clear by a reference like "In another and perhaps older version of the story" (35).

"Every person is . . . like no other person." In the third panel of each section the author gives expression to his own special vision. These entries are composed of memories of personal experiences, sensory impressions, and portraits of family members. The figures who loom large are Momaday's grandfather, his grandmother, his father. The descriptions in this category, unlike those in the second category, are not of cultural practices but rather of the author's responses to the natural world and to the places and people he has known. The past invoked here is the personal past, the memory of incidents and impressions: "I have walked in a mountain meadow" (23); "Once I went with my father and grandmother to see the Tai-me bundle" (37); "One day late in the afternoon I walked about among the headstones at Rainy Mountain Cemetery" (45).

This level of experience also has its own characteristic language. It is first the language of the senses: "I have seen," "I have heard." Then it is the language of reflection: "I looked and thought," "I remembered." In many places the authorization of this information seems tentative; the phrases "I think" and "it seemed" recur. But at other times the authority of this mode of experience is asserted forcefully: "now I see the earth as it really is" (17); "I know of spiders" (27); "In my mind I can see that man as if he were there now" (47); "I know what it is, on a hot day in August or September, to ride into a bank of cold fresh rain" (67).

By structuring the narrative into three-part sections, Momaday encourages us to think about the kinds of knowledge we have access to and the authority on which that knowledge is founded. But his presentation is not a reductive one. He makes clear, especially toward the end of the book, the subtle and complex relation between these levels of meaning. As the author moves through his narrative, the distinctions between the parts of the sections become blurred, and interdependencies are displayed. Personal experience turns back into myth, and the author's own story assumes the didactic function of the traditional tales.

This merging of modes occurs in several permutations. In an interaction between the second and third categories of experience, the historical mode acts on the author to energize his faculties of imagination and interpretation. Material that appears in the second frame inspires reflections in the third. An example is the passage in section 15 dealing with the artist George Catlin. The second panel presents facts about Catlin's work with the Kiowas and his conclusions about them. In the third part of the section Momaday describes one of Catlin's pictures, the portrait of Kotsatoah. This description quickly becomes an interpretation, however, as the author imaginatively projects the character of Kotsatoah: "he knows beyond any doubt of his great strength and vigor . . . there is a look of bemused and infinite tolerance in his eyes." Catlin's painting exists in the cultural realm, but the author's response makes it an important part of his personal world.

There is a similar movement between the second and third parts of section 20. The second part recounts an incident that happened in 1861, when an old man of the tribe, Gaapiatan, sacrificed a fine horse to ward off the smallpox sweeping the community. In the third part the author meditates on that event and identifies with his remote predecessor: "I think I know how much he loved that animal; I think I know what was going on in his mind."

This movement between the historical and personal modes becomes an actual fusion in section 22. There the historical data records the theft of a fine Kiowa horse by a Pawnee boy. That the event belongs in the historical mode is attested by the time reference: "In the winter of 1852–53." But in the last sentence of the account the author's interpretation of the event becomes a part of the event itself: "The loss of that horse was a hard thing to bear."

Even more interesting is the relation between the first and third parts of the sections that develops as the narrative progresses. Mammedaty, who has been previously introduced in the third panel as a member of Momaday's family, appears in the first panel of section 21 in a mysterious encounter with a boy on the plains. The story has definite echoes of the earlier stories in the mythic mode, which recount strange events with supernatural overtones. Mammedaty appears to have earned a place in the company of heroic progenitors whose exploits are recalled in the traditional tales. But in the third part of section 21 the same story appears in the personal entry: "Mammedaty saw four things that were truly remarkable. This head of the child was one, and the tracks of the water beast another." The indicator "this" refers the reader back to the first part of the section. The mythic and personal modes are here exploiting the same source. Furthermore, the story about Mammedaty, which has shifted to the mythic mode, now in section 22 receives the same notation as the previous mythic stories: "This is how it was."

Finally, all three modes of knowing are brought together in the person of Aho, the author's grandmother. She becomes a kind of synthesizing force in the narrative; in section 23 she is responsible for what is found at both the mythic and historical levels. In both these passages strange occurrences surrounding the Tai-me bundle are recounted. The first panel begins with the statement: "Aho remembered something, a strange thing"; the second records that "Aho remembered this." Aho brings together the separate strands of knowledge, and what she remembers also achieves the force of universal truth: "This is how it was."

What emerges from this analysis is an appreciation of the mysterious and complicated ways that human beings generate and communicate meaning. What also emerges is a sense of the importance and power of the creative artist in this process. The figures and symbols created by Momaday form a part of the human inheritance and may ultimately move from their place in the third category to a place in the first. They may be transformed from objects of personal reference to objects of universal reference, to be shared and studied by people everywhere. This is the meaning of the beautiful buried woman in the last section. She began as part of the family lore: "Mammedaty used to know where she was buried" (82). She had a location that might have been uncovered by historians and anthropologists studying Kiowa culture. But now "no one knows" where she lies. She has transcended her origin in the world of event and fact and has been made by Momaday into a symbol of his precious heritage. On this level of significance she continues to inhabit the minds of readers.

Through its formal complexities, *The Way to Rainy Mountain* offers an occasion for students to consider profound questions about what we know and how we come to know it. Looked at from this point of view, Momaday's text not only enriches our understanding of the author's relation to the Kiowa tradition; it also enriches our understanding of the means through which we come to know ourselves. "There are on the way to Rainy Mountain many landmarks, many journeys in the one" (4).

The Way to Rainy Mountain: Structure and Language

Robert L. Berner

The American Indian vision of reality, as has often been said, is traditionally structured in four parts. The four directions and the four seasons are models in space and time for patterns in myth and legend, in political and social structures, in religious practice, and in everyday life. The Cheyennes' Maheo, like the creator in many earth-diver myths, was assisted by four birds in the creation of the world. The Hopis, like many other Pueblo peoples, emerged into this world after journeying from the fourth world below. The sky worlds of the Winnebagoes belonged to Hare, Turtle, Trickster, and Earthmaker. Many other examples could be cited, and it is possible that Momaday's four-part division of Abel's story in *House Made of Dawn* derived from his awareness of this tradition.

In teaching *The Way to Rainy Mountain*, we should remember the universality of this characteristic preoccupation when we examine the element that may give students the greatest difficulty at first reading—the sequence of legends, historical glosses, and personal recollections that compose Momaday's three-stage history of the Kiowas. These three divisions ("The Setting Out," "The Going On," and "The Closing In") and the three-part structure of each of the twenty-four sections that make them up suggest that Momaday has chosen to ignore traditional Indian methods in this book. In fact, the question is much more complicated. For one thing, in sentence structure, use of examples, and even the Al Momaday illustrations, as Mick McAllister has shown, the book reveals subtle four-part patterns (22–23). But more important, Momaday's decision to give the core of the book and its twenty-four sections a three-part structure is related to what is probably his primary intention—his conception of language.

A convenient approach to traditional Indian four-part intellectual structures is the vision of the Sioux holy man Black Elk as it is outlined in the third chapter of John G. Neihardt's *Black Elk Speaks*. This vision is complex in its patterns of symbolism, but perhaps for that reason it offers students an easy means of understanding how an Indian religious philosopher could define the place of human beings in the universe and in time.

Black Elk understood the four directions, the four seasons, and the four stages of life as metaphors for one another. The east, because it was the direction of the morning star, was associated with understanding and wisdom, and because the sun rose there, it was the direction of the Great Spirit. Therefore it symbolized birth and the rebirth of the year in the spring. The south was the direction of growing things and of physical strength because it was associated with summer and with youth. The west, the direction of bad weather on the Great Plains, was associated with lightning and thunder and thus with the destructive powers of nature, but because the lightning brought rain, it was also associated with nature's life-giving powers. As the direction of both creation and destruction, therefore, it symbolized autumn and maturity, the stage of human life beyond the youthful vitality that precedes old age. Finally, the north, symbolizing winter and old age, was associated by Black Elk with "the power to endure," and thus with strength of character and mind.

What we see in this quaternity is an interrelationship of two pairs of contrasting elements. The east-west axis contrasts the Great Spirit with the creative and destructive powers of nature, while the north-south axis contrasts physical strength with strength of character and mind. To put it another way, Black Elk's vision relates the spiritual and material aspects of the world to the mental and physical qualities of humankind, as shown in Figure 1.

Figure 1

North
Winter
Old age
Mind, character, endurance

West		East
Autumn		Spring
Maturity		Infancy
Nature's power to		Wisdom, understanding,
create and destroy		the Great Spirit

South
Summer
Youth
Physical strength

While the religious and philosophical structuring of the world and of human experience in most Indian cultures may lack the complexity of detail that Black Elk, using traditional Lakota conceptions, achieved in his description of his great vision, the use of the four directions to define four aspects of tribal awareness is common. The Cherokees, for example, associated the four directions with two contrasting dualities. Whereas the north was associated with defeat and trouble, the south was the direction of peace and happiness. By contrast, the success and triumph associated with the east was balanced against the west, which was associated with death (Hodge 325–26). While this scheme may lack much of the subtlety of the concepts diagramed above, it is certainly similar.

The Zunis did not understand the four directions as Black Elk did, probably because the New Mexico weather was different from that of the Great Plains. The spring rains came from the west, and the cold wind of fall blew from the east; they reversed Black Elk's east-west axis. For the Zunis the seasons moved from the west through the south and east to the north. And because they were a peaceful people, without the warrior ideal of the societies of the Great Plains, they associated warfare with winter and the north. Summer (and the south) were associated with medicine and husbandry. But the Zuni conception of the east-west axis resembles Black Elk's: the east was spiritual and was associated with magic and religion, whereas the west was associated with hunting, that is, with the exploitation of wild nature (Cushing 188–89).

But despite these differences, there are enough similarities to show that, like Black Elk, the Zunis saw their world in terms of two contrasting relationships: the opposition of the spiritual and material aspects of the world (magic and religion versus hunting) and the opposition of the mental and physical activities of humankind (medicine and husbandry versus warfare). Though the Zuni year moved counter to Black Elk's, its seasons symbolized the movement we have seen: from spirit (east) through physical activity (north) and the activities associated with wild nature (west) to the summer activities of the mind (south).

The religion of the Kiowas, as it is delineated in *The Way to Rainy Mountain*, is understood in relation to two objects of veneration, the ten bundles of the Talyi-da-i ("boy medicine") and the Tai-me bundle. The former originates in the myth of Sun Boy, the child of the Sun who was raised by Grandmother Spider and who became "half-boys."[1] The Talyi-da-i, in one version of the myth, came into existence when one of the twins disappeared beneath the waters of a lake and the other converted himself into the ten bundles of the Talyi-da-i as a kind of eucharistic gift to the Kiowas. While Momaday makes no reference to the four elements of the story, it is clearly based on two contrasts. One, corresponding to Black Elk's conception of east and west, contrasts the Sun, the god who is the lord of the sky world above, with Grandmother Spider, the maternal figure associated with the natural world. The other, of the physical brother who enters the natural world while his brother remains among the Kiowas as a source of spiritual strength and endurance, at least partially resembles the north-south contrast as Black Elk understood it.

The other myth that provided religion to the Kiowas had to do with the appearance among the people of Tai-me. That creature, half animal and half bird, remained among the Kiowas, in the form of an effigy that was kept concealed in its bundle and was only exposed during the Sun Dance. This myth apparently appears later than that of Sun Boy as a development of the Sun Dance. Tai-me is the spiritual presence among the people of the sun itself, and the buffalo, the sacrificial animal of the dance, is the embodiment of the sun's physical presence. In other words, what we see in this structure is a trinity that bears comparison with the Father, the Son, and the Holy Ghost.

But by implication the missing fourth element in this structure is the buffalo herd itself. The Sun Dance was performed for various reasons—as an act of thanksgiving, as a means of tribal purification—but one of its chief purposes was to ensure success in the hunt. A single buffalo, as the sun's physical self, was sacrificed, and the Tai-me effigy represented the sun's spiritual self, but the dance was performed to achieve mastery over the buffalo herd. The Kiowa hunters could not be certain of success in the hunt if they did not prove themselves worthy in the Sun Dance. This presumably is the meaning of the story of the two hunters who find the mysterious meat outside their lodge in section 11; because it had not been sanctified by the Sun Dance, apparently, the hunter who ate it turned into a water monster, that is, became part of nature, while the other, wiser hunter was able to return to his people.[2]

In this connection, it is worth comparing the Kiowa trinity (sun, buffalo, Tai-me) and the buffalo herd, as well as the elements of Black Elk's vision that resemble it, with Jung's discussion of the Christian Trinity. Jung insists that the unconscious mind can be understood in terms of four "functions" and that psychological deformation is the inevitable result of repressing one for the benefit of the others. The Christian Trinity, Jung believes, is by definition a deformation of this sort because it ignores an important fourth element, Satan, and thus it excludes the natural world, the realm that Satan is assumed to represent, from the structure ("Psychological Approach"). The Kiowa religion, like Black Elk's, did not exclude the natural world; nature was not the enemy, outside the structure, but part of the structure.

The usual pattern in the twenty-four sections of the three major divisions of *The Way to Rainy Mountain* is (1) a Kiowa legend, presumably a story told to Momaday by his grandmother Aho, or at least associated with her because of her tribal identity; (2) a historical or ethnographic commentary on the legend; and (3) a personal recollection somehow related to the legend or the commentary or both. This pattern of legend, history, and autobiography can be compared with the three major divisions themselves. "The Setting Out" deals with the mythic origins of the Kiowas and with their acquisition of their religion. "The Going On" deals with the Kiowas in history, in their great heyday on the Southern Plains. Finally, "The Closing In" records the decline of the Kiowas, the end of their independence, and their final reduction to a condition in which they can be known only in memory and verbal tradition. The movement from legend through history to personal recollection, therefore, ends in a condition in which only the imagination—which is to say, only language—can restore the Kiowas to meaning. In other words, *The Way to Rainy Mountain* can be understood not only in the three movements—origins, heyday, and decline; or, legend, history, and personal recollection—but in a fourth movement, which is the work of art itself, Momaday's book.

Everything Momaday says about language in *The Way to Rainy Mountain* supports this reading of its structure. The journey of the Kiowas, the prologue says, is "preeminently the history of an idea, man's idea of himself, and it has old and essential being in language" (4). In "The Setting Out," the Kiowas name themselves from their experience of emerging into the world (17; sec. 1). The tribe splits, and the exiles are given a name (18; sec. 2). They acquire dogs when a hunter is saved from his enemies by a talking dog (20; sec. 3), and the brave *Ka-itsenko* ('Real Dog') warrior society originates in words spoken by a dog in the dream of the society's founder (21; sec. 3). Grandmother Spider comforts Sun Boy with a song (26; sec. 6), and her magic word saves the brothers from the giant's cave (32; sec. 8). Finally Tai-me first appears to the Kiowas in a magical moment as a voice (36; sec. 10). All these examples show the truth of Momaday's repeated assertion in "The Setting Out" that a word possesses sacred power and "gives origin to all things": "By means of words can a man deal with the world on equal terms," as Aho did when she said her word *zei-dl-bei,* which was her "exertion of language upon ignorance and disorder" (33; sec. 8).

In "The Going On," language continues to serve the Kiowas, though they have achieved such power on the Great Plains that they hardly need it. The arrow maker could kill his enemy because of the Kiowa language (46; sec. 13). The Kiowas do not fear Man-ka-ih, the storm spirit, "for it understands their language" (48; sec. 14). The man who is threatened by the strange steel-horned buffalo hears a voice that tells him how he can save his life (54; sec. 16).

But in "The Closing In" the stories are of defeat and disappointment, and, significantly, language cannot save the Kiowas from the destruction of their independence as a tribe. Two brothers who are captured by the Utes escape only because of one brother's skill and bravery (66; sec. 19). A great hunting horse dies of shame when its rider turns it away in a charge (70; sec. 20). Mammedaty shoots an arrow at a rogue horse, misses, and hits a second horse (76; sec. 22). And, finally, Tai-me falls to earth, and this mystery is probably related to the suggestion that sacred bundles become heavy when the people do not pay them a proper respect (80–81; sec. 23).

The movement we see here is from a magical time when language creates the culture of the Kiowa and gives meaning to their world through a time when language still works to preserve them in their prosperity and independence to the final defeat when language, like the Tai-me bundle, has fallen to earth. This movement suggests a conception of language itself. The Kiowas define their origins in myth, and myth originates in the tribal imagination. Language begins in the need to name the objects of the world, and every name begins as a metaphor. But just as the Kiowas emerge from myth and legend into history, so words lose their metaphorical power and lapse into mere denotation. Finally the words fall to earth, the Kiowas die as an independent tribe, and a modern Kiowa, Momaday himself, is left with the fragments of their experience as it exists in memory and in the scattered accounts of historians and ethnologists. But this is not the end, because the Kiowa journey, beginning in the emergence into the world from a hollow log, beginning, that is, in myth, does not end in the graveyard at Rainy Mountain. It ends and begins anew in Momaday's book, in his imaginative restoration of the Kiowas. The three major divisions suggest a structure of beginning, middle, and end—the birth, life, and death of the Kiowas—but it is the artist's task to create a fourth stage in their journey, beyond the Rainy Mountain cemetery to new life in a work of art. Language begins as metaphor, evolves into denotation, and may die if the poet does not breathe new metaphorical life into it.

The Way to Rainy Mountain must be seen as a profound work of literature, the meaning of which is well within the conventions of a traditional American Indian vision of reality. The structure that we see in Black Elk's vision of the interrelationship of the directions, the seasons, and the ages of humankind is the structure of movement in Momaday's book, in the Kiowa story it tells, and in the conception of language that informs it.

The structure of the interrelationships of all of these elements — (1) Black Elk's vision, (2) the Sun Boy myth, (3) the Tai-me myth (and the Christian Trinity it resembles), (4) the structure of *The Way to Rainy Mountain* itself, and (5) the stages in the life of language — can be seen in Figure 2.

Figure 2

	Summer	Autumn	Winter	Spring
(1)	South Youth Physical growth	West Maturity Nature's power to create and destroy	North Old age "The power to endure"	East Birth, rebirth Widsom, understanding
(2)	Twin who entered the lake	Grandmother Spider	Talyi-da-i	Sun
(3)	Sacrificed buffalo (cf. Christ)	The buffalo herd (cf. Satan)	Tai-me (cf. Holy Ghost)	Sun (cf. God)
(4)	"The Setting Out"	"The Going On"	"The Closing In"	*The Way to Rainy Mountain*
(5)	Metaphor (myth, legend)	Denotation (history)	Death of language (memory)	Poetry, i.e., new metaphor

A careful examination of this chart and of the way its elements relate to one another both horizontally and vertically will provide both the teacher and the student of *The Way to Rainy Mountain* with a variety of insights into the book, its structure, and the characteristically American Indian vision that it expresses. Students should always be reminded that Indian literature is not part of a vanished past that is "quaint" and finally valuable only to sentimentalists. In fact, this literature is particularly relevant to the age in which we live — an age when we must seek alternatives to values that many people believe may have led us astray. Whatever the complexities that initially present themselves to the reader, *The Way to Rainy Mountain* is accessible and easily adapted to a variety of classroom situations. Momaday's conception of language, which is implicit in the book's structure, should provide teachers of literature with ways of describing poetic language: how myth may be considered the poetry of the race and how fresh metaphor can be distinguished from cliché. Furthermore, as the chart shows, the book's structure—like the structure of Black Elk's vision that informs it—reveals remarkable similarities to the Christian definition of divinity. The analogy should be obvious to every student at the same time that it shows how the American Indian vision provides a valuable alternative to the radical opposition of divinity and the natural world that is inherent in the premises of Christianity.

NOTES

[1] Momaday presumably calls the boys twins because Mooney, apparently his primary source, calls them "twin brothers" (239). Maurice Boyd makes the point that the Kiowas understood them as "half-boys," that is, as "two halves of the original son of the Sun" (2: 5).

[2] Boyd collected another version of this story in which the hunters receive the meat because they deliberately wish for a buffalo in a vision. The rest of the story basically resembles Momaday's, but it emphasizes the sorrow of the hunters' parting, and Boyd suggests that the myth commemorates the early separation of the Kiowas and the Crows (2: 131–33).

The Way to Rainy Mountain:
Internal and External Structures

William Oandasan

I have taught contemporary American Indian poetry for the Council on Educational Development at UCLA. The council offers courses that are not available in the regular curriculum and are not taught by the regular faculty. For example, I am an American Indian poet, and there were no American Indian faculty members in the English department at UCLA when I taught there. Since the council does not confer a degree, the students who enroll in these classes are usually interested in educational enrichment, in courses related to but not required for their majors or minors, or in general course electives. Most of them have not previously studied American Indian subjects. *The Way to Rainy Mountain* is well-suited to these students, to the institution, and to teachers with or without backgrounds in American Indian studies.

For the first class meeting I usually have the students read *Rainy Mountain* and at least the first two or three chapters of *House Made of Dawn*, because the end of the second chapter, "The Priest of the Sun," finds a counterpoint in the introductory material of *Rainy Mountain* and pertains to Momaday's journey toward self-identity in *Rainy Mountain*. Then I draw attention to the poems "Headwaters" and "Rainy Mountain Cemetery," which begin and end the book, and to the relation between the log in the first poem and the stone in the second. I present next a brief, informal lecture covering the general themes of the three major divisions of the book, concluding with the suggestion that there is a fourth, unseen part of the three-part design of each section of the divisions. (I discuss this fourth part later in the essay.) After a short description of the "many journeys in the one" of the prologue (4), I introduce this fourth part. Because this part involves reader participation, I often end the first class session at this point, emphasizing the need for students to review *Rainy Mountain* for the following class. The second meeting consists of a detailed textual discussion of the important sections of the divisions, sometimes closing with a quick review of the significance of the "many journeys in the one" and their convergence in sections 23 and 24, their confirmation in Momaday's vision of ancient Ko-sahn in the epilogue's language, and how this significance relates to language, memory and imagination, cultural tradition and change, and individual and tribal identity. If a third class meeting is required, an oral reading of the book, presented in relation to the fourth, unseen part of each section, can enliven the reading experience through dramatization and student participation.

This approach to teaching *The Way to Rainy Mountain* depends heavily on my understanding of the book's internal structure. The "gross structure" (McAllister 21–22) of *Rainy Mountain* is triadic:

"Headwaters"

Prologue
Introduction

"The Setting Out"
"The Going On"
"The Closing In"

Epilogue

"Rainy Mountain Cemetery"

Herein are three major divisions and three prose narratives, all within beginning poem-prologue-introduction and ending epilogue-poem. Similarly, there are three illustrations for each division, in addition to a beginning and an ending illustration. The division titles suggest the three main episodes of the Kiowa story, and each of the twenty-four sections consists of three parts, which correspond to the three journeys, or times: the mythic, the historic, and the biographic. The content of these themes changes emphasis in "The Closing In" from tribal culture and historic commentary to family memories and stories (Nicholas 154). The change allows Momaday to reestablish his collective, Kiowa identity and to confirm his individual, modern identity in sections 23 and 24. These identities are confirmed by a vision of Ko-sahn derived from the language in the epilogue.

In the journey toward his identity, Momaday must resolve three dialectics: traditional Kiowa culture versus Kiowa society today; his collective, Kiowa identity versus an individual, modern identity; and "traditional" versus "creative" mythology (Nicholas 150; J. Campbell, *Creative Mythology* 93). The conflicts that weave through *Rainy Mountain* are resolved in sections 23 and 24 and tied together at the end of the epilogue. Two compelling examples of the attempt to bring the oppositions into harmony are found in sections 10 and 16. Although Momaday uses memory to align his personal life with Tai-me, the central symbol of the Kiowa culture, by moving the sacred image in section 10 from mythic to historic time and to personal experience, this is not yet a confirmation of his journey or a resolution of the dialectical conflicts of his life. In section 16 Momaday traces the buffalo—the animal representation of Tai-me, the sun and spirit of the Kiowa people—to a personal experience with a buffalo that gave him the feeling of "what it was to be alive" as a Kiowa (55). But this experience is not yet one of spirit crystallized by imagination into language whereby his quest for balance is fulfilled.

In sections 23 and 24 Momaday resolves his conflicts in a conversion of "personal and cultural experience, poetry and myth" (Nicholas 156). In section 23 he understands and experiences—through memory, renewed respect, and an act of imagination—what Tai-me has meant to the Kiowa people and culture, a meaning that is symbolized in language by the "great iron kettle" at Aho's house (81). In section 24 Momaday links the mythic tone of the first part with the poetic creation of the third part by opening them with the same words, while maintaining a respectful relation with the historic second part.[1] However, after finishing *The Way to Rainy Mountain*, Momaday had second thoughts on what he had accomplished; it was then that Ko-sahn "stepped" from his "language" of the epilogue as a "vision" and "restored" his "faith" in his people, in the immediate accomplishment, and, most of all, in himself, a modern Kiowa with a reestablished connection to his tribal traditions (Nicholas 156–57; Momaday, "An American Land Ethic" 99–100).

The Way to Rainy Mountain can also be studied in terms of four-part structures. One quadripartite organization "provide[s] transitional devices and a means of cross-referencing themes and motifs" (McAllister 22) and can be found throughout the details, motifs, and counterpoints of the book. For example, consider the four beginnings in the "many journeys in the one": the "hollow log" in "Headwaters," "The journey began . . . " in the prologue (3), the journey that began when Momaday "returned to Rainy Mountain in July" in the introduction (5), and the beginning in the third part of section 1 of "The Setting Out" (17). "Structuring by fours can also be found in the larger units of the book" (McAllister 23):

    (A)- "Headwaters"
    (B)- Prologue
    (1) - Introduction
    (2) - "The Setting Out"
    (3) - "The Going On"
    (4) - "The Closing In"
    (B)- Epilogue
    (A)- "Rainy Mountain Cemetery"

Although the narrative structure of the introduction falls into three general parts, they are not distinctly separated like the three-part structure of each section. Nor do the three parts of the introduction correspond, like the sectional parts, to the mythic, historical, and personal.

A second quadripartite organization exists. "The alternating ordering into four, which is asymmetrical, is suggested by the summary of the prologue" (McAllister 23; prologue, pts. 2, 3):

    (A)- "Headwaters"
    (B)- Prologue
    (B)- Introduction
    (1) - "The Setting Out"

(2) - "The Going On"
(3) - "The Closing In"
(4) - Epilogue
(A)- "Rainy Mountain Cemetery"

The four beginnings in the first four parts provide textual support for this quadripartite organization (McAllister 23–24).[2] If these beginnings are crucial to this quadripartite organization, then this design would seem more appropriate:

(1) - "Headwaters"
(2) - Prologue
(3) - Introduction
(4) - "The Setting Out"
(1) - "The Going On"
(2) - "The Closing In"
(3) - Epilogue
(4) - "Rainy Mountain Cemetery"

While textual evidence certainly substantiates the existence of the first four-part organization, there is little textual evidence to support the second, alternate, asymmetrical quadripartite organization. Nevertheless, one can assume that what follows the four beginnings is historic, and this sequence is clearly perceived and underlined by the first and last illustrations and poems. The counterpoints between the poems are the images of the log and the stone, and the counterpoints between the illustrations are the two images of the seven stars, representing many beginnings and endings. These counterpoints signify the differences between the mythic and historic. McAllister divides the book's eleven illustrations into mythic (first five) and historic (last six), an arrangement to which he ingeniously applies interrelated systems of threes and fours to explain the functions of the illustrations (24–30). This division, however, may be too confusing for students to grasp in their initial readings.

A simpler, but not ingenuous, way to divide the illustrations to suit a quadripartite organization might be as follows:

(A)- 1st (Devil's Tower)
(1) - 2nd (cricket in a circle)
(2) - 3rd (spider)
(3) - 4th (water creature)
(4) - 5th (storm horse)
(B)- 6th (buffalo head)
(1) - 7th (buffalo and hunter)
(2) - 8th (buffalo skulls)
(3) - 9th (peyote bird)
(4) - 10th (horse impaled by arrow)
(C)- 11th (falling stars)

The functions of A and C are self-evident, and the functions of the first and second groups of four are naturally mythic and historic. B, the buffalo illustration, serves as a crucial pivot between the mythic and historic halves of *The Way to Rainy Mountain*; it also illustrates section 16. This section shows the transition of the buffalo, the animal symbol of the spirit of the Kiowa people, from mythic to historic to personal. Significantly, the buffalo in the illustration consists of both mythically fabulous and historically representative details: its angular horns, rectangular eye, and lightning motifs are fabulous; the face, especially the nose and mouth, is realistic — almost personal.

This quadripartite organization can be perceived also as a dyad consisting of the mythic and the historic and a beginning and an ending. The dyadic organization would not be guided by a principle of dichotomous order, even if the different beginnings of the journey start in separation. The dyad tends to be dialectic because the "many journeys" synthesize in the coalescences of the different identities, the oral and the written, the first and last poems and illustrations, and the other oppositions at the end of "The Closing In." In this dialectic synthesis the "many" become the "one," and within the "one" there are the "many."

As the overview of my class procedure indicates, an awareness of external — especially intertextual — structures can help students to understand *The Way to Rainy Mountain*. One crucial external structure is *House Made of Dawn*, in particular the "January 27" sermon of Tosamah at the end of "The Priest of the Sun" (117–25). The sermon, a variation of the introduction to *Rainy Mountain*, is titled — not surprisingly — "The Way to Rainy Mountain." At this point in *House Made of Dawn*, one could turn to *Rainy Mountain* as another chapter, or subchapter, of the novel.

Tosamah's and Momaday's similarities deserve close attention. The description of Tosamah can apply to Momaday: "big, lithe as a cat, narrow-eyed, suggesting in the whole of his look and manner arrogance and agony" (*House* 85; Velie 58); and Abel's friend Benally describes Tosamah (and Momaday) aptly: "He's educated. . . . [He] doesn't come from the reservation" (*House* 137). Although Momaday did live on the Navajo and Jemez reservations in New Mexico when his parents were Bureau of Indian Affairs employees, his experience was primarily an outsider's, and consequently he did not share the consciousness of a reservation resident. Furthermore, Tosamah expresses some of Momaday's anti-Indian sentiments from the days of his youth at Jemez pueblo (*House* 135–36; Velie 59). Hence, one is not surprised to learn that a man named Abel did live as a neighbor to Momaday at Jemez and that this man informs, through Momaday's memory, aspects of Abel's character. Although Tosamah is not a "caricature" of Momaday, he does "reflect one side" of him (Velie 59).

Another important similarity is the existential-tribal identity of Tosamah and Momaday. While Tosamah, a Kiowa, is a "priest" in the Native American Church, the peyote way is not conventionally Christian nor is it a traditional

American Indian religious practice. The church is, in part, an American Indian way to maintain a ritualistic religious life while living in the modern world. Yet, for Tosamah and for Abel, the return, respectively, to Rainy Mountain and to Tolawa pueblo is a remedy for their need to be complete in their self-identities. Like Momaday, who proceeds through his "many journeys in the one" toward his whole identity in sections 23 and 24, Abel begins to realize his identity when he returns to the pueblo to resume his life there, while Tosamah, for Momaday, is shed in Los Angeles in *House Made of Dawn* as a "side" of Momaday. The "Rainy Mountain" sermon, then, is a departing point for the "many journeys," with references that parallel and contrast with Abel's final return to the pueblo and the medicinal results.

Students also need to become aware of the Kiowa oral tradition, which is the fourth, unseen part of the three-part design of each section of *The Way to Rainy Mountain*. One reason this book defies easy literary classification is that it is derived partly from the oral traditions of the Kiowa people and partly from Momaday's own writing hand. As a professor of English, Momaday participates in a literate tradition, while at the same time the Kiowan oral tradition, which informs so much of *Rainy Mountain*, has been entrusted to him. The act of reading allows the reader to participate in the life of the printed word. When the class reads the sections collectively, readers participate more closely in the tribal experience, which is the foundation of the book.[3]

Nearly all students find the class reading rewarding. Before or after the reading, a brief discussion of section 13 can be fruitful. Besides examining the life-and-death consequences in this section pertaining to knowledge of the Kiowa language and besides dramatizing and discussing oral traditions in the class readings (Fleck 7), students can consider the power of the spoken word in oral cultures and the parallel power of the written word in literate societies. The point is that, whether one lives in an oral or a literate world, the lack of committed participation can deprive one of the literature passed down through the ages, of the effective means of communication, of the magic and vision that imagination makes possible through language, of the perception of how language created order from chaos, and, as in the story of the arrow maker and his family, of the ability to survive in a world that is occupied at times by danger and enemies.

Other comparisons may also be useful to students; for instance, they might consider the relation between Tosamah's sermon on John and the concepts and uses of words in *The Way to Rainy Mountain*. Or, students can trace the evolution of the introduction to *Rainy Mountain* from journalism (an essay in the *Reporter*) to fiction (a sermon in *House Made of Dawn*) to poetic-mythic prose as a journey in creative writing aimed at the creation of tribal and self-identities. For additional cross-disciplinary possibilities, see the "Other Works" and "Background Studies" sections of part 1 of this volume.

An awareness of how Momaday reuses his material and of how autobiographical contexts come into play opens up possibilities for many discussions.For example, Momaday's Billy the Kid suite, which shows his early identification with cowboys and his attitude toward Pueblo Indians, can be cited as one source for Tosamah's attitude toward Abel, and Tosamah's character can find sources in Momaday's involvement in the Native American Church and the American Indians in Los Angeles (Momaday, "Growing Up," "Cherish the Legend"). The relations between the various forms of *Rainy Mountain's* introduction and Momaday's essay "Man Made of Words" also suggest possibilities for examining broad and complete networks of external structures. The gestalt for the (loosely) modular nature of his writing and the relevance of his writing to periods in his life must be understood with references to Momaday's integrated view of the world and to his self-identity. For Momaday's creative fiction and poetry are testimony to the unique, developmental interaction between the literary and Kiowan worlds.

Of course, cross-referencing the internal and external structures points to the complex but often clearly delineated interrelations of Momaday's works and life.

The Way to Rainy Mountain expresses one American Indian's ability to establish his identity and art on many levels at once. It is a statement also of his people and of all peoples who desire to maintain ties with their cultural heritages. It serves as a beacon in the night directing those torn between their heritages and the fast, confusing life of the twentieth century; it serves as well as a model for young American Indian authors who are dedicated to careers that promise self-fulfillment but who are burdened with feelings of doubt and isolation. The revitalization of one's spirit in the warm earth of one's culture can give new purpose and direction to living habits if one respects and understands what has survived the test of time and assault. For students encountering American Indian culture for the first time, *The Way to Rainy Mountain* helps explain how and why American Indians have persisted over the centuries since contact with Europeans and have continued to identify even to the present with the ways of their ancestors. For not only do the ancient ways offer American Indians reasons to go on in the face of overwhelming odds, they also show us all how to surmount alienation in a fragmented world and how to avoid nuclear holocaust through communion with all life forms.

The Way to Rainy Mountain is a statement of one of the highest aspirations of humanity. As art, it expresses the promise of possible perfection in an imperfect world. It is an example of how memory provides information that imagination, through language, transforms into an essential expression of human consciousness; for, by maintaining contact with the past, memory can locate the present and chart the future; consequently, the knowledge of life evolving from the inanimate toward a growing awareness of its place in the universe has become imaginable. Thus, the fear of a nuclear winter has not undercut the hope that humanity can reestablish its ancient roots in its mythic and historical relations with the land, as Momaday has done in *Rainy Mountain,* so that life can continue to flourish on this planet.[4]

NOTES

[1] In "The Closing In" the third parts of each section also seem to link the poetic and the prosaic as they progressively become more and more like prose poems.

[2] Mick McAllister does not consider Momaday's reason for traveling to Rainy Mountain in July (intro. pts. 2–5) to be an impetus for the journey that begins in voice 3 of sec. 1. Rather, McAllister focuses on the retelling of the myth of emergence from the hollow log (prologue, pt. 2) as the third journey motif before the fourth journey that begins in section 1.

[3] The teacher should, however, caution students against believing that they have actually duplicated a tribal activity or that, by understanding *Rainy Mountain*, they can obtain a Kiowan outlook.

[4] Appreciations are extended to the Dorland Mountain Colony for providing the solitude to write this narrative.

Image and Silence

Helen Jaskoski

> The storyteller . . . creates himself, and his listeners,
> through the power of his perception, his imagination,
> his expression, his devotion to important detail.
> N. Scott Momaday, "To Save a Great Vision"

Literary analysis, I believe, is not something we do to a text but something
we do to ourselves. As a result of reading, minds may change; texts remain
themselves. The book creates its reader. This essay focuses on how *The Way
to Rainy Mountain* creates its reader: the expectations it holds out, the
challenges it presents, the models it provides. I maintain that *The Way to Rainy
Mountain* is fundamentally a meditative work: it is much more like a lyric
poem than like a chronologically ordered narrative. The demands it makes
on the reader are those of lyric: a meditative recognition of parallels, sym-
metries, internal resonances—in short, of circularity and reflexivity rather
than the forward thrust of motive-action-consequence typical of narrative. To
be comprehensible, the book requires cultivation of silence and of visual as
well as verbal attentiveness, and—paradoxically—it challenges us to participate in completing its meaning.

This essay suggests some ways to cultivate stillness and attention. It discusses the models Momaday presents and suggests an approach to *Rainy Mountain* through its parallels with visual art, its illustrations, and its two framing
poems. I emphasize receptive silence as crucial to understanding and experiencing the book; however, specific methods of achieving this attitude will
depend on the temperament and wishes of the instructor; on the size, subject, and composition of the class; and on many other circumstances. This
discussion articulates principles, then, instead of describing particular methods
in detail.

In *The Way to Rainy Mountain* Momaday the narrator talks about language
as the paramount human gift, a gift that permits expression of and access to
the consummate work of the imagination. But silence is the necessary condition for meaningful language. In any conversation, only one can talk; the other
must know how to receive, in silence, if words are not to be mere noise. The
narrator of *Rainy Mountain* does not explicitly discuss this necessary condition of silence but rather shows it to us, primarily in the "other" Momaday
we encounter, the character the narrator creates as he recollects significant
moments in his own life.

While the narrator's voice dominates the text, Momaday as character is never
presented as talking. Rather, we perceive this boy, youth, and man again and
again in attitudes of intense, silent, watchful contemplation: watching while
his grandmother prays by the light of a kerosene lamp (a scene in which mean-

ing transcends language), gazing reverently at the Tai-me bundle, observing a boy eating liver from a freshly butchered calf, looking into his grandmother's arbor, staring at hypnotically moving boughs appearing to sail overhead in a blue sky, walking alone in Rainy Mountain cemetery, listening to the story told by the aged Ko-sahn. The aggressive questioning we sometimes mistake for a search for meaning is absent here: instead, precise observation and "devotion to important detail" characterize the way this man approaches the world. The birds he hears or watches are not undifferentiated creatures but the male pine grosbeak, the bobwhite, the meadowlark, the robin; horses are a small red roan, a spotted horse, a black-eared horse, a small bay, a proud hunting horse that died of shame. The natural world is a world we make significant by paying attention.

The book itself is a small world also, and it, too, requires attention. The narrator's voice must be heard, and it is important to hear as much of the text as possible, whether read by the author on a tape or by the instructor or students. Attentive listening is equally important. Sometimes I ask students in a class to close their eyes, put down anything they are holding, and quietly observe the darkness for two or three minutes before listening to a passage. Hearing in this posture makes a difference. Sometimes before or after we discuss the book I give the following assignment: "Find a place, preferably outdoors, away from all forms of mechanical sound reproduction (tv, stereo, Walkman, radio, tape). Close your eyes for fifteen minutes and listen carefully. Then describe that place as exactly as you can from what you heard." Sometimes, too, Socratic questions can free people from looking for certain things and enable them to look at what is before them. Questions might include, What expectations did you have of this book (plot? adventure? conflict? linear sequence? chronology?)? Where would you shelve it in the library (i.e., what genre do you think it is? fiction? autobiography? folklore? other?)? Where do you think it starts and ends (prologue and epilogue? poems? titles? covers?)? What do you think about the illustrations? about the divisions and parts? Chances are that many students in any given class have not noticed these things.

The attentiveness I have been describing resembles the expectations we have of paintings and lyric poems much more than it does those we have for ordinary narratives with their linear plots and chronological time sequences. In structure and design, *The Way to Rainy Mountain* resembles a picture, or a series of pictures framed within each other. A diagram of the structure looks like Figure 1.

Figure 1

front cover

   title

     Full title and author

     Acknowledgments

     Dedication

     Contents

   title

   poem: "Headwaters"

     Prologue

      Introduction

        "The Setting Out"   R

                                      U

          I: [1, 2, 3]   N

                                      N

         II: [1, 2, 3] . . . XI   I

                                      N

        "The Going On"   G

          XII . . . XVIII   T

                                        I

        "The Closing In"   T

                                        L

          XIX . . . XXIV   E

     Epilogue

   poem: "Rainy Mountain Cemetery"

   design note

back cover

Whether an instructor lectures and draws diagrams or asks questions and waits for "discovery," it is worthwhile to spend a little time on the front matter enclosed within two otherwise blank title pages. These opening pages remind us, for one thing, that *The Way to Rainy Mountain* is the work of many hands. On the cover and full title page, N. Scott Momaday's name appears prominently, with the name of the illustrator, Momaday's father, below. The author's parents, Al and Natachee, are named in the dedication: besides contributing the illustrations, they participate as recipients, those to whom, first of all, this book is offered. Also named, in the design note at the end, is Bruce Gentry, the book's designer. Taking a minute on this last item is not so trivial as it may seem: many readers do not see the different typefaces and therefore do not distinguish the tripartite divisions of the sections (1–24) constituting the three center parts of the book. Finally, in the acknowledgments, we learn of anonymous "kinsmen" who told the author the legends and lore within the text. We as readers, then, are also in the debt of these unnamed relatives and elders, for in his book Momaday offers us what they have given him. The book represents a giving back as well as a giving out: Momaday learned much of Kiowa lore from his father (Schubnell 144), and *The Way to Rainy Mountain* offers back his father's gift transformed.

The patterning in the second part of the book, the journey part that begins with the first poem, is more intricate. The divisions and subdivisions form a set of nested frames, like nested boxes — or like the sacred objects described within the text, the Talyi-da-i and, especially, the Tai-me. Medicine bundles such as these contain precious and powerful objects carefully wrapped with sweet herbs in layers of special cloth and leather bindings. They are no longer opened; like the woman buried in the beautiful buckskin dress (82), they represent a buried beauty and power, and they are inaccessible to the modern viewer, who can no longer provide the context necessary for manifestation of their holiness. In a sense, *The Way to Rainy Mountain* is like a new kind of medicine bundle, made for a world in which writing turns words into physical objects.

We can compare the succession of parts within parts to a picture seen through a doorway of a wall with a mirror showing a view out a window. The inward journey through memory and imagination follows this pattern of image within image. In section 2, for example, Momaday the narrator remembers and describes Momaday the protagonist watching pronghorn antelope in Wyoming moving slowly across the plain, and then he remembers himself remembering at that time having previously seen against the hills a frightened buck leaping (19). The description of Momaday remembering himself remembering an old memory is like the later picture of himself as a boy gazing into his reflection in the water. The narrator takes us into the (no longer) "secret place" where we see at once with a kind of doubled vision: we look at the boy looking at his reflection, while we see both what he sees ("my mind fixed on the wings of a dragonfly") and does not see ("the great open land . . . a stone's throw away") (31).

Moving through the book and reading the parts in turn is something like looking at a frieze of pictures around a room. (It reminds me of going round the Elgin marbles room at the British Museum, not least because the bas reliefs of Lapith and centaur evoke the reverence for horses in *The Way to Rainy Mountain*. There is the same sense of a chaotic, violent, even tragic event, charged with heroism and glory, yet contained within the cool precision of the worked stone and the symmetry of the room itself.) One can move

around the pictures in order, pause, go back, see how figure and design repeat, regroup, change, or echo. This is a good way to consider *The Way to
Rainy Mountain*, moving through it, then pausing, going back, working around
and through the different themes. The approach will be new to many students and may require some explanation.

Such a procedure for looking at books or pictures requires an engaged
reader or viewer. Successive and reflexive parts are not connected by authorial
bridges: there are no labels, no little "editorials" to explain why one thing
follows another. Rather, the method of *The Way to Rainy Mountain* resembles
that of collage. In collage, materials of different kinds from different sources
come together to form the picture through their arrangement and variety.
There is no attempt to hide or disguise the nature or origin of each contributing piece; on the contrary, it is essential that each piece retain its original
identity as newspaper or cloth or dress pattern or nail or wood, so that the
viewer sees the materials in their essential materiality, as well as participates
in the picture by "putting them together" with sight and imagination into
a single image (Wolfram). So in *The Way to Rainy Mountain*, the author's words
and memories, the stories of his unnamed relatives, passages from the anthropologist James Mooney, Al Momaday's illustrations, Bruce Gentry's selection of typefaces and arrangement of text and white space on the page—all
require recognition of their unique wholeness and identity, and all demand
of the reader a participatory act in "putting the story together."

The eleven black-and-white drawings can tell us something about the kind
of participation that is expected of us. (One advantage in centering a classroom lecture or discussion on the pictures is that they provide occasions for
silent attentiveness, as students may be given unhurried minutes to look carefully at what is there.) As Mick McAllister notes in his detailed discussion
of the book's illustrations, the first and last illustrations balance each other,
like the poems that enclose the text. In the first picture, the seven sisters escaping from their metamorphosed brother have ascended to form the stars
of the Big Dipper and be "kinsmen in the night sky" to the Kiowas (8). The
picture illustrates the tale in the prologue, though the identification of the
fast-growing tree with Devil's Tower, which is pictured in the illustration, is
not made explicit but left for the reader to put together. Story and picture
also parallel the tale of the girl who ascended a tree to become bride of the
Sun (22), and this tale begins the sequence (secs. 4–9) that relates the Kiowas to the children of the Sun through the Talyi-da-i. The bear, whose loss
of language first warns his sisters, reminds us of the arrow maker who knows
his enemy by his lack of language (44), and both tales contrast with that of
the dangerous tornado horse, whom the Kiowas do not fear because it shares
their language (48).

In the final drawing seven stars fall from a cloudy sky onto five tents lined
up at the bottom of the page. The reference is to the meteor shower of 1883,
which, Momaday says, "marks the beginning as it were of the historical period

in the tribal mind" (epilogue 85). The first and last pictures mark, then, beginning and ending: from myth to history; from story to science; from living stars, women, and kin to lumps of rock, geology, and meteors; from earth to sky and back to earth. The way is circular.

The drawing following the introduction, of the cricket seen against the moon, makes an explicit statement about circularity. The insect inside the circle recalls the insect in "Headwaters," the poem that opens the journey, in which the speaker sees "A log, hollow and weather-stained, / An insect at the mouth," and both images then in turn echo the origin story of the Kiowas coming out of a hollow log. Most important, however, this picture of the cricket illustrates not an object but an act of seeing: "Once I looked at the moon and caught sight of a strange thing. A cricket had perched upon the handrail, only a few inches away from me. My line of vision was such that the creature filled the moon like a fossil. It had gone there, I thought, to live and die, for there, of all places, was its small definition made whole and eternal" (12). The figure is like the bat in Buson's haiku:

> The bat flits and flutters
> In the moon
> Over the plum-blossoms.   (Blyth 290)

Like Emily Dickinson's "minor nation" of insects in the grass, the cricket has no definition, no "being," save in the seer's "line of vision," in the power of the storyteller's perception.

This emblem of cricket in moon is a mandala, a kind of symmetrical design of worldwide provenance, and as such it is related to other illustrations in the story and to the emphasis on silence, concentration, and the mind's journey. The mandala serves in some Eastern religious traditions as a focal point for concentration of the mind in meditation. Often a circle divided in some symmetrical way, the figure finds its most well-known form in the yin-yang circle of the Tao and the quartered circle. It can, however, be any figure, or even a natural object, like a rose, whose form suggests symmetry, harmony, and a union of opposites. The mandala is above all "a vehicle for concentrating the mind so that it may pass beyond its usual fetters" (Arguelles and Arguelles 13–14). It is a means—a visual way.

Two other illustrations in *The Way to Rainy Mountain* are also forms of mandala: the tarantula following section 6 and the bird in flight following section 21. The three taken separately and together suggest sets of opposites and their reconciliation in the imagination. The cricket, a creature of earth, has "gone to live" in the moon, recalling the seven sisters who became stars and the woman who married the sun: unions of heaven and earth.

The tarantula represents Grandmother Spider, who lives in the earth and whom the brothers (Momaday calls them twins) eventually leave, as the Kiowas left dark forests to live on sun-filled plains. While the tarantula calls to mind Kiowa origins in the earth, the bird images a relation to the sky: swift, soaring, arrogant freedom and power. The figure leads us to Mooney's elo-quent description of the impact of the horse on Kiowa life (60) and to the Tai-me, "a human figure dressed in a robe of white feathers" (36), by which the Kiowa "shared in the divinity of the sun" (6).

At a different level all three mandala emblems are one side of another dyad, when contrasted with the remaining six illustrations. While the mandala can signify unity of opposites, its circularity and balance make it an icon of still-ness, silence, patience, receptivity—the earth with all its female connotations, the great mother of all (Azcuy 42–43). Opposed to the circle is all that is angular, uncontained, impetuous, arrogant, possessive, male. In the middle sections of *The Way to Rainy Mountain*, the illustrations image just these "mas-culine" qualities. Six figures refer to and represent accounts of violent muta-tion, unbridled power, impetuosity, kidnapping, heroism, and destruction and death: the water monster, storm horse, steel-horned buffalo, speeding hunter, skulls, and arrow-stricken horse. These are emblems of warrior and hunter, of courage and risk, attributes of an ideal of masculine life, as opposed to pa-tience and acceptance.

There is throughout *The Way to Rainy Mountain* a tension, a suspicion and wariness and conflict, between these opposing forces of earth and sky, Grand-mother Spider and Sun, female and male. The conflict between Grandmother Spider and Sun Boy reflects the tension throughout the book: "She saw that the ball was full of arrows, and she knew then that the child was a boy and that he would be hard to raise. Time and again the grandmother tried to cap-ture the boy, but he always ran away. Then one day she made a snare out of rope" (26). The snare of rope, the hollow log, the storm cellar: from these must the proud hunter desperately escape. The golden age of the Kiowas, as Momaday depicts it, centers on and celebrates the works of males. It is a world in which "the lives of women were hard" (58), where women are men's possessions, to be stolen, traded, given away, thrown away, or simply left to freeze, finally to serve men, having gossip as their compensation. Many feminists (students or not) dislike the book on first reading, finding little to admire in the vision of a people whose men appeared to leave all modest, nurturing qualities stuck with a pregnant woman in a hollow log, in order to make war "their sacred business" (6). The explicit masculine bias requires an instructor to confront the difficult question of the relation of moral and aesthetic values. These "male" and "female" themes seem intractably at odds.

Yet both sets of images are in the book, and both are honored. One ap-proach to reconciling and harmonizing these opposing ideas is to see them as part of the relation between language and silence, motion and stillness, storyteller and listener. Momaday identifies the "masculine" ideal of domin-ion and potency and pride with language, by means of which men can "deal with the world on equal terms" (32)—although a factual account of "the mean and ordinary agonies of human history" (3) tells us otherwise. Language is the responsibility and the power of the storyteller—the "sender of words," in Black Elk's phrase—whose function, Momaday says, is sacred ("To Save a Great Vision"). Such a word sender is N. Scott Momaday the poet, shaping his vision with eloquence and certainty and authority.

There is another Momaday, though, as we have seen: "the man made out of words," the character whom the words create, who recollects, regards, imagines, who contemplates painting, photograph, landscape, with devotion to important detail, and then moves beyond to the more perfect world of imagination. In this figure is seen the patience, receptivity, attentiveness, and silence of that other — "female" — side of life. This meditative man lives most vividly in the two poems that embrace and enclose the intricate, circling steps of the journey and that model for the reader the attitude the poet finally explicitly recommends.

Both "Headwaters" and "Rainy Mountain Cemetery" present the figure of a silent observer, witnessing and remembering and, above all, seeing what is before him with perfect attention. In each, the speaker stands silent, gazing at a particular landscape, conscious of the sun seeking its zenith, meditating on the mystery of mortal human life in such a vast and magnificent universe. In "Headwaters" the speaker reflects on the power of the upwelling ground water rising imperceptibly against the base of the marsh plants. He moves in his imagination beyond the physical water pushing implacably and placidly out, to reflect on its violent underground artesian sources. We remember the hidden power of the Tai-me bundle, making a great noise when it fell, or Momaday gazing at Catlin's portrait of Kotsatoah, willing the figure to walk toward him (53). And, we remember the shape of the book, with its "wild and welling" stories of heroism, betrayal, violence, bloodshed, games and races and hunts, its tales of turbulent life, contained within these two measured meditative poems.

At the end of the book, "Rainy Mountain Cemetery" returns us to the starting point of the journey, back from the infinite prairies to the final earth. In earlier passages Momaday describes standing in Rainy Mountain cemetery, walking among the headstones with names of kin on them, and shows the reader a single inscription (58):

> KAU-AU-OINTY
> BORN 1834
> DIED 1929
> AT REST

Paradoxically, it is in the written poem rather than at the graves themselves that the old Kiowa tradition is observed: "the Kiowas would not speak the name of a dead man. . . . The dead take their names with them out of the world" (33). Although the word *name* is repeated in the poem four times within ten lines, that name is never spoken; it remains the "nominal unknown," the mere tracing of a shadow on rock. We, like the speaker, hear only "the wake of nothing audible" and never learn who might be addressed in the poem—

Aho, or Kau-au-ointy, or Mammedaty himself, whose presence is so vivid throughout the book that I am always surprised to find, each time I reach the epilogue, that he died before the author's birth. The imaginary listener in the poem exists and is addressed, not in the grave, but in the heart and the imagination: he or she lives within and by means of this silent vision.

To write, to use language, Momaday believes, is not only a sacred but a moral act. At the last step of his journey he offers a moral for his story in the often-quoted lines beginning "Once in his life a man ought to concentrate his mind upon the remembered earth" (83). The passage sums up much of what we have seen thus far: it presents once again the figure of one contemplating a landscape in silence, the arc of the sun, the angle of the seer's vision. But most important, it asserts that the real way to Rainy Mountain takes us to the landscape within. It is to the *remembered* earth one gives oneself, to that landscape "in . . . experience" that one "ought to imagine" in touch and in sound and that one "ought to recollect" in all its changing lights. This is that landscape of wonder to which "the journey, intricate with motion and meaning" leads us: that condition of the spirit "where every time and place / Will take your thought for grace" (Bogan).

The Way to Rainy Mountain is a compelling work, but one most difficult to talk about, for at every turn it reaches beyond its powerfully felt and meticulously observed world and invites the reader to participate in what is ultimately a visionary experience beyond the reach of language. The book challenges all readers: living as we do immersed in a continual racket, we may find it difficult to perceive, acknowledge, and respond to a demand for silence. Young people may at first find the venture incomprehensible. Used to filling up the classroom hours with language, teachers and students may become acutely uncomfortable with silence. Yet, in taking up this challenge and attempting to experience this dimension of silence in *The Way to Rainy Mountain*, we not only experience the book more completely but, I believe, become better readers of all literature.[1]

NOTE

[1] The author acknowledges financial assistance received from the California State University Fullerton Foundation while this article was being written.

CRITICAL CONTEXTS: THEMES

Momaday and the Evocation of Identity

Gretchen M. Bataille

The Way to Rainy Mountain can be used for undergraduate studies as a vehicle for understanding N. Scott Momaday's approach to defining the elusive nature of "Indianness." Momaday has said he does not think of himself as "an Indian writer" despite the "evocation of the Indian world" in his work ("Interview," with Abbot, 31). This seeming contradiction is often difficult for students to understand, particularly those for whom American Indian literature is a departure from the usual classroom fare. When students are told that Momaday defines an Indian as an idea of the "self" ("Man Made of Words" 162), their confusion multiplies. Most students truly believe that they know what an Indian is; *The Way to Rainy Mountain*, however, disabuses them of their fantasies.

Students, particularly college students who have chosen to take courses in American Indian literature, are frequently mystified by the process of discovering their own identities. As college classrooms are increasingly populated by students with diverse backgrounds, confrontation with personal and public ethnicity becomes more common. The stereotypes of stoic Indian warriors or sultry "princesses" are destroyed when Indian students in Lee jeans and fraternity sweatshirts are in class with white students from Sioux City and Taiwanese engineering students. Each must wonder who the other is as fervently as each seeks to confirm his or her own identity. This is just the sort of class for which *The Way to Rainy Mountain* is appropriate.

In reading *The Way to Rainy Mountain* students become the audience for a series of stories, historical accounts, and personal memories. Initially students have a difficult time with the structure of the book, because they do not fully comprehend they are a part of it. They wonder why there are only three parts to each section when, as Robert Berner emphasizes in his essay in this volume, the number four is repeatedly stressed as significant in Indian literature and religion. Momaday divides each section into three voices, providing students with the opportunity to become the fourth element, the audience, interpreters of the meaning of the oral tradition through time.

I have taught *The Way to Rainy Mountain* in both undergraduate and graduate literature courses, as well as in an interdisciplinary undergraduate course in American Indian studies. This introductory course for students who plan to minor in American Indian studies allows for only a few weeks out of the semester to be spent on literature. I teach the course with David M. Gradwohl, a professor of anthropology. Gradwohl presents the material on archaeology, language, physical types, culture areas, and music. I am responsible for lectures on Indian identity, literature, religion, media images, and contemporary issues. Guest lecturers introduce students to Indian education issues, visual arts, and issues confronting Indians in Iowa.

A combination of materials, approaches, and themes, some of which are used throughout the course, are particularly valuable for teaching students about American Indian identity in general, Kiowa identity in particular, and broader concepts of cultural and ethnic identification: (1) audiovisual aids help students "see" and "hear" the land and people that define Momaday's identity; (2) legal testimony helps them to understand the complexity of the Indian identity issue; (3) information about contemporary American Indian literature introduces them to how Momaday's "colleagues" approach this theme; (4) biographical material about Momaday and his names transforms the general issue into a more particular and personal case; and, possibly most important, (5) a knowledge of an "Indian" worldview—especially the concepts emphasized in Momaday's poem "I Am Alive"—enables students to see the rich networks of personal and tribal experiences that helped him to imagine the identity articulated in *The Way to Rainy Mountain*.

During the first week of the course we show the film *More than Bows and Arrows*, which is narrated by Momaday. Students learn a great deal about the historical and political background of Indians in this country and are introduced to Momaday. Early in the course I discuss the stereotypes of American Indians perpetuated by mass media and miseducation and show the slide program *Inside the Cigar Store* (Bataille). Later in the course, after students have begun to read *The Way to Rainy Mountain*, we show a videotape of Momaday's lecture "The Man Made of Words," delivered at Iowa State. Because both of us believe in the impact of visual images as well as aural experiences, we also use a variety of audiovisual aids during the remainder of the course. Photographic slides of Devil's Tower and the surrounding terrain are useful to the students, as is the picture of Tai-me that appears in the Bureau of American Ethnology material collected by James Mooney on the Kiowa (facing 242).

In my initial lecture on Indian identity, I explain to students the various ways Indians have been classified, pointing out that biological, cultural, and social definitions are often at odds. I quote testimony from 1954 California hearings during which the California State Interim Committee on Indian Affairs sought unsuccessfully to answer the question "What is an Indian?" (Forbes, *Indian* 1–3). Jack Forbes's brief story "Only Approved Indians Can Play: Made in USA" demonstrates the ironies of Indian identity and provides a transition from legal definitions of Indianness to literary interpretations.

When I begin the section on literature, I know I have only a short time to cover a great deal of material, almost all of which is new to the students. After a lecture on the basics of the oral tradition, in which I incorporate the reading of several short myths and tales, students are expected to plunge into their reading of *The Way to Rainy Mountain*. When they return for the first class period devoted to the book, they admit their confusion.

At this point, a discussion of several important characteristics of contemporary American Indian literature often helps students to overcome their confusion. American Indian literature is significantly different from canonic literature in its focus and in the history of its evolution. Contemporary American Indian literature has evolved from an oral tradition reflecting and interpreting a particular worldview. Alfonso Ortiz defines this worldview as "a distinctive vision of reality which not only interprets and orders the places and events in the experience of a people but lends form, direction, and continuity to life as well" (qtd. in Beck and Walters 5). One crucial aspect of how this process occurs is expressed in the identity themes of the fiction. The search for identity and the concern with names appears in Leslie Marmon Silko's *Ceremony* as Tayo learns about his relation to the land and to the people of Laguna. In Momaday's *House Made of Dawn* Abel returns to Jemez to take his place among the runners. James Welch uses the unnamed narrator of *Winter in the Blood* and the pointedly named Jim Loney of his second novel, *The Death of Jim Loney*, to emphasize the isolation of both characters as they search for their place in contemporary America. Silko echoes Momaday's philosophy: "We are taught to remember who we are: our ancestors, our origins. We must know the place we came from because it has shaped us and continues to make us who we are" ("Old-Time Indian Attack" 213). The "working out" of this search for identity marks much of modern American Indian literature.

An acquaintance with contemporary Indian fiction helps students to understand *The Way to Rainy Mountain*, but to appreciate fully Momaday's identity formation, students must confront his own life story: PhD from Stanford University, Pulitzer Prize winner, and a Kiowa who spent much of his boyhood at the Jemez Pueblo in the Southwest. Here is an author who fondly remembers the many dogs around his grandmother's house in Oklahoma, who was sent to a military school in Virginia to prepare him better for college, and who can recall his awe at seeing the sacred Tai-me bundle. Momaday's parents, both teachers at Indian schools in the Southwest, expected their son to know English as a first language at the same time he participated in traditional activities with his Pueblo schoolmates. As an adult Momaday lectured in Europe and attended Kiowa gourd dances. (For more biographical information, see Schubnell's essay in this volume.) Initially, few students can understand the contradictions, mostly because they expect ethnicity to be fixed in time and place. Knowledge of Momaday's life undermines this simplistic notion.

A person is known by a name, and the complexity of identity is demonstrated by Momaday's several names. N. Scott Momaday, a name derived from the Kiowa Mammadaty and linked to the white man George Scott, was also called Tsoai-talee, Tsotahah, Red Bluff, and Rock-Tree Boy. Born in 1934 in Lawton, Oklahoma, his birth certificate identified him as Navarro Scotte Mammedaty, and the Kiowa Indian census verified his "Indianness" as seven-eighths degree (Schubnell 13). But it is not blood quantum that defines Momaday as an Indian. Identity is a combination of factors: myth, ancestors, place, and imagination. Momaday's Kiowa name, Rock-Tree Boy, links him with the geological formation vividly recalled in stories of the Kiowa migration. In this way he identifies with a place along the historical migration trail of his people. In his imagination he could become Aho, he was Theodore Scott, he knew the old woman Kau-au-ointy, and he could evoke the presence of Ko-sahn by saying her name. In *The Names* Momaday provides his personal statement about identity—who he is and how closely linked he is to those who came before. He dedicates the book to "those whose names I bear and those who bear my name." In the preface, he writes, "a man's life proceeds from his name."

Now students should be ready to move from the particulars of Momaday's life and names to the broader concepts of Indian identity and worldview defined in his poem "I Am Alive."

> You see, I am alive.
> You see, I stand in good relation to the earth.
> You see, I stand in good relation to the gods.
> You see, I stand in good relation to all that is beautiful.
> You see, I stand in good relation to you.
> You see, I am alive, I am alive.   (14)

Momaday celebrates life; he does not take it for granted. The repetition of "I am alive" leaves no doubt. He first acknowledges the landscape, the reality of earth and sky: "I stand in good relation to the earth." Momaday says in *The Way to Rainy Mountain* the landscape forces "your imagination [to come] to life" (5), but students sometimes have a difficult time evoking the landscape of a place they have never seen. Those who have never seen the Yellowstone River, Devil's Tower, or Rainy Mountain need visual images to help them "see" what Momaday is describing. Al Momaday's illustration of Devil's Tower provides a skeletal view of the tree that grew into a rock, placing the Big Dipper in the sky. Unless students have seen the movie *Close Encounters of the Third Kind* or visited Devil's Tower, they probably cannot project a visual image from the artistic rendering. Actual photographic prints or slides of the monolith force students to consider how and why stories were created: to fulfill the human need to explain the nature of the universe (see *Devil's Tower*). Although Momaday knew of the places through stories, he needed to confirm their reality, to "touch" the landscape and to imagine its past and his destiny. Momaday needed to experience the landscape, the terrain that his grandmother knew "in the mind's eye" just as Ko-sahn knew of the falling stars. He traveled the fifteen hundred miles of that ancient migration of the Kiowa people and describes Devil's Tower, where "the core of the earth had broken through its crust and the motion of the world was begun" (8).

The real beginning of the Kiowa story, however, was much earlier and is recorded in myth: "I stand in good relation to the gods." The religious stories of the Kiowas incorporate American Indian symbolism and values, but they also reflect universal religious symbolism and important concepts of language. The story of Devil's Tower and the transformations of a boy to a bear and girls to stars link the Kiowas with the night sky; ultimately their destiny is determined by the falling stars. Mammedaty's grandmother Kau-au-ointy was born the year after the stars fell, linking Momaday's family to a long history. The woman descending from the sky is killed with a gaming ring, the hoop of life but also the circle bringing death, for death too must be acknowledged as a part of life. The mysterious origin and powers of the Kiowa hero-god, the androgyny of this new hero, and the presence of the nurturing Grandmother Spider determine the mythic quality of their stories. The account of the two boys and other Kiowa stories reinforce Momaday's attitude about the relation between language and religion. For example, the boys learn early the power of language and use words to escape the smoke of the giant's cave (32).

For Momaday the word is sacred, it defines and gives shape to reality. Words are sacred precisely because they define reality and give voice to the imagination. Aho's use of *zei-dl-bei* to ward off evil is an attempt to direct reality or confront the unknown. The Kiowas talk to the storm clouds, and their stories acknowledge the unclear origins of language: "it comes from nothing into sound and meaning" (33).

The Way to Rainy Mountain describes the Talyi-da-i, or boy medicine, and Momaday's awe of the objects of religious veneration. His experience seeing the Tai-me bundle evoked the holiness of birth and death, the complete circle of life. Students are exposed to the synthesis of religion in Kiowa life as Momaday refers to traditional beliefs, peyotism, and Christianity as symbiotic in the lives of American Indian people. The universal religious symbolism of water is significant in Kiowa life from the beginnings at the headwaters of the Yellowstone River to the storms on the Plains. Momaday sees his own reflection in the pool of water, one of the boys disappears into the water, and water is a part of the peyote ceremony as well as of the sacred vision of Mammedaty. Momaday uses water imagery when he describes the "water-like touch" of his great-grandmother's (Keahdinekeah's) hand (35) and finally the deathlike silence of the dawn, which is "cold and clear and deep like water" (47).

Momaday says of the Kiowas, " . . . they had dared to imagine and determine who they were" (4). Imagination is the defining principle of identity. The aesthetic sense is critical, for it is the ability to imagine: "I stand in good relation to all that is beautiful." The power to imagine ourselves and to create our own realities is what Momaday communicates in *The Way to Rainy Mountain* and in his other writings. In "The Man Made of Words" he says, "We are what we imagine. . . . The greatest tragedy that can befall us is to go unimagined" (167). The issue of identity is significant in Momaday's personal life, important as a theme in modern American Indian literature, and a significant factor in any definition of ethnicity.

The "you" of Momaday's line "I stand in good relation to you" is more than his community and his Kiowa ancestors. Certainly they are crucial in determining who he is, but Momaday makes clear that his community crosses time and space as well as racial barriers. *The Way to Rainy Mountain* shows the integration of the individual with a tribe, but it also shows the integration of a place and a past. The coming together of these elements in stories constitutes identity for Momaday and gives an identity to those Kiowas who have gone before him and to Kiowas in generations to come.

Scholars in ethnic studies are confronted always by the elusiveness of identity and the demands to define the undefinable. Analyses focus on the forces of assimilation and the necessity for acculturation, and scholars debate the existence of the "melting pot" or "salad bowl" as metaphor for the American population. Scientific and biological definitions of blood quantum have little meaning, however, when one does not know the stories, the language, or the religion of a given people. Jokes about "apples," "oreos," or "bananas" are in-group ways of emphasizing that identity is more than skin deep. Race has been used and continues to be used as a political statement, sometimes for positive ends, but more often to perpetuate discrimination or point up differences. Although discrimination and prejudice can force a group to become stronger, as they probably affected the Kiowas when they were at war with various other tribes and the United States government, ultimately identity is forged within the group. The values and memories from the past determine identity in the present. In the same way, Momaday's childhood experiences determined his adult perceptions.

The structure of the sections in *The Way to Rainy Mountain* tells students of at least three ways of perceiving reality: mythologically, historically, and personally. But separation of mythology from the historical and personal proves to be untenable, for Mammedaty, a real person and Momaday's grandfather, is ultimately a part of all three voices. In section 21 the three voices become one, and in section 23 Aho too becomes a part of Kiowa myth. A story, according to Momaday, is the result of imagination being superimposed on the historical event ("Man Made of Words" 169). The Mexican captive Kau-au-ointy survives as a Kiowa because of the stories, and Momaday's mother, Mayme Natachee, created her own identity as an Indian from her imagination and from her links across time to the Cherokee Natachee who had married her great-grandfather, I. J. Galyen. The lives of Momaday's ancestors cannot be separated from the stories about them. Even the anonymous woman "in a beautiful dress" who is buried south of the pecan grove exists as long as that dress is imagined; Kiowa heritage survives in those who continue to have the vision. Momaday reminds the readers to "concentrate [their minds] on the remembered earth . . . " (83).

Genealogy is cumulative, as is storytelling, and both define an individual, a culture, a time, and a place. In *The Names* Momaday writes, "Notions of the past and future are essentially notions of the present. In the same way an idea of one's ancestry and posterity is really an idea of the self" (97). In *The Way to Rainy Mountain* Momaday practices what he describes in his autobiographical recollections, and in the execution the reader is invited into the storytelling process. The story of the Kiowas is an evolutionary process from the myth of the birth of the tribe through a mossy and weather-stained hollow log to the final poem about Rainy Mountain cemetery, which condenses all the periods of Kiowa history into two stanzas. Momaday says, "The first word gives origin to the second, the first and second to the third, the first, second, and third to the fourth, and so on. You cannot begin with the second word and tell the story, for the telling of the story is a cumulative process, a chain of becoming, at last of being" (*Names* 154). This philosophy explains why *The Way to Rainy Mountain* proceeds chronologically and geographically from the beginning, but the story is a series of concentric circles as time and lives go on, finally, as Momaday describes it, closing in on the essence of "being" that identifies him as a Kiowa.

In "Native American Attitudes to the Environment" Momaday says, "we are all . . . at the most fundamental level what we imagine ourselves to be" (80). The assumption that one can "choose" an identity cannot be taken too glibly, however, for such pseudo-Indianism has alienated many tribal people who are increasingly vocal about "white shamanism" (Hobson). In *The Names* Momaday provides his own view of his choice. He "imagines" himself a Kiowa, but he does not deny the Ellis, Galyen, and Scott of his heritage. What he shows students is that finding one's identity is a personal quest, a going forth to discover "who and what and that we are" ("Man Made of Words" 167).

Although the students in the interdisciplinary introductory course are seldom English majors, the course evaluations always indicate that they enjoyed reading *The Way to Rainy Mountain* and that, after class discussion, they began to understand the book and, more important, they began to understand more about "Indianness." The book appeals to them initially because it is short and looks easy; finally they like the book because they had to work to understand it and because they believe they learned something about who Momaday is and who they are.

Discovering Our Natural Resources
in Language and Place

Norma C. Wilson

The Way to Rainy Mountain is the one text I use each time I teach American Indian literature. There are two major reasons the book is indispensable. The first is Momaday's emphasis on the spoken word, especially storytelling. The second, no less important, is his emphasis on the land. Momaday presents a convincing and creative argument for esteeming the spoken as the most powerful form of literature, just as he argues for a new-old reciprocal relation to nature that we must maintain if we are to survive. In Momaday's work the language and the land come together into an intense kind of unity through the human imagination; and a story is born like a culture—it emerges through imagery into the world of light, providing some link between the earth and the cosmos above and beneath it.

In the American Indian literature course, I often encourage Native American students to write about their cultures, their stories, their land. To be fair to non-Indian students, I also require Native Americans to respond to the literature directly, to demonstrate their reading and understanding of assigned works. But I structure the course requirements in such a way that students are both tested on their knowledge and allowed to write creatively. I have found that Native American students bring an important dimension of knowledge to the course. Lakhota or Kiowa or other Native American students can give the classroom discussions a vitality and a validity that would otherwise be lacking. Their presence invites the rest of the class to take the literature more seriously and to ask serious questions about it. This effect on the other students' attitudes is as important as the Native Americans' experiential knowledge. Teachers need to respect this knowledge, for not only can it lead to more meaningful classes, it can increase the feelings of self-worth and capability in Native American students by showing them that their lives and their cultures are worth studying and writing about.

Most of the Native American students at the University of South Dakota grew up on or near one of South Dakota's Indian reservations, and as a result they have had greater access to their culture than has Momaday. Yet they are not given to criticizing him for being an urban academic who writes as often about the Pueblos as about his own Kiowa people, probably because they so respect him for the respect his writing has brought to Indian people. Momaday's writing has demonstrated the subtlety and complexity of Indian circumstances and experiences, past and present. And he has written in language that has a grand, clear style.

During the fall semester of 1978, a Lakhota student, Eileen Le Beau (now Eileen Peacock), and a Ponca student, Gloria Gaspar (now Gloria Chytka), were inspired by Momaday's book to write about their own Native American and French ancestries. The following excerpts are from their essays, which first appeared in my article for *English Notes*. I am grateful to these writers for their contributions to my essay.

From "Red," by Eileen Le Beau

I remember my Grandmother told me about the color red. She said it was one of the four basic colors of the Indian people. More importantly, it was also a sacred color from which the Lakhota people believed the quality goodness was derived. . . .

In the 19th century, a Frenchman ventured south from Canada to Dakota territory. He and his brother were leaders of a fur trapping expedition. The reason for this explorer's decision to separate from his party is not clearly known. Yet, his journey southward was to predestinate the history of certain members of the Two Kettle band of the Teton Sioux located at Cheyenne River. This group of Lakhota people welcomed him and adopted him into their tribe. His adoption rites gave him full entitlements and privileges as those of any natural full-blooded Lakhota. He was given the name Ogle Ša, which means "red shirt." He later married a member of the Two Kettle. His French name was Antoine Le Beau—my great, great grandfather.

From the time I was old enough to know myself, I was aware of a tangible feeling of my family. . . . My Grandmother was instrumental in helping me discover myself as a Le Beau. . . . As a result, I feel good about myself. . . . I have found my "red pathway." (7)

From "MeLe," by Gloria Gaspar

One of the minor chiefs of the Ponca was a man called "Nabawonton." This was translated in two ways, depending upon the translator—Fleet Eagle and Treads on Two. Born in 1780, he was a son of Smoke Maker. Fleet Eagle was a powerful man and could travel as far as 100 miles a day by foot. He had two sons, Thomas and Frank, and a daughter by the name of High Feather.

Francois La Charite was a French-Canadian trapper. He traveled the rivers of South Dakota and Nebraska trapping. He met and married High Feather. They had a daughter they named MeLe, born in 1840. Francois liked to travel on the riverboats and gamble with the many men who traveled up and down the rivers.

During the years of 1854 and 1855, a man from Ohio traveled the riverboats selling his handmade diamond willow canes and pipestone pipes. His name was Justus P. Sherman. He, also, liked to gamble. . . . Francois eventually lost one hundred dollars to Justus. He did not have the money to pay the debt. He decided to give his daughter, MeLe, as payment for the debt. Justus was pleased with his arrangement.

Justus and MeLe were married in August, 1856 at Omadi, Nebraska. They farmed on land near Rulo, Nebraska until 1867. They then moved to the farm near Niobrara, Nebraska. They remained in close contact with MeLe's relatives, the Ponca. . . .

During the years of 1876 and 1877, the government made treaties with the Poncas and eventually moved most of them to Oklahoma — Indian Territory. MeLe, her family, and many of her close relatives stayed behind. They built a community house south of Niobrara and held weekly meetings there, where they kept their Ponca traditions alive.

. . . .

I remember hearing this many times as a child. MeLe La Charite Sherman was my great-great-great grandmother. My grandmother still has a tortoise shell comb that MeLe used to wear in her hair. Eventually that comb will be mine to pass down to my daughter and grand-daughters.

. . . .

In 1969 my parents moved to Verdigre, Nebraska, which is 12 miles from Niobrara. We went over and looked at the old Ponca Community House. It is slowly falling to ruin, as there is no one to care for it. As I stood outside the building, I could still hear the songs and chants of the Ponca as if they were there singing for my benefit. We visited MeLe's grave, where she is buried with one of her sons and a grandchild . . . in all of her traditional Ponca finery. She is buried not far from her final home, on a bluff overlooking the river. . . .   (8–9)

These two responses to *The Way to Rainy Mountain* differ in content and form, but both students were clearly impressed with Momaday's sense of the power of the spoken word and, especially in Gaspar's case, the power of the land.

Another highly satisfying teaching experience also involved students' awareness of the power of the spoken word and a sense of place. When I taught a Native American literature course at the University of Oklahoma in 1976, two Kiowa brothers who were enrolled in the course invited the class to their home to meet with their Kiowa grandparents, Jenny and Cecil Tsa-toke, who lived near Carnegie. Thus the class was able to travel to Rainy Mountain and to experience the Kiowa culture for themselves. The stories the Tsa-tokes told us were not, as we had expected, versions of those told by Momaday. Jenny Tsa-toke told us a story about her grandfather, Tsai-con-gai (Black Bear), who led other Kiowas to safety when they were fleeing the US Cavalry. The point of the story was not that the Kiowas were finally subdued and forced to give up their nomadic life; it was the grandfather's service to the other warriors in the face of danger and death. The Kiowas escaped from the soldiers by taking refuge in a cave discovered by Tsai-con-gai. But after leaving the cave, the warriors were faced with bitter cold. Snow was falling and they were freezing. By killing several buffalo, Tsai-con-gai was able to provide food and hides for the men. Later, performing even more heroically, he built a fire and swam with each warrior across a river. In the family's stories, he became a super hero able to save his people from death, from enemies, and from the harsh natural elements.

There are no stories about Tsai-con-gai in Momaday's book. This story and the many others the Tsa-tokes told us made it clear that *The Way to Rainy Mountain* contains only a part of the oral tradition of the Kiowas. Perhaps more important, the experience showed us that the oral tradition is still very much alive in the voices of Kiowa people. Ten years have passed since my class traveled to Rainy Mountain and stood there on the top looking at the flat land all around—ten years since we listened to the stories told us by the Tsa-tokes. The experience had a lasting impact. We had touched the place and heard the voices. *The Way to Rainy Mountain* made us want to do that.

Momaday's book has helped my students and me to have a more complete understanding of who we are in relation to the land, to spoken stories, and to one another. *The Way to Rainy Mountain* invites all its readers to discover their natural American resources in language and place.

Beneath the Stars: Images of the Sacred

Susan Scarberry-García

The opening illustration in *The Way to Rainy Mountain* depicts an enraged bear rearing against Devil's Tower and gazing up at his sisters, who have just become the stars of the Big Dipper (9). The closing illustration, also by the author's father, depicts a cluster of tipis beneath a night sky that is exploding in star showers (87). These two mythic events demarcate crucial episodes in Kiowa religious history and signify the awesome and sacred relationships that exist between the Kiowa people and the natural world. Such sacred events are acts of cosmic participation between the life forces of sky and earth, and, when recalled through story, they become models of human involvement with the dynamic processes of nature. N. Scott Momaday's text then becomes a paradigm in itself for the personal involvement in narrative that is critical to the interpretative process of analyzing and teaching Native American Literature. Teaching the text cannot be separated from the teachings of the text.

This essay discusses Momaday's presentation of Kiowa sacred events in the narrative and suggests ways that the spiritual dimensions of the text can be intelligibly introduced into the classroom. Since many readers will approach the text from a secular, urbanized perspective, skeptical of the value of sacred myths and confused by the Kiowa view of sacred space as a vertical corridor of power and by the incorporation of the "ordinary" within the "sacred," it is essential that teachers initially guide these readers in connecting their lives meaningfully with the natural world.

One way to begin this process is to emphasize how the "natural" can be sacred. At the same time that "sacred" indicates something out of the ordinary, worthy of great respect, in Native American cultures sacred experience is thought to be continuous with ordinary experience. Lame Deer's well-known example of the steam of a Sioux cooking pot also being the breath of Grandfather (Wakan Tanka, the Great Spirit) is appropriate here. Lame Deer says, "We Indians live in a world of symbols and images where the spiritual and the commonplace are one. . . . What to you seems commonplace to us appears wondrous through symbolism" (96–97). "Symbols" from the natural world such as stars, bears, or rock formations unite ordinary and extraordinary reality and personal and collective visions, because these life forms have been continuous from the time of mythic creation. In *The Way to Rainy Mountain* Momaday draws on his knowledge of myth to present events that have either personal or tribal meaning or both. His grandfather Mammedaty's experiences reveal that a sacred moment "is filled with an intangible but very real power or force, for good or bad" (Allen, *Sacred Hoop* 72). Mammedaty learns to trust the medicine power of the natural world, and his stories of encounters with strange beings are teaching stories about receiving knowledge from unusual sources.

Mammedaty "saw things that other men do not see" (39). Among his visionary experiences was the sight of a mole making a mound (73). A seemingly commonplace event in the country, the incident takes on a sacred character for Mammedaty, who acquires personal knowledge of animal ways from momentarily participating in the mole's life. Mole is wary and no doubt notices Mammedaty but trustingly shows him the secret origin of the refined earth. Mammedaty acquires both knowledge and significant personal power because of his attentiveness and his desire to learn more about mole behavior. The circular mole ring is an expression both of perfection and of the wholeness of the experience. Mole is important to watch because he has knowledge of the underworld, the place of origin of the Kiowas before they traveled upward through the hollow cottonwood log onto the present earth surface. In a way, then, Mammedaty's experience with Mole reconnects him to the inherent power in his ancestors' emergence story. The pattern of curiosity, revelation, and transformation that Mammedaty becomes absorbed into when he witnesses the mole blowing fine powder in a circle on the ground is analogous to the process of inquiring and of receiving knowledge from the text itself.

When the sacred center of the Kiowa world shifted from the mountains to the plains over two centuries ago, the culture underwent many transformations as it adapted to new circumstances. One dimension of Kiowa reality that continuously renews and integrates the culture is hierophany, or the manifestation of the sacred experienced through a personal or tribal vision at a power spot in the landscape (Eliade, *Myth of Eternal Return* 4, 59). Hierophanies occur, for example, in the canyon where Tai-me first appears (36), at Devil's Tower when the Big Dipper is created (8), near the pecan grove when Mammedaty sees the alligators (73), and during the Sun Dance preparations when the old woman brings the bag of sandy earth into the medicine lodge (88). These appearances of the sacred in landforms, deities, animals, and celestial phenomena establish a pattern of revelation and transformation for the culture. The point of contact with a god or divine power creates sacred geography and sacred stories of the experience for the Kiowas. Momaday has imagined *The Way to Rainy Mountain* as an extension of the process of events in sacred space giving rise to sacred stories that order and revitalize the world.

The dimension of the sacred in the text is, of course, difficult to comprehend, but an understanding of it is, I believe, essential to penetrating to the heart of the book. Since the religious qualities of the text will be foreign to most students' personal experience, discussion must be grounded in Native American cultural distinctions that contextualize the narrative. Resources such as Alan Dundes's *Sacred Narrative: Readings in the Theory of Myth* and Peggy Beck and A. L. Walters's *The Sacred: Ways of Knowledge, Sources of Life* demonstrate that myths are not primitive or inferior explanations of natural phenomena but literary foundations of truth for indigenous cultures. James Mooney's *Calendar History of the Kiowa Indians* provides a well-documented ethnographic history of the religious customs of Momaday's people, and the recent two volumes of Maurice Boyd's *Kiowa Voices* present Kiowa myths and legends, as well as tribal history, from many storytellers' perspectives.

Once students have been provided with these background materials, the instructor could open a discussion about revelation in religious experience. Especially helpful here are Sam Gill's introductory pieces on vision quest, pilgrimage, and the Plains tribes in *Native American Religions* (97–105, 161–71). Using these readings, the class can begin to contrast native religious systems with other established religious practices (e.g., Judeo-Christian). Particularly germane to studying the Momaday text would be a discussion focusing on Native American ritual acts, including sacrificial ritual, and individual vision experience. By engaging in such a discussion, students will inevitably begin to uncover Euroamerican assumptions about the character of religious experience and realize that dominant Western views have historically stereotyped Native American religions as cultural anomalies.

To encourage an attitude of open-mindedness about Kiowa beliefs, teachers can ask students to recollect and share any unusual religious revelations or inexplicable experiences that they or close family members may have had. By telling their own stories, they not only enter into the spirit of the text but also discover that "unaccountable" strange events, such as the appearance of the alligators (73) or the disappearance of one of the Sun Boys into the lake (35), sometimes have their counterparts in the non-Indian world. The biblical story of Jonah being swallowed by a whale for three days while on a journey to Tarshish exemplifies a mythic marvel intellectually accessible to most students. My own personal experience of uncannily knowing that I was going to find a tooth on the beach at Santa Barbara—and then walking twenty-five yards to discover a large canine incisor—may not be replete with much discernible meaning, but it convinces students that the world is infinitely complex and surprising. When events such as these are discussed in a cross-cultural comparative framework, the skeptical resistance against accepting Native American spiritual knowledge as truthful is partially broken down. Students can be educated to realize that the spiritual symbols in the narrative have an organic connection with events in Kiowa mythic history and that the powerful eruptive reality of myth rooted in a specific landscape continues to shape the lives of contemporary Native Americans. The common ground for discussing the text is broadened even further if students are encouraged to tell stories about their personal ties to specific places, particularly rural areas where the character of the land can be seen to shape the values and religious beliefs of the people who live there.

When I teach students about the sacred symbolic events in *The Way to Rainy Mountain*, I use Mircea Eliade's model vision–sacred space–center–integration to explain the dynamics of the full event of religious transformation (*Myth of Eternal Return* 5, 12–27). Vision is prized among the Kiowas (Boyd 2: 93). In a comment about religious visions, Davíd Carrasco notes, "When a vision takes place in a specific geographic place that place becomes the 'Center of the World'" (3). The experience of being at the center of the world is personally and culturally integrating or spiritually balancing, denot ing a space where sky, earth, and the underworld come together on a vertical axis. These three cosmic regions constitute the "zone of the sacred, the zone of absolute reality" that is filled with the power of the creation of the world (*Eternal Return* 17). This special power spot, often containing religious objects, becomes a point of communication between human beings and the deities, a place that is periodically visited to renew personal or tribal spiritual energies. The integrating powers of the center are made available to the tribe through visions that contain inspiration, messages, energy, and medicine.

The prologue to *The Way to Rainy Mountain* introduces the concept of the center with the words: "Tai-me came to the Kiowas in a vision born of suffering and despair. 'Take me with you,' Tai-me said, 'and I will give you whatever you want.' And it was so" (3–4). Tai-me's story is told more fully later on in the text (36–37), but this early reference to her centers the narrative in religious reality of the greatest magnitude, for Tai-me has, as promised, continuously maintained the Kiowas' life for centuries. The following introduction to the book describes the land around Rainy Mountain, Oklahoma. Momaday remarks, "Your imagination comes to life, and this, you think, is where Creation was begun" (5). Although the Kiowas did not originate near Rainy Mountain, the Oklahoma plain is their sacred homeland. Shortly after this vivid description of place, the narrator mentions the people's origins farther north: "According to their origin myth, they entered the world through a hollow log. From one point of view, their migration was the fruit of an old prophecy, for indeed they emerged from a sunless world" (7). The link between the beginnings of the tribe near the Yellowstone's headwaters and their transformed life in the southern Plains suggests that there can be multiple sacred centers of the world, even for one people.

Yet another sacred center exists for the Kiowas. Devil's Tower, known as Tso'-saw in Kiowa, is also described in terms of creation imagery (Boyd 2: 93). This place, "Rock Shelter," is revisited by Momaday, who observes: "At the top of a ridge I caught sight of Devil's Tower upthrust against the gray sky as if in the birth of time the core of the earth had broken through its crust and the motion of the world was begun" (8). Devil's Tower is especially significant for understanding how sacred space gives rise to sacred stories. The story of the seven sisters and their brother is an imaginative projection of the Kiowa ancestors that accounts for the scored monolith and the seven stars of the Big Dipper. When the brother turns into a bear and chases his sisters partway up Devil's Tower into the sky, he makes possible the creation of the Kiowas' "kinsmen in the night sky" (8). "And since the Kiowas are symbolically identified through kinship with the seven star sisters, it is as if the tribe is finally freed of its long association with mountain wilderness, as bear retreats" (Scarberry-García 82). Yet an image remains. "The scored bark around the huge tree — a vertical image of the Kiowas' emergence log — is the incised mark of the bear's story. And the rising stump, a striking image of regenerative growth, like the old log, signifies passage into another life." The details of the story all point toward transformation as a central theme. "Thinking of bear as the active agent who brought about these transformations in earth and sky is a means of accounting for the massive energy that created this upheaval" (Scarberry-García 82, 81).

Momaday prominently places this vision story, along with the emergence myth and the story of Tai-me, near the beginning of *The Way to Rainy Mountain*. These stories taken together constitute the core of his sacred trust as one of the Kiowa tribal storytellers. In a class discussion of this cluster of myths, it is important to ask the students how these stories are related. Once students recognize transformation and the creation of a new cultural reality as the themes, they will better understand one of the organizing principles of the book. Devil's Tower, it can be seen, is yet another center of the Kiowa world that remains essentially mysterious, and the activity of ordering the cosmos through placement of a new constellation (the Big Dipper) integrates celestial space with earthly space.

The central textual image of what Eliade calls the "irruption of the sacred" is the Kiowa emergence story, which establishes the people's knowledge of their identity and history. Momaday's brief version of the emergence in *The Way to Rainy Mountain* (sec. 1) can be contrasted to a longer version in *Kiowa Voices* (Boyd 2: 14), which includes mention of the culture hero Saynday's role in helping the people come out. In both versions the circumscribed sacred space of the hollow cottonwood log opens up to a larger landscape, "the world." A mythic concern with ascension and vertical space is transformed into a narrative interest in horizontal space as the people spread out. The narrator's informal, yet matter-of-fact, authoritative voice relates that the people were emerging one by one from the underworld until a pregnant woman blocked the opening so that no one else could get out. Thus, the theme of suffering and death in the midst of birth and life is introduced at the start of Kiowa experience. The conditions of life are such that anguish will be ever-present as an aspect of the people's life road. This origin story, like all creation myths, becomes a paradigm for the unfolding patterns of future experience. As the narrative beginning for Kiowa life, the emergence story serves as a point of departure for the people's long journey between sacred centers.

Before the Kiowas left the northern mountains, they already had as part of their oral tradition the story cycle concerning the son of the sun who became two boys. Sections 4–9 of *The Way to Rainy Mountain* tell the extended mythological story of the transformation, maturation, and family of the beautiful girl-child who becomes the grown woman lover of the sun, who had first approached her as Redbird. This sacred story cycle expresses multiple hierophanies. The woman and the sun are replete with spiritual power, as are their children and the old spider-snake couple. That the "boy medicine" is still with the Kiowas testifies to its sacred staying power.

A number of elements in the "twins" story relate to the concept of the center and to the topography of sacred space. In the classroom one might ask students to imagine mapping the "home terrain" for the mother, for the twins, and for the old couple, as one means of discovering what is sacred about them.

The mythological family—father, mother, and boys—has knowledge of earth and sky. One of the boys, the one who disappeared in the lake, has knowledge of sky, earth, and watery underworld, as does Grandmother Spider. This personal knowledge of the vertical "zone of the sacred" gives them access to spiritual power that is used to counter the bad medicine of the giants or the deadly harm of the bears (Boyd 2: 8). Trespassing outside the boundaries of culturally described space has not only cost the mother her life (when she fled back to earth) but also nearly cost her sons theirs when they ran over the hill chasing the rings into forbidden territory. The disobedient boys' adventures, or journeys away from the center (home) where grandmother remained, emphasize the alluring destructive side of ring power, whereas the bifurcation of the boy by the ring emphasizes the creative side of the ring as a vehicle of increase. The mother's death by the ring makes life possible for her progeny and, through them, for the Kiowas. Sun Boy (Tah'-lee) becomes the Half-Boys who are doubles of each other but not exactly twins (Boyd 2: 5). When one boy descends into the lake, it is as if his submergence is a sacred reversal of the Kiowas' emergence out of the original center. The boy's return to origins is a model of the completion of the life cycle. The other brother's transformation into ten medicine bundles—Sun Boy medicine—was his way of offering his Sun father's (Pahy) spirit power to the Kiowas forever (Boyd 2: 51). In terms of the center, the myth of the Half-Boys is spiritually integrating and culturally renewing whenever the medicine bundles are present. Praying over the bundles is a performative event that recognizes that the space surrounding them constitutes yet another sacred center of the world (35).

When Tai-me suddenly appears to the starving Kiowa man (36), a hierophany occurs. It is not coincidental that she reveals herself in a canyon, amidst a storm, on the fourth day of the man's journey for food and vision. The sacred four represents a fulfillment after several days of seeking, and the thunder and lightning are powerful natural elements representing the terror, yet the utter necessity, of spiritual and physical transformation. In discussing the Tai-me sequence, teachers may find it useful to ask students where Tai-me appears and how she is described. Most of the students will remember something about her appearance, but few will recall her startling voice emerging out of the landscape. It is the voice of the center speaking. The instructor could ask the students how language is transformative here, as elsewhere in the text, and how this passage could be compared to the talking-dog and the storm-horse stories.

The introduction suggests another version of the origin of Tai-me. The sacred Sun Dance doll was acquired from the Crows on the northern Plains (6). After having come indirectly from the Crows, through an Arapaho family, Tai-me was stolen for two years by the Osages (Boyd 2: 48–50). This theft was potentially devastating, because Tai-me was a central focus of Sun Dance observances, which brought communal healing and revitalization.

The two versions of the coming of Tai-me—either through her appearance in the canyon or her presentation as a gift of the Crows — are not incompatible accounts of her origins, as they might seem. The presence of Tai-me sacralizes the canyon, and, likewise, the presence of Tai-me, newly brought to the Kiowa camp by the Arapaho, sacralizes the Sun Dance lodge. Her presence in both places is the sign of spiritual assistance arriving for the needy Kiowas. It is as if Tai-me can appear as a mediator with multiple selves to aid the people in different ways and places (Scott, "Notes on the Kado" 350–51). Tai-me orients people to the sun, and whether that orientation first began in a "great canyon" following a rain storm or in a medicine lodge during a dance, Tai-me became rapidly absorbed into the Kiowas' symbolic religious system as if she had always been with them. When Momaday himself goes with his elders to see the Tai-me bundle, he is struck by "a great holiness all about in the room, as if an old person had died there or a child had been born" (37). A hierophany occurs as Momaday offers the figure a piece of red cloth. Momaday's gesture is sacred because it is the old way of showing veneration, as Ko-sahn had done before the Sun Dance began (86). And when the Tai-me bundle had fallen unexpectedly near Aho, Momaday's grandmother experienced the sacred power in things that have an inexplicable life of their own (80).

After students have been sensitized to the "extraordinary" in an ordinary mole's mound making and to the theme of the sacred in the stories of Devil's Tower, the emergence, and Tai-me, they should be able to discuss other passages from these perspectives. They can, for instance, see that the peyote ritual is a conscious attempt to evoke the sacred (38–39), that the storm cellar opens into another world (49), that the black-eared horse is a sacred offering (71), and that the bones of Little Red are probably stolen because they still possess a sacred vitality and strength (77). Students should by now realize that beings imbued with a high spiritual quality (e.g., peyote and horses) are customarily treated with great respect.

The last sacred event that is described in *The Way to Rainy Mountain* is the awesome meteor shower of 13 November 1833 (85). The epilogue opens and closes with star images. Momaday discloses in his memoir *The Names* that the elder Pohd-lohk told him about the importance of this event to Kiowa tribal memory. Momaday says that his name giver Pohd-lohk kept a ledger of drawings constituting a calendar history of the people. "He [Pohd-lohk] opened the book to the first page, and it was *Da-pegya-de-Sai*, November, 1833, and the stars were falling" (*Names* 48). The event of the falling stars was so pivotal in Kiowa consciousness that it presaged a different trajectory for the people — a "new emergence" into deteriorating times. Yet this cataclysmic event is sacred because it is a powerful, mysterious vision that mythically defines space and relations between earth and sky. The event is terrifying because it signifies a world uncentered and shattered.

In Momaday's account of the event, "The falling stars seemed to image the sudden and violent disintegration of an old order" (85). This "strange commotion of the stars" was spiritually unbalancing, heralding as it did the coming disasters of warfare with the US Army and the government's enforced suppression of traditional Kiowa religious practices (Momaday, "Night the Stars Fell"). Since the bundles were not strong enough medicine to stop the star fall and avert catastrophe, it must have appeared that the vertical "zone of the sacred" had ruptured. Instead of feeling related to the stars, the people were, for a time, disconnected, cowering beneath them.

The falling-star episode is so compelling that students readily become engaged in discussing its symbolic significance and its relation to the Sun Dance sequence. The star imagery is sustained by references to meteors, Venus, the moon, and the sun. Students can be asked why the star stories serve as a fitting close to the book. The instructor can press the students to develop theories about why Kiowa tribal memory is so fascinated with star stories and star events.

An excellent example of a star event as hierophany is the annual Sun Dance described just before the epilogue ends. Ko-sahn, the ancient Kiowa woman, recalls that in her youth she witnessed an old woman bring "a bag full of earth on her back" into the medicine lodge, as part of the preparations for the Sun Dance. This memory stretches back one hundred years to tell of the "certain kind of sandy earth" necessary for the dancers (88). Clean wet sand is brought into the medicine lodge by the members of an old women's society, who heap it around the center pole and sweep it smooth (Scott 362; Spier 441). This ritual activity is a means of consecrating space, of defining a center or focal point for ceremony. The digging tool that the old woman holds is a "woman's root digger" made of ash with an eagle breath feather attached (Scott 350). Her stock binds her to the powers of earth and sky. And through her act of bringing the sand, her extreme old age is linked to the dancers' spirit of youth. "The dancers treated themselves with buffalo medicine, and slowly they began to take their steps. . . . And all the people were around, and they wore splendid things—beautiful buckskin and beads" (88).

In a writing course for Indian students in the T.R.I.B.E.S. Program (Tribal Resources in Business, Engineering, and Science) at the Colorado College, a Kiowa-Caddo student, Carol Botone, delivered an oral report on section 4 about the child-woman ascending the growing tree after Redbird. Botone said, "The Kiowas worship the skies and everything that's real tall, real big and high." This insight about Kiowa spiritual orientation opens the perspective about sacred space from which this essay has been written. From the emergence climb to the rising redbird tree, to the rising "stump" of Devil's Tower, to the center pole of the Sun Dance, the Kiowas have been gazing upward, centered in their primary mythic direction. The star fall, of course, represents an inversion of this upward impulse, and it is perhaps all the more terrifying accordingly. In Kiowa culture, events focused around a rising vertical axis are centering.

Perhaps the main problem in teaching this concept of vertical centering is trying to introduce ideas of the sacred to students who are immersed in our contemporary secular culture. If sacred events in the journey story are seen as imaginary fables — rather than as life-giving religious stories — then the loss in comprehension of the text is immeasurable. There can be no genuine learning from the text if this most fundamental level of understanding how to see the text according to a sacred perspective is bypassed or overlooked.

To help students appreciate the book from a sacred perspective, I ask them to give an oral report and write a paper. The oral presentation discusses the central theme of one section, the relationships among the three parts of the section, the relationships with other sections, and the spiritual dimensions of the experiences related by the narrator. The written assignment of a two-page paper (and "rewrite") is based on Kenneth Roemer's model ("Inventive Modeling" 769, 778–79). In three voices, each student describes a personalized view of a landscape, either home ground or some other well-known place. The first voice is the mythological or storytelling voice that customarily develops spiritual concerns in the narrative. The other two voices develop historical and contemporary views of place. Both Indian and non-Indian students seem to favor the oral assignment — even though at first it is more challenging to them because few are used to public speaking. Talking through the story involves the students in the narrative in a compelling personal way. Discussing Redbird's role in tribal mythology, for instance, necessitates according him a certain kind of personhood, and this is a first step in realizing the sacred quality of his being. Through participating in these exercises, students come to see how the energy of sacred events maintains life even in the face of cultural genocide and inspires literature.

A recurring pattern in all N. Scott Momaday's writings reveals that the structure of sacred events is rooted in both mythic and ordinary reality (Scarberry-García 21). Through the use of repetition, parallelism, and symbolism (devices from oral tradition) Momaday retells portions of his people's sacred stories and finds his place in them. The journey that he undertakes is his means of achieving personal wholeness or spiritual balance. What interests Momaday is the process of coming to know the sacred, the ultimate source of knowledge.

The Way to Rainy Mountain is not a sacred text, but it imparts the sacred. Momaday as storyteller-author-teacher is concerned with the process of acquiring knowledge and passing it on in a memorable way. Those who teach *Rainy Mountain* may find the book empowering, because the very act of teaching the text requires that one enter the centering sacred space of the story long enough to experience the magnetism of small moments like a mole's breathing or grandiose moments like the beginning of a meteor shower. Teaching *The Way to Rainy Mountain* is a means of accessing power to ponder the patterns of events unfolding daily beneath the stars.

PEDAGOGICAL CONTEXTS: COMPOSITION COURSES

Gathering the Past: *The Way to Rainy Mountain* in Freshman Composition Courses

Lauri Anderson

In spring 1984 eleven instructors at Suomi College decided to use *The Way to Rainy Mountain* as a source text for the four hundred students in freshman composition. A tiny Finnish Lutheran private college in Michigan's Upper Peninsula, Suomi generally typifies many open-admissions two-year institutions. Most of the students are enrolled in vocational programs and show little interest in humanities courses. Most have very limited knowledge of history, geography, the arts, and literature, read below college level, and have weak writing skills. Consequently, Suomi requires that all entering freshmen take an English placement test. About forty percent are placed into LL103 College English (equivalent to university freshman composition) and about sixty percent into LL101 Basic English (remedial). In each of these classes the students write essays and a term paper. Each class also heavily emphasizes reading. Texts are chosen for their ethical or moral content because the college sees the student's ability to make sound ethical judgments as an important educational objective.

Suomi instructors considered *The Way to Rainy Mountain* one of the few texts that would be useful with the full range of our students. The reasons were several. All students could be intellectually stimulated by the book's multiplicity of narrative voices, complexity of structure, and fluidity of style. The text is short, has several clearly defined themes, and has an inherent interest for our many students who are from second- or third-generation American families whose older generations speak a language other than English. Although Finnish Americans are the single largest student group, most students are from the other ethnic groups that make up the population of Upper Michigan—Croatians, Italians, Cornish, and Native Americans (Ojibwa from the Keweenaw Bay Reservation, where only the very old still speak the language). About ten percent are blacks from Detroit or other large cities. Of these students many have parents or grandparents who, while not speaking a language other than English, did grow up in a radically different environment—the rural South.

The Way to Rainy Mountain explains Momaday's discovery of those nearly severed cultural roots that define Momaday as a twentieth-century Kiowa and as an American. Because the Finnish American archives are located at Suomi College, we hoped to encourage our students, through a study of *Rainy Mountain*, to examine their own roots—to discover family histories that, once written, could be valuable additions to those archives. We also hoped to receive from non-Finnish students some essays worthy of inclusion in the local-history section of the college library. In particular, we hoped that the Ojibwa students would produce materials of value to the tribal archives at the tribal center. We were secondarily interested in Momaday's theme of intercultural conflict and its effects since a study of this theme fulfilled our humanistic objective of teaching ethical decision making.

Our primary aim in using *Rainy Mountain*, however, was to examine the process whereby Momaday gathered and integrated the materials for his book. We planned that, as an outcome of this examination, students would gather their own materials. Through interviews and historical research (using the library and archives), they would compose essays that traced their roots to immigrant or Native American ancestors. Because the main objective of our composition classes is to train students to write clearly and concisely whenever they need to communicate in writing, we did not expect them to recreate the multiplicity of voices of *Rainy Mountain* or to write prose or poetry in the mode of Momaday. Instead we expected a well-researched, interesting, and carefully written chronological history of the family and the family's environment. This research had the added advantage of preventing the unconscious plagiarism that had always beset our attempts to teach the library research paper. Few of our past students had been able to discern the difference between actual research and the mere copying and combining of materials from multiple sources.

In preparation for this assignment, students purchased several notebooks to be used for interview questions and answers, thoughts pertaining to the assignment, and class notes. Instructors reserved books in the library about Momaday, Plains Indians, and Indians in general. The reserve list included Ralph Andrist; *Black Elk Speaks*; Dee Brown; Matthias Schubnell; Leslie Silko, *Storyteller*; John Terrell; Alan Velie; and James Welch. We also made available a number of texts that showed a writer's strong feeling for a piece of land, for example, Bruce Chatwin's *In Patagonia*, Henry David Thoreau's *Walden*, Ed Abbey's *Desert Solitaire*, Michael Arlen's *Passage to Ararat*, and Isak

Dinesen's *Out of Africa*, one of Momaday's favorite works.

Classes initially spent several days discussing *Rainy Mountain* as a work of literature and as a testament to what the Kiowa nation has lost since its surrender to the United States Army. Then students were asked to make suppositions about the process whereby Momaday set to work to create the book. How, we asked, do you suppose that Momaday got the ideas that went into the final draft? What was the probable source of the three distinct voices (the storyteller's, the historian's, the poet's) in the main part? Were the opening and closing poems and essays composed in the same way as the voices of the main part? We did not ask students to research Momaday's process. In fact, our library contained only two texts about Momaday—Schubnell's *N. Scott Momaday* and Velie's *Four American Indian Masters*. Neither would have answered with surety our questions, though Schubnell does offer some important insights into the composing process. Instead, we wanted students to arrive at their own conclusions, to think through to the method that they themselves might have used if they were Momaday.

Students came up with a surprising variety of hypothetical approaches to the composition of *Rainy Mountain*. Most agreed that the storyteller voice came either from a storyteller that Momaday had remembered listening to in his youth or from a storyteller that Momaday had consulted when he decided to write the book. For most students, at least one member of the family served as a family historian and mythologizer and knew a great deal about grandparents, great-grandparents, aunts, and uncles. Many students seemed aware that much would be lost if this person were to die without passing on that knowledge. Several indicated that the family's best-known storyteller was already dead.

All the students felt that Momaday's historical voice came out of textbooks he had consulted. The equivalents for the students would be local histories compiled by the city historical society; histories of Finland and other countries of ancestral origin; community histories by interested local citizens who self-published; histories by local ethnic, union, and political organizations; and interviews with professional historians from Suomi and from a nearby university.

Students disagreed about the origin of the poet's voice. A few suspected that Momaday had imagined the whole thing—that he had written these passages at a desk. Others were sure that Momaday had actually traveled (probably by car) to some appropriate point on the edge of the northern Plains and then had either walked or driven south to Rainy Mountain. Most students preferred the romantic vision of Momaday walking hundreds of miles across the Plains. One student envisioned him with wire cutters so he could snip his way through the fenced-in farms, thereby reopening the Plains to the buffalo and nomadism. Another wondered if Momaday stopped at a supermarket to get a plastic-wrapped package of buffalo steaks to cook over an open fire behind the motel where the student envisioned Momaday staying the night. Several suspected that Momaday might have been arrested for trespassing somewhere en route if he had tried to walk all the way.

There seemed to be general agreement that the opening and closing poems and essays were composed either earlier or later than the main part. Students also generally agreed that these were academic exercises carefully written and rewritten at a desk. They felt that the poems were imaginative reworkings of stories that Momaday had heard from a tribal historian, and several were intrigued that the essays seemed to be a mixture of all the voices of the main section.

Students were now prepared for a writing assignment based on their knowledge of *Rainy Mountain*, their suppositions concerning Momaday's composition methods, and their new awareness of sources that they themselves had available for similar research. Each student was asked to research family history with the intent of producing an essay that, in particular, reviewed those aspects of family heritage that had been lost or transformed through the process of Americanization. Students were urged to interview family historians, to do historical research in the library or elsewhere, and, if pertinent, physically to retrace their families' roots by visiting ancestral homes, recreation sites, and work sites. Abandoned copper mines where grandparents worked are scattered all around the college.

Many students wrote more about themselves than about their ancestries. Several wrote bleak tales of growing up in one of the isolated back-road Upper Peninsula communities haunted by the effects of alcoholism and economic deprivation. Some of the most interesting autobiographical writings came from the mixed-blood Native American students. Susan LaFreniere's description of her school days typifies these writings:

> I still don't understand why my friends and I had to fight so often. Many times I came home from school with scratches, bruises, and a bloody nose. I'm still not sure whether it was because of my Indian blood, my Finnish blood, or my French-Canadian blood. Maybe it was all three. Some people didn't like any of those groups and, on any given day, I never knew whether I'd be called a squaw, a Canuck, or a Finlander.

This young woman wrote several pages about her grandmother, a respected herbalist who was one of the last in the family to speak Ojibwa. Susan noted that in her grandmother's day there were no "fake Indian powwows to draw tourist dollars from all around" and "few people lived off government welfare checks and government grants."

Students enjoyed discovering what life was like in the foreign countries of their ancestries at the time of the ancestors' leaving. Many learned why their ancestors came here. Darren Baumgarten's description of why his great-grandparents came to America is typical:

> The Czar was convinced that Finland should not be given special privileges that were not enjoyed by other parts of the Russian Empire.

Finland's constitutional rights were thereafter violated and such in-
justices as censorship of literature and drafting of men into the Russian
army became intolerable to the Finnish people. The northern provinces
began to suffer economically during the same period. These factors
caused the sudden departure of many individuals for America. Two of
these individuals were Heikki and Marion. Heikki was born and raised
on a small farm that could no longer support his family. He and his
brother left for America to escape the draft into the Russian army. Marion
had to leave because her homestead was taken over by the Russians during a campaign.

Darren also learned that his great-grandparents came from a province in Finland where there was a strong Swedish influence, explaining why, even today,
the Finnish of Darren's Minnesota parents is laced with obsolete Swedish
loanwords.

Student papers were peppered with similarly odd but fascinating bits of
information. Fay Chaudier learned that her grandfather took his politics so
seriously that anyone he suspected of being a Democrat was not allowed into
his yard or home. Judy Mayo discovered to her horror that in Sweden in the
1870s her great-grandmother had "to stand before the church congregation
every Sunday during her pregnancy" because her child was not her husband's.
Judy also discovered that her grandparents had sung in a local opera house.
To her chagrin she found that no one in the family remembered the name
of her grandfather's second wife.

These few examples suffice to show the written results of using *Rainy Mountain* as a source text for student research into family history. Other results
were positive as well. Student interest remained high throughout the project, from the initial discussion of *Rainy Mountain* to the final drafting of the
papers and the reading of the papers aloud to the class. This high interest
presumably accounts for the better-than-average writing. Students wished to
make their families interesting to me and to their classmates. They were also
required to do some original research and to gather together all the data into
a logical order. Overall, students spent more time and effort on this project
than they normally do on research papers, did more writing and rewriting
than is usual, and showed a great deal of pride in the finished essays. The
college also gained some family histories for the archives. *The Way to Rainy
Mountain* acted as an inspiration and as an intellectual catalyst in leading many
students to discover their rich and varied heritages — to search out answers
to that age-old question of who they are.[1]

NOTE

[1] I would like to thank Suomi College and the students who let me use the material quoted in this essay.

From Israel to Oklahoma:
The Way to Rainy Mountain,
Composition, and Cross-Cultural Awareness

David Hoehner

Although I have used *The Way to Rainy Mountain* as a model to teach composition in several writing courses, my most comprehensive and successful experience was in an unconventional interdisciplinary liberal arts program named the Utah Plan. Under this program a small group of freshmen students (generally those who academically placed in the upper levels of their high school classes) begin their course work by taking the required university writing class and the first of a three-quarter humanities sequence called the Intellectual Tradition of the West (ITW), a core course that examines representative Western literature and ideas, beginning with Greek and Hebrew texts. The instructors of these two classes form a team-teaching unit, coordinating reading and writing projects and occasionally conferring on students' writing progress. During the quarter that I taught the composition segment, the texts used in the two courses contained similar ideas and themes; all the texts were read and discussed by both teachers, enabling us to reinforce each other's central topics and teaching strategies and thus develop a valuable sense of continuity between the two classes.

My goal was to develop an effective heuristic procedure that would prepare my students for a range of college writing assignments over the next four years and to do so in a way that would also help expand their cultural awareness and their sense of the relation between literature and culture. I chose *The Way to Rainy Mountain* as the course's principal model for writing both because of my past successes with it in teaching composition and because of its thematic parallels with material in the *Odyssey*, the Bible, and other ITW texts. We spent nearly five weeks using it as a model to lead students to inventive writing processes and new discoveries and, to a lesser degree, as a basis for discussions of grammar, usage, and style. Students wrote two (graded) drafts of a paper, a midterm examination, and several daily exercises during those weeks.

Most of the writing skills my students learned and practiced during the first two weeks of the course would be reconsidered on a more technical level when we began our study of *The Way to Rainy Mountain.* In the first few classes we therefore moved quickly as we surveyed purpose, audience, close reading, and so on; applied those elements directly; and summarized and paraphrased short essays. We then examined formal techniques used in writing comparison-and-contrast papers, including simple analogy formation and the use of symbols to reveal or illustrate unseen relationships. These lessons prepared students for both the first essay assignment and Momaday's use of these techniques in *The Way to Rainy Mountain.*

To provide examples of how students might find topics and methods for writing the comparison-and-contrast papers and to present cultural themes and ideas that they would repeatedly encounter during the quarter, I asked them to photocopy a number of readings from world literature and religion. These readings included short selections from various American Indian mythologies, the Koran, the Hindu Vedas and Upanishads, and the Chinese Tao Te Ching, as well as modern selections such as the "creation of white people" poem from Leslie Silko's *Ceremony* (132–38), prophecies from Frank Waters's *Book of the Hopi* (333–34), and passages from Gary Zukav's *Dancing Wu Li Masters*, a book that investigates connections between Hindu scriptures and modern physics. My students, meanwhile, had read Hesiod's *Theogony*, Genesis, and part of the *Odyssey* in ITW, and they found they could list and discuss several thematic parallels among the different readings. Many of the selections, for example, contain themes of emergence, creation, journey, and sacrifice and also speak of the importance of words in defining and preserving both culture and self. All these themes would resurface in *The Way to Rainy Mountain*, thus helping to demonstrate a borderless, timeless continuity in thought and perception among world cultures. In addition, we had considered many contrasting views of reality, and I asked students to consider where myth ends in literature and culture and where reality begins, in order to prepare them for Momaday's unique structural approach to these concerns in *The Way to Rainy Mountain*.

During the third week, with the comparison-and-contrast paper behind us, we began examining the themes, inventive process, and sophisticated writing techniques of *The Way to Rainy Mountain*. I opened the discussion with a mention of oral traditions, exemplified by the *Odyssey*. This topic led us into a discussion of Native American storytelling and, in turn, to an overview of Indian thought and culture, including the Sun Dance, Anglo stereotyping of Indians, and students' impressions and images of the roadside jewelry stands on the nearby Navajo and Hopi reservations. We next discussed Momaday's life, his writings, and his influence on other Native American writers. I finished the session by reading selections from Momaday's memoir *The Names* (a practice I would continue over the weeks), which is thematically similar to *The Way to Rainy Mountain* and contains some of his most descriptive and impassioned writing. I also handed out a list of books that I had put on reserve at the library. These works were written by Indians or about Indian thought and culture and included several volumes of Indian stories and historical accounts.

Momaday entices us to read his text in a traditional manner, from the opening poem through the sequential historical development to the closing poem. A careful reader, however, eventually discovers that the concluding sections of the book cannot be fully appreciated without returning to the opening sections—that the text has no conventional beginning or ending but follows an intertwined or circular pattern. Although I waited until the class had read through *The Way to Rainy Mountain* before examining this aspect of it, our early discussions involved the symbol of the circle. The prologue and introduction contain many symbolic cyclical themes and images, such as the representation of life and death, or emergence and decline, by Aho and a baby; the changing seasons; and Momaday's ongoing journey and his containment of both the past and the present through memory, imagination, and stories. Learning to discern Momaday's development of cyclical themes and images was an important first step in recognizing the wider structural processes that he applies to the paragraphs, to the twenty-four sections and three major divisions of the text, and to the text as a whole.

The paragraphs in the prologue and introduction not only reveal a historical progression, often beginning in a past time and concluding in the present or near-present, but also often end with new or different sorts of beginnings. The second paragraph of the prologue provides a typical example of this pattern. It first describes the origins of the Kiowa tribe, then mentions their demise, moves back to the historical events that led to that demise, and concludes on a note of continuance, as if a new story were about to begin. This circular structure is reemphasized when each section is read in its entirety, as each progresses through a sequence of stories, histories, and reflections, revealing the place of history, imagination, and memory in continuing and renewing the story, and thus the life, of the Kiowa people. Furthermore, the prologue and introduction give a strong overview of the entire central story in *The Way to Rainy Mountain*, preparing students for the book's unusual tripartite structure and suggesting contextual strategies and organizational formats to consider in their writing projects.

We next considered Momaday's development of symbol and metaphor through imagination, memory, and illustration. The introduction affords a fine model for this part of the writing process, because it contains both concise illustrations and most of the symbols used in the central text of *The Way to Rainy Mountain*. To give my students experience applying these skills, I asked them to select a place, a season, and a symbol and to free write a description by drawing on memory and imagination. They took their writings home, revised them, and repeated the process the next day by describing another season. I then asked them to select one of those writings and to combine their descriptions with narration by introducing human characters whose actions could be developed sequentially. I also wanted the symbols to reveal a relation among the season, place, and character. For example, the image of summer sunshine on a mountaintop might symbolize growth in both the landscape and the character and thereby lead the reader and the writer to new insights and perceptions. Through this process my students were learning to apply multiple writing skills to a single situation in order to communicate an idea or image clearly and visually.

Before moving to the central text of *The Way to Rainy Mountain*, I gave out the "Rainy Mountain Project" assignment. Students were asked to write a short, informal introduction, structured as either an overview or as an outline of their projects, including a thesis statement or a mention of their main idea, and to write three "chapters" of text following Momaday's tripartite approach. They needed to select a topic that could be explored in all three voices and to develop a general organizational strategy (chronologic, symbolic, thematic, etc.) that fit the subject matter. For the first voice students needed to retell a story or a few interrelated myths (from oral or written sources, including novels, short stories, journals, or interviews) in a concise, summarized form and to cite their sources. For the second, objective voice, students had to research their main topics, bringing in historical facts or other documentation related to their subject matter, and to paraphrase and footnote that research. This section was to emphasize definition and factual illustration and to serve as a link between the storytelling voice and the personal voice. The third voice was to bring together the symbols and themes found in the other voices, to apply personal memories and observations, and to further explore the patterns, analogies, and associations developed in the other sections.

Although I did not limit my students to Momaday's exact method, I did suggest that they consider those most basic symbols and aspects of their lives: significant persons, landscapes, objects, and experiences. Students were encouraged to explore every aspect of their subjects, to consider critically their most unquestioned beliefs and ideas, to brainstorm and free write, and to jot down every possible metaphor, analogy, symbol, illustration, or thought that might help link chapters and voices into a unified whole. I also said they should think of the voices as three ways of approaching a single topic, of saying similar or related things, while remembering that each format has its own methodology.

At about the same time I gave out the assignment to my writing class, the ITW instructor assigned a paper asking students to write about an "odyssey" or journey that they had undertaken in their lives, in relation to the ideas explored in that class. The odysseys could be either actual trips to other places, coupled with the meanings those experiences held for the students, or they could be imaginative, intellectual journeys connected in some way to the ITW texts. In either case, this assignment helped students gain experience for the Rainy Mountain Project because it asked them to practice similar writing techniques in a traditional essay format. It also made the students take another look at the ITW texts in relation to *The Way to Rainy Mountain*, and many of them used this paper as a stepping-stone to the Rainy Mountain Project.

By now my students were overwhelmed with ideas and memories, and it was time to start organizing those ideas around specific voices. As we began examining the central text of *The Way to Rainy Mountain*, we discussed important family stories that would fit the context of the first voice and suggest ideas for the others. For instance, many of my students' ancestors were Mormon pioneers who crossed the Plains in the nineteenth century to settle in Utah, and most of these students had inherited interesting stories (listened to or read in journals) that could easily be used in the first-voice position. In addition, we discussed uniquely American mythologies that could, if researched, apply to students' projects. Such American legends as Billy the

Kid and Buffalo Bill were examined for mythological trappings, while personages and movements such as robber barons, the construction of the railroad system, "movie Indians," and California gold strikes, with the associated cases of tribal genocide, were explored with an eye toward dispelling illusions.

Selecting American myths for critical evaluation had significant effects. Once again, students were confronted with the questions: How do myth and reality interact to create or define a culture? What is the place of literature and history in our cultural lives? These questions were reemphasized by the "Going On" and "Closing In" portions of *The Way to Rainy Mountain*, as students noticed that Momaday refuses to overromanticize Kiowa culture and history. They saw that the reality and horror of the Kiowas' situation must be explored along with its beauty and idealism for Momaday to develop an honest, multidimensional picture of his people. In turn, students designed their early drafts, first, by separating fact from myth (basic research was helpful at this stage), while considering how the two worked together to form a humanistic whole, and, second, by attempting to combine the two elements following Momaday's tripartite approach in order to say more than they might in a single-voiced structure.

Another method I used to teach organizing and unifying techniques and to strengthen paragraphing, sentence-structure, and analytical skills was to select certain voices from *The Way to Rainy Mountain* and dissect them a symbol or image at a time and then to ask students to imitate the process in their writing. The personal voice in section 9 affords a simple example of this procedure. Momaday begins by telling a story of interaction between members of two previous generations (his father and great-grandmother). The spiritual symbols of a shrine, an offering of cloth, and a medicine bundle are then presented. The importance of words and memory are shown through the old woman's praying, Momaday's retelling of his father's story, and the relating of his own story. The symbolic Rainy Mountain Creek is mentioned, as well as an old house and the circular symbol of his great-grandmother's baby-like skin. Sound, touch, and reverence also play a role, and there are succinct descriptions and metaphors as well. The point is, each of these symbols and images helps form this one voice into a unified, deeply meaningful memory, while exploring both the sacred and the commonplace and reemphasizing the circularity of the book's structure. Momaday never loses his audience, because these symbols can easily be traced to the other voices in section 9 and are repeated with variations in the following section. Investigating this procedure also helped my students condense their often lengthy sketches by demonstrating how every word and image can grow organically out of others and easily lead to new voices and connections.

I reinforced these writing methods and introduced others by letting my class write a sample Rainy Mountain Project paper on the blackboard. Students would come up to revise sentences for tone and style and to select effective words, metaphors, and definitions, or they would simply discuss analogy formation and organizational approaches from their seats while I wrote on the board. Since the subject chosen for the sample paper was contemporary rock groups, the exercise again brought students closer to elements of their own cultures and time. Through memory and imagination we selected concert halls and outdoor festivals as places or landscapes; tales of "legendary" musicians as our stories or myths; and lyrics, instruments, and life-styles as symbols. Research sources ranged from *Rolling Stone* magazine to album covers.

As we approached the paper deadline, I held personal conferences with each student and had students work together in groups of two or three so that they could improve their editing skills and further develop the possibilities of their projects. The results were intelligent and diverse papers. One writer summarized and retold sections of Kipling's *Jungle Book* for his story, researched animal and "feral-child" studies for the second voice, and in the personal voice explored his own experiences growing up with animals. Another became involved with Aztec culture and blood sacrifice, drawing connections among various world religions, the Aztecs, and her own reflections on womanhood. A third student selected passages from the works of George Sand, Sylvia Plath, and Emily Dickinson to discuss her own artistic growth in a male-dominated society. Still others gathered stories from grandparents and old journals about emigrations to the United States and the West, which they considered in relation to their present cultures, activities, and a variety of other topics.

Completion of the papers, however, did not mean we were through with either the Rainy Mountain Project or with Momaday's works. It was now time to practice essay-exam writing, and, as we had spent considerable time discussing Momaday's love of words and the significance they hold for him, we turned to his essay "The Man Made of Words," exploring it in conjunction with the Bulgarian writer Elias Canetti's essay "The Writer's Profession." Canetti similarly discusses the relation of words and stories to the survival, continuity, and transformation of cultures, drawing examples from many of the works students had read in ITW. Canetti's essay helped to reemphasize the point that, although the structure of *The Way to Rainy Mountain* is unique and inventive, its themes are common to many cultures. The exam involved ideas and questions explored in both classes during the first six weeks of the quarter, asking students to discuss the writers' and their own views on such topics as cultural and personal metamorphosis, emergence and regeneration, the relation of literature to culture, and the idea that a culture's myths are always real and always vital to that culture.

The following three weeks gave the class a distancing break from both the writing project and *The Way to Rainy Mountain*, but I advised my students to keep working on their papers. Although revision (including the addition or rejection of voices) was a natural part of the first stage of the project, for the final grade students were expected to revise their three three-voice sections, on the basis of new observations and the comments I wrote on their first drafts, to write two additional sections in the manner of the last sections of *The Way to Rainy Mountain*, and to formalize and expand their introductions. The fifth section was to be written entirely in the first-person present tense — as a culmination of the symbols and themes presented in the other sections, as a suggestive completion of a journey or a stage in a "circle," and, I hoped, as an insightful realization of the self. The last week of the course was given over to workshops, conferences, and a reconsideration of "The Man Made of Words," the last sections, the epilogue, and the circular structure of *The Way to Rainy Mountain*.

The final drafts were refreshingly thoughtful and original, and students' writing skills had improved markedly over the quarter. We had journeyed through ancient and modern world literatures; examined such subjects as history, folklore, and geography; and considered a wide range of ideas, methods, and exploratory procedures. In a sense, students wrote two essays. On the one hand, the tripartite structure of the sections helped them investigate their topics from three different though interrelated viewpoints and thus to discover fresh insights that they may not have found by writing conventionally structured essays. The formalized and extended introductions, on the other hand, made students return to a conventional format; by using a single voice to blend narration, research, and reflection, they could tell basically the same story found in the body of their papers. Now, however, their introductions were flush with new discoveries and insights. Taken together, the two classes helped students to gain a deeper intercultural understanding and self-perception, as well as develop personal writing processes — including invention, design, research, and revision — that could be applied to all future college writing assignments. By following Momaday's heuristic, students had further learned to see the value of their experiences, to explore those experiences in writing, and to enter the experiences of writers from other times and cultures. They had thereby discovered a nearly unlimited supply of resources and inventive techniques to draw on in future writing situations.

College Composition:
An Experience in Ethnographic Thinking

Suzanne Evertsen Lundquist

The Way to Rainy Mountain is an excellent tool for teaching literacy. By literacy I do not mean merely the acquisition of skills, the learning of formulas for decoding and composing texts. I mean also a way of connecting with one's history, society, and culture through language. In this sense, literacy becomes an ethnographic concern — it involves the mythos, logos, and ethos of a culture and concerns how an individual relates to that culture.

In a course dealing with ethnographic thinking the composition teacher takes what is essentially a moral position. On the one hand, as in preliterate societies, the teacher's efforts to improve reading, writing, and thinking can provide a means through which students more successfully apprehend and transform reality (Mackie 2). Literacy, in this sense, is liberating; it improves mental capacities and allows students to deal on equal ground with others who are literate. On the other hand, increasing literacy, as is often seen in cultures where a certain level of literacy has been long established, also tends to isolate individuals and fragment societies. When exposed to new views of the world, individuals may find their own views challenged. It may be necessary for them to reconstruct their old concepts of reality in the light of new knowledge and new perspectives. If individuals engage in such reconstruction without the benefit of a coherent ethos, mythos, or logos to connect them with others, extreme individualism can result (see Oxenham 112–13). Reality, then, becomes a verbal construct, the composition instructor an iconoclast.

Momaday transcends the naïveté of preliterate societies, as well as the ambiguity of long-established literate cultures, in a process that involves the mythos, logos, and ethos of his people. In *The Way to Rainy Mountain*, he makes a journey "with the whole memory, that experience of the mind which is legendary as well as historical, personal as well as cultural." Momaday, in this process, couples the "imaginative experience [with] the historical" as equal realities in the unfolding of individual, as well as communal, identity (4). The imaginative experience incorporates the individual capacity to make meaning — to create reality. This capacity comes about, however, through understanding how others have made meaning before us. The whole journey and the whole memory are represented in *The Way to Rainy Mountain* in three entities that are separate yet connected: the origin of an idea in myth and legend (the mythos); historical episodes that bring the mythic reality to life or reasoned expositions that comment on the mythic reality (the logos); and, finally, autobiographical reflections on the first two (the ethos). The first two paragraphs in each of Momaday's twenty-four sections could only be retrieved through the verbal world, from other human beings or texts. The autobiographical paragraphs, however, demonstrate how Momaday makes personal meaning from the mythic and historic. The ethos, then, comes through Momaday's showing the traditions living within him—shaping, forming, and creating his sense of self. Momaday, after all, shows the values, the ethos, of his people and thereby establishes his own identity and value. Language becomes a vehicle for recovery as well as discovery.

Such a process of recovery and discovery has been called "ethnographic thinking." According to Jay Robinson, writing programs in colleges and universities should invite students to "develop as ethnographers of thought—as careful and reflective participant-observers, critical thinkers of their own thoughts" (493). The result of such a process would be the capacity to make meaning that is satisfying to each individual. I believe that this is what Momaday has done in his works—poems, novels, essays.

If students can accept the journey that Momaday sets forth as archetypal, they must also understand the vehicle for that journey—language. University students seldom ask themselves what they think about the role of language in their lives; like a familiar landscape, language has always been there. One way to help students ask themselves about their attitudes toward language is to compare popular assumptions about language in Western societies with assumptions in a non-Western culture like the Kiowas'. Beginning where Momaday generally begins, with the power of words, this essay describes how I incorporate *The Way to Rainy Mountain* into a university composition course.

Phase One: The Power of Words.   We first examine short essays that define the powers and limitations of language. Using the metaphor of landscape, the students see how, in S. I. Hayakawa's terms, their experience with the "verbal world" (knowledge coming from schools, newspapers, books, television, family, and friends) ought to correspond to their "extensional world" (the world of firsthand experience) "as a map does to the territory it is supposed to represent" (31). When this correspondence does not occur, the result may be a "false map" of reality. False maps cause mental illness, personal and cultural fragmentation, prejudice, and war. A brief examination of how Helen Keller discovered words shows students what life without language might be like. We then move to the assertion made by several scholars that modern humankind suffers from "semantic aphasia": "that numbness of ear, mind and heart—that tone deafness to the very meaning of language—which results from the habitual and prolonged abuse of words" (Madox 296). By way of contrast, we study, in three works of Momaday, how Native Americans tend to view the power of words. These works, or excerpts from them, include *House Made of Dawn* (57, 87–89), "The Man Made of Words" (particularly the notions drawn from Margot Astrov and Momaday on language and imagination), and *The Way to Rainy Mountain*. Exposure to the substantive force of language for Native Americans—language used to heal, to grow crops, to ward off evil, to bring about change in private and public life—helps university freshmen to examine their assumptions about the power of language.

Phase Two: Language and Worldview.   Students soon begin to realize that the established literate and preliterate traditions represent different ways of viewing the world. Studying several more essays by or about Native Americans, with especial attention to "Seeing with a Native Eye" by Barre Toelken, helps students understand how each culture sees things in "programmed ways" (Toelken 11). Worldview is then understood to be a constraining as well as a liberating factor in a student's attempts to deal with the world. At this point, students become receptive to grammar as more than a series of tedious exercises. They begin to see that "the grammar of a language is its theory of reality": "The world is grasped through language. But in its use by a speaker language is more than that. It is a version of the world, offered to, imposed upon, exacted by, someone else" (Kress and Hodge 7, 9).

Phase Three: Ethnographic Thinking—The Way to Rainy Mountain as Model for a Writing Assignment.   We now begin to explore genre and the traditional modes of developing thoughts (definition, process, classification analysis) as more than just "intellectual coigns of vantage but as ways of being in the world, ways of framing, seeing and establishing reality" (Geertz 147–63). As students explore myth (as defined by Eliade, *Myth and Reality* 1–20), fantasy (Le Guin, *Wizard of Earthsea*), a psychology text (Frankl, *Man's Search for Meaning*), ritual drama (Sophocles, *Oedipus Tyrannus*), a physics text (Gardner, "Brief History of Astronomy"), and the like, Momaday's journey is clarified. Students learn to recognize and to imitate, from their own experiences, paragraphs that also explore the relations among myth/legend, history, and personal experience. Of particular importance is an understanding of what myths are. We define myths as those sacred texts or traditions that explain the intervention of supernatural beings into human affairs. The purpose of such intervention is to establish order out of chaos—to bring about natural objects (the earth, a mountain, plants, animals), to establish laws, or to explain why a human being is "a mortal, sexed, and cultural being" (Eliade, *Myth and Reality* 6). Essentially, myths are sacred creation stories considered true by the cultures that own them. The Book of Genesis, the Koran, and *Black Elk Speaks* are examples of such sacred texts. These pieces of literature hold central or core positions in generating the worldviews of the Judeo-Christians, the Muslims, and the Sioux.

With this in mind, I ask students to take one subject, as Momaday does, and look at it from three different perspectives. They write only three paragraphs. In the first paragraph they must show the mythic or legendary origins of an idea; in the second they write a historic, objective, or scientific commentary on the subject; in the third students set down their personal reflections on the first two paragraphs. Momaday's section 10 on Tai-me is exemplary for illustrating this process. From the narrative (mythic) introduction of Tai-me into Kiowa existence to overcome famine ("'Take me with you,' the voice said, 'and I will give you whatever you want'" [36]) to the objective description of the Tai-me ("The image itself is of dark-green stone, in form rudely resembling a human head and bust, probably shaped by art like the stone fetishes of the Pueblo tribes" [37]) to Momaday's personal commentary about seeing the Tai-me bundle on a ceremonial tree ("There was a great holiness all about in the room, as if an old person had died there or a child had been born" [37]), the process involved in ethnographic thinking is made evident.

The following student response to this assignment was written by Dale Hunt (a student of genetics at Brigham Young University). He explores his experience with the myth of a universal flood from his Judeo-Christian heritage. He first shows, from the biblical text, the idea of a universal flood dating to the time of Noah. He then makes a scientific observation about a universal flood, drawing on principles from geology and genetics. The two versions are in conflict. The third paragraph shows Hunt's personal reflection on that conflict. (Hunt gave permission to reproduce his work.)

Mythos

In the days of Noah the people of the earth were very wicked. God wanted to destroy the whole earth with a flood. He told this to Noah and commanded him to build an ark. He also told Noah to preach to the people and to warn them about what was going to happen, but they would not listen. Noah built the ark and put in it two of every kind of animal. Then he, his wife, his three sons, and their wives also entered the ark. God sent rain for 40 days and nights, and opened the fountains of the deep. After the rain stopped, water covered the whole earth. The flood that God sent had wiped out everything and everyone everywhere on the earth except the occupants of the ark. After nearly a year the waters receded enough for Noah to find dry land and to open up the ark for his family and all of its other passengers to leave and repopulate the earth.

Logos

The study of geology is in many ways the study of the history of water as it relates to the earth. The study of population biology is largely the study of genetic diversity as it changes over time in a population. In geology almost nothing is easier to see than the effects of water, including cataclysmic events such as floods. In population biology it is very easy to assess and accurately document the genetic diversity of a population and to calculate the fluctuations of that diversity. If there ever was a flood involving the whole earth and every population of every organism on the earth, geology and population genetics would be the most reliable sciences for proving that it occurred and for documenting its effects. It would have left evidence in the rock formations in every part of the world. It would be discernible in every population of every organism in the world. Neither science has ever found any evidence for a universal flood.

Ethos

> I read in the Bible that Paul declared that the Gospel of Jesus Christ had finally been preached in all the world. I read in the Bible that the waters of Noah's flood covered the whole earth. I knew Paul hadn't been to China or Japan, Mexico or Chile. What did he mean? This lead me to conclude that the Bible could originate from a geographically localized people and yet be spiritually universal. Its spiritual universality is not dependent on its scope in terms of space, time, or description. Noah's flood didn't have to cover the whole earth as we know it. It had to cover Noah's world, as floods have at different times and in different places covered, cumulatively, the whole earth. The purpose of the flood story is much less to describe with scientific accuracy a particular event than to repeat in a different way the theme of all religious writing—God's ways and how man is affected by them.

I emphasize that it is Momaday's technique in *The Way to Rainy Mountain* that allows students to see their responsibility in the process of understanding and creating their own views of the world through language. Always, the students are asked to keep the "rhetorical stance" in mind (Booth): that they are saying something about aspects of their world that they know well and saying it to some other human being who cares what they think and write.

I am amazed how often students, even those classified as remedial, can write significantly and convincingly, wanting to understand and then own ideas, wanting to enter into true "dialogical thought" (see Freire, *Pedagogy of the Oppressed, Education*). Momaday's *The Way to Rainy Mountain* serves for me as well as my students as a specific example of how ethnographic thinking is possible.

Phase Four: Evaluation.   A freshman composition class in ethnographic thinking should not be, is not, a course in existential thought, in moral or cultural relativism, or in individual over community consciousness. By finding the origin of their assumptions, of their ways of being in the world, students can liberate themselves from the dogmatism that circumscribes their world and shuts them in. Finding mythic roots can serve several purposes. It is hoped that students will begin to see that blind adherence to mythic thinking is what creates the tensions in India between Hindus and Muslims, in Ireland between Catholics and Protestants, and in the Middle East between Jews and Arabs. True ethnographic thinking should not prescribe ways of being in the world; rather it should free students from being controlled by forces they have not yet recognized. "When genuine myth arises into consciousness," claims Ursula Le Guin, the message is always, "You must change your life" ("Myth and Archetype" 45). True myth should bring about a transformation, not only in individuals, but in cultures as well. True myth makes us all more aware of our connections to our higher selves, to others, to nature, and to our god or gods.

I concur with Margaret Donaldson, who writes,

> the point to grasp is how closely the growth of consciousness is related
> to the growth of the intellect. The two are not synonymous—but the
> link with intellectual growth is none the less intimate and profound.
> If the intellectual powers are to develop, the [student] must gain a mea-
> sure of control over his own thinking and he cannot control it while
> he remains unaware of it.   (129)

Robert Bellah, using Paul Ricoeur's terms, suggests that a fundamental purpose of education is to move students from "primary naïveté," which involves
taking or assuming a worldview and its values without being aware of doing
so, to "secondary naïveté," which involves being exposed to critical thought
that does not totally undermine primary naïveté but holds out the "possibility that once again the symbols may speak, and we may be able to live in
their grasp" (113). Bellah indicates that as students come to realize that various texts are interpretations of reality or vehicles for comprehending or trans-
mitting reality, they are then free to transcend the problems of the
contemporary university (fragmentation, indoctrination, vocationalism) and
discover new ways of becoming whole human beings (115). The moral implications of this idea are vast. (See also Bellah et al., *Habits of the Heart*; and
Hesburgh, "Future of Liberal Education.")

Momaday's journey to Rainy Mountain allowed him to achieve just such
a victory. He was able to expose himself to the mythos (symbols), history, and
values of his cultural genealogy and to come away with what he called "man's
idea of himself . . . as crucial and complete as it ever was. That is the miracle" (4). Such benediction and healing seem to be appropriate aims in the
process of making meaning in a fragmented world. They might also be proper
aims of programs teaching literacy.

PEDAGOGICAL CONTEXTS: LITERATURE COURSES

Journey into the Wilderness:
American Literature and *The Way to Rainy Mountain*

J. Frank Papovich

The vast landscape of the North American continent has played an important role in the development of an American literature—whether written by
Americans of native or nonnative background. Building on this distinguish-
ing trait, I have organized a thematic introduction to American literature of
the nineteenth and twentieth centuries. Including works by Native Americans with those of non–Native American writers provides students with an
exciting and important contrast by which they can better perceive not only
the mainstream literary response to the landscape but also some of the general
characteristics of the American Indian view of the natural world.

As a student of American literature, Momaday has himself provided a starting
point from which students can distinguish between these two literary traditions. Contrasting the nineteenth-century American romantic perspective with
the perspective of the Native American, Momaday has observed that the "nature poets"—many of whom had studied "botany, astronomy or zoology"—
conceived of themselves as observers who placed "a kind of 'esthetic distance'"
between themselves and the landscape. In contrast, the Native American traditionally conceived of nature "as an element in which he exists. He has existence within that element, much the same way we think of having existence
within the element of air" ("Native American Attitudes" 83–84).

Perhaps the most frequently mentioned nineteenth-century literary observer
of the natural world was Henry David Thoreau, whose writings have influenced countless students of the environment. Because he was so success-

ful in evoking a sense of the landscape that has appealed to Americans, Thoreau provides students with an important focus for considering the relation between native and nonnative views of the land.

To Thoreau, nature was valuable in part because of its distance—both physically and psychically—from society. Society stood in opposition to the freedom offered by nature, a freedom to escape from the responsibilities of social existence. On 3 January 1853, Thoreau wrote in his journal: "I love Nature partly because she is not man, but a retreat from him. None of his institutions control or pervade her. . . . There is a prairie beyond your law. Nature is a prairie for outlaws" (*Journal* 445–46). Nature is separate from human beings and independent of their participation. The prairie or the rising sun might illustrate a spiritual lesson, but neither depends on humankind for its strength or well-being. Furthermore, society often hemmed Thoreau in with its "dirty institutions," and people pressured him "to belong to their desperate oddfellow society" (*Walden* 115). Thoreau's social ethic is one of withdrawal from institutions and society in search of individual purity. His trip to Walden Pond was made because he preferred "not to live in this restless, nervous, bustling, trivial Nineteenth Century, but to stand or sit thoughtfully while it goes by" (*Walden* 218). Although Thoreau's response to the land was more complex than I have suggested and certainly more sympathetic than the typical response of his time, its evocation of freedom from society and history was characteristic of the romantic response to the wilderness landscape.

The romantic reaction to the wilderness as a place to escape from society is reinforced by a passage that I excerpt for my students from Josiah Gregg's *Commerce of the Prairies*, first published in 1844. Gregg, one of the first white Santa Fe traders, concluded his memoirs with sentiments similar to Thoreau's. After retiring to Missouri, he wrote that he often felt "a pang of regret" about leaving the "western plains." He explained his emotions by claiming that "the wild, unsettled and independent life of the Prairie trader, makes perfect freedom from nearly every kind of social dependence. . . ." This land of "no government—no laws" was contrasted to "life in civilization," where freedom is "invaded at every turn, by the complicated machinery of social institutions . . . (185–86).

In Gregg's text, students can discover many of the characteristic aspects of the American romantic encounter with the landscape. The frontier—"untrammelled" nature—is a place of "high excitement," a "wild" and "unsettled" place that "makes perfect freedom from nearly every kind of social dependence an absolute necessity of . . . being." The landscape is unique because of its irresistible tendency to disrupt a person's social responsibilities and stimulate a sense of total freedom. There are no fellow beings or societies to "propitiate." Indeed, Gregg, after a brief stay among the civilized, will again, as he himself predicts, spread his bed "with the mustang and the buffalo" and live among the "little prairie dogs and wild colts, and the still wilder Indians—the *unconquered Saboeans* of the Great American Deserts" (186–87). The Indian was seen as the ultimate free person, unconstrained by all meaningful social institutions.

Even James Fenimore Cooper's creation of the mythic Leatherstocking was predicated on a notion of the wilderness and its inhabitants as the prehistorical prelude to an ordered and civilized society. Natty Bumppo personifies all the good aspects of the wilderness, of humanity apart from society. As Cooper wrote in *The Pathfinder*, he was an "example of what a just-minded and pure man might be, . . . amid the solitary grandeur and ennobling influences of a sublime nature . . ." (135). While the force of Leatherstocking's character frequently subverts Cooper's thematic development, often because of the strength of Natty's relation to the landscape, Cooper could never break free from the dualistic romantic perspective of a sublime and solitary nature set against a corrupting society.

After considering the writings of Thoreau and Cooper, students can often deduce a basic pattern of the European-American response to the land developed in detail by Leo Marx in his essay "Pastoral Ideals and City Troubles." Marx describes a symbolic, three-part narrative movement: retreat, exploration, and return. In this pattern, the protagonist retreats from a complexly organized and alienating community. Next the protagonist explores the natural world with its possibilities of a simpler, more harmonious way of life. Marx describes what students have already seen in Cooper, Gregg, and Thoreau:

> [I]nvariably, there is an idyllic interlude when the beauty of the visible world inspires him with a sense of relatedness to the invisible order of the universe. During this episode, . . . he enjoys an unusual feeling of peace and harmony, free of anxiety, guilt, and conflict. (95)

But life beyond the community is nearly always disrupted by either the intrusion of technology—the machine—or the "fear of psychic freedom" in the "anarchic" wilderness. These limitations finally lead to the return to the community. The movement toward the open landscape is a search for a "sense of relatedness . . . that is unavailable in the social environment" (101).

Such an analysis offers students several points by which to contrast native and nonnative attitudes toward the land. The movement into the wilderness depends on the perceived divorce of society from nature, on an alienating, technological space from which the narrative movement is initiated, and on the romantic perception of the wilderness as possessing transcendent meaning, as offering "a sense of relatedness . . . unavailable" in society. This perception in turn arises from a view that humanity and notions of social reality are separate from the landscape. Marx notes that the movement to the wilderness "discloses the necessarily individualistic, transient character of the satisfactions that such an escape provides." Such an escape also releases the central figure from "the painful omnipresence of history" (109–11).

In *Rainy Mountain*, by contrast, students see a landscape that is neither a "retreat" nor an anarchic threat. Native American ethical relations with the

natural world are typically predicated on a landscape peopled with social beings. There is no "psychic freedom" as such in this animistic environment
but rather a complex set of traditionally defined reciprocal relations. Momaday's journey into the landscape of his Kiowa ancestors may be marked by
his attaining a greater sense of peace or harmony, but this sense is not achieved
through the simplification of his social relations or through a sudden and pas-
sive escape from anxiety. The missing "sense of relatedness" sought by many
heroes in American literature is at the core of *Rainy Mountain.*

Unlike most earlier American authors, Faulkner, particularly in "The Bear,"
comes close to describing an animistic environment. The wilderness Old Ben
inhabits has an existence independent from and even antagonistic toward those
who presume to possess the land by purchase. Faulkner's wilderness is pos-
sessed only by those who live, who survive, on the land. Ike McCaslin comes
closest to recognizing this principle and living his life on such terms. And
students often admire Ike's repudiation of his landed inheritance — associated
as it is with ancestral corruption and bondage.

But though Ike as a young man achieves communion with the living landscape, he finally fails — in both "The Bear" and "Delta Autumn" — because he
cannot communicate his personal knowledge to others in the society. This
failure comes in part because Ike's cultural traditions, unlike those of Sam
Fathers, are of little value to him, are, in fact, opposed to the conception of
humankind's relation to the land that he has received from Sam. Ike's knowledge does not allow him to create order and establish a meaningful sense
of continuity with the past. If Ike has been set free, his is a freedom divorced
from the painful though necessary responsibility of personal, family, and cultural past that Faulkner sees as crucial to the establishment of a proper relation to the land.

Several recent non–Native American authors provide a contemporary comparison to Momaday, for they have developed a spiritual perspective of landscape similar to that of many Native American writers. Such authors as Wallace
Stegner, Wendell Berry, and Gary Snyder not only appreciate the wilderness
as a spiritual resource but also approach it with "an implicit and essential
humility, a reluctance to impose on things as they are, a willingness to relate
to the world as student and servant, a wish to be included in the natural order rather than conquer nature" (Berry, "Secular Pilgrimage" 401). (For discussions of other similar attitudes expressed by contemporary authors, see
Lattin's examination of Chicano fiction in this volume.)

I include on my reading list selected essays from Berry's *Continuous Harmony* and Stegner's *Sound of Mountain Water.* Snyder's work offers a wide
range of appropriate selections, including his poetry in *Riprap and Cold Mountain Poems* and *Myths and Texts* and his essays in *The Old Ways.* Yet among
the variety of responses to the landscape apparent in American writers, only
a few, and those most recent, approach the perspective of *Rainy Mountain.*
And all are without the long tradition that lies behind Momaday's response
to the land. *The Way to Rainy Mountain,* then, is a particularly appropriate

text to include in a survey of American literature because it is concerned with issues and experiences that are important to the national literary tradition.

In attempting to characterize a general American Indian response to the landscape, Momaday emphasizes the key role of animism, reciprocity, and tradition. He asserts that the relation between human beings and the landscape is "a matter of reciprocal appropriation: appropriations in which man invests himself in the landscape, and at the same time incorporates the landscape into his own most fundamental experience" ("Native American Attitudes" 80). In an essay entitled "I Am Alive . . .," Momaday writes, "In the case of the American Indian the idea of the self is based upon a number of equations. . . . The first of these relationships is a perception of the landscape. . . . Only in reference to the earth can he persist in his true identity" (14). For the Kiowa tribe and for Momaday, the central place of reference is Rainy Mountain.

Momaday's choice of this grassy knoll in the Wichita Mountains of Oklahoma is significant not only because it marks the geographical center of Kiowa land but also because it symbolizes the fruition of the Kiowas' cultural identity as buffalo hunters of the southern Plains. His journey to Rainy Mountain is a search for individual identity within both the natural world and ancestral tradition.

The introduction to *Rainy Mountain*, combining elements of legend and history, unfolds from Momaday's personal experience of the landscape. It begins with an evocation of Rainy Mountain, in which the mountain becomes a place of origins, both personal and tribal: "To look upon that landscape in the early morning, with the sun at your back, is to lose the sense of proportion. Your imagination comes to life, and this, you think, is where Creation was begun" (5).

The loss of the "sense of proportion" that Momaday experiences, however, is less an isolated individual response than a personal response to a cultural landmark intimately connected to the traditions of a people. In the introduction, Momaday's grandmother, Aho, most clearly displays the synthesis of time, cultural imagination, and landscape that is crucial to *Rainy Mountain*. As Momaday notes, "The journey is an evocation of three things in particular: a landscape that is incomparable, a time that is gone forever, and the human spirit, which endures" (4). Although Aho had never traveled far, had lived her many years "in the shadow of Rainy Mountain, the immense landscape of the interior lay like memory in her blood. She could tell of the Crows, whom she had never seen, and of the Black Hills, where she had never been" (7). As a child, she had participated in the annual summer Sun Dances and had "a reverence . . . a holy regard" for the sun, the greatest Kiowa spirit power. Born in the final years of Kiowa independence, she was a last link in a fragile inheritance that Momaday saw rapidly fading. By journeying along the Kiowa migration route back to Rainy Mountain, Momaday hoped "to see in reality what she had seen more perfectly in the mind's eye . . ." (7).

It is the nature of the journey to Rainy Mountain, though, that the integration of the individual with the cultural identity occurs only gradually through Momaday's imaginative experiencing of the landscape in terms of traditional culture. For instead of presenting a static example of the difference between Native American and non–Native American views of the natural world, the personal or third voice of *Rainy Mountain* undergoes a gradual shift away from an essentially separate sense of self and landscape to an integrated historical awareness of the traditional reciprocity between humanity and environment.

While this shift can be traced through many individual sections, in the classroom I generally focus on a few key passages that mark clear transitions in the development of this perception.

The first section provides an overview of the shift. The perspective in this third voice moves from the details of the environment—the meadows of "blue and yellow wildflowers"—to a general view of the distance—"the still sunlit plain . . . nothing but the land itself, whole and impenetrable." Then there is a sudden change of perception. Details begin to coalesce into a whole of "perfect being" in space and time (17). Set in the context of the legend of Kiowa emergence, this vision establishes the connection between individual and community.

The second division, "The Going On," focuses less on myth and origins than the first division does and more on the legends and events of a developing material culture. Here, the personal voice continues observing the landscape but moves through description toward a more abstract understanding of the wider significance of the landscape. In section 13 the personal voice evokes the arrow maker of the legend by introducing Cheney, petitioner of the sun. Momaday believes that Cheney prayed to the sun "because it was appropriate that he should":

> In terms of his own understanding, the sun was the origin of his strength. He understood the sun . . . similar to the way someone else understands the presence of a deity. And in the face of that recognition, he acted naturally or appropriately. Through the medium of prayer, he returned some of his strength to the sun. ("Native American Attitudes" 83)

By this point, Momaday has come to share something of Cheney's knowledge. He sees Cheney "in my mind . . . as if he were there now." And as Momaday implies in this passage—"I know where he stands and where his voice goes on the rolling grasses and where the sun comes up on the land"—and reveals explicitly elsewhere—"there, in the early summer, I have seen the sun rise out of the ground an immense red-orange disc, scarcely brighter than the moon, beautiful and strange and health-giving" ("Morality" 34)—he has both symbolically and literally "stood where Cheney has stood." Cheney's perception of the landscape is an older example of what Momaday's becomes. Like Momaday's vision by the end of section 1, Cheney's sight "extended far beyond the physical boundaries of his time and place. He perceived the wonder and meaning of Creation itself. In his mind's eye, he could integrate all the realities and illusions of the earth and sky . . ." ("Vision"). Both men perceive the landscape with physical and spiritual reality in single focus as a result of the commingling of individual and cultural experience. For Momaday, this way of seeing is an important step on the way to Rainy Mountain. As Aho had seen "perfectly in her mind's eye," so her grandson has begun to see.

In the third part, "The Closing In," Momaday completes the shift away from description toward informed observation. The personal voice in each of the sections asserts knowledge, understanding, or the possession of "powerful medicine."

Marking a culmination of the response to landscape in *Rainy Mountain*, the third voice of section 19 reiterates the connection not only between men and horses in the first and second voices but also between humankind and the landscape. Here Momaday links the enduring cultural tradition with an invigorated personal present by remembering his youth, his horse, and an intensely felt landscape. This section presents three distinct and essential experiences. Power, imaginative freedom, and enthusiasm for the cultural moment resound in the account of the legendary brothers, but they are cut off at the high point of tribal achievement by the destruction of the captured Kiowa horses. After the buffalo culture was destroyed, however, something remained. In Momaday's personal experience lies the reinvigoration of that something, a recognition of a personal and social self defined in terms of human interaction with a symbolic cultural landscape.

The personal voice of the final section, 24, summarizes Momaday's attitudes toward the natural world. This passage, similar in its confident tone to the personal voices of sections 13 and 19, begins with a variation of the first line of the legend: "East of my grandmother's house . . . there is buried a woman in a beautiful dress" becomes "East of my grandmother's house the sun rises out of the plain." The shift in the main clause from burial to sunrise, with its evocation of Cheney's ritual sunrise prayer, indicates a renewed vitality brought to the traditional ways — especially the ways of viewing the landscape — by a culturally significant act of the imagination. In the legend, Momaday sees the buried woman not in literal reality, as he had intended to see the "immense landscape of the continental interior" at the beginning of his journey, but "more perfectly in the mind's eye" — just as Aho had known the landscape of the Kiowa migration "like memory in her blood" (7).

The voices of legend, history, and personal reminiscence gradually merge as Momaday completes the journey. And in the epilogue, the tribal memory of legend, history, and landscape is embodied in the person of Ko-sahn. Much as Aho had, Ko-sahn too had realized both cultural and individual experience "in the one memory, and that was of the land" ("Man Made of Words" 166). She becomes a spiritual mentor for Momaday, for as she both carries traditional knowledge in her memory and is carried by that tradition into existence beyond her lifetime, she provides a resolution to the question of time's erosion of a material culture and the endurance of the spirit. Unlike the view in much of American literature, Momaday's understanding of his place in the world comes not through isolated meditation in a largely inanimate, esthetically distanced environment but through participation in a landscape teeming with profoundly significant life, with horses and buffalo and bear as well as with water and wind and star beings. And his understanding also comes upon the voices of human beings — of relatives like Aho and Cheney and Kosahn. They provide him, through their existence and their remembered stories, with an understanding of the people's relation to the landscape and of the transmission of that relation.

The Way to Rainy Mountain not only provides students with an outstanding single-text introduction to Native American literature but also takes its place most appropriately in a survey of American literary responses to the land.[1]

NOTE

[1] Several passages in this essay originally appeared in my article "Landscape, Tradition, and Identity in *The Way to Rainy Mountain*," *Perspectives on Contemporary Literature* 12 (1986): 13–19. Reprinting is by permission of the editor.

Momaday's Pastoral Vision in the Contexts of Modern Ethnic and Mainstream American Fiction

Vernon E. Lattin

One should not approach *The Way to Rainy Mountain* in isolation. One should bring to teaching the work a whole set of experiences about other ethnic and mainstream American literatures, so that students can see *The Way to Rainy Mountain* within this larger context. In the prologue Momaday sets the parameters for his real and imaginative journey and in so doing describes an appropriate way to study his book: "It is a whole journey, intricate with motion and meaning; and it is made with the whole memory, that experience of the mind which is legendary as well as historical, personal as well as cultural" (4).

If one keeps this sentence in mind, one is more likely to approach the work from a broader point of view. I teach *Rainy Mountain* along with Momaday's novel *House Made of Dawn*, making extensive references to other Native American and Chicano writers and to mainstream American novels. In this manner, Momaday's pastoral vision can be sited correctly within the mythic and pastoral quest of American literature.

American literature has traditionally reflected what Annette Kolodny calls America's "oldest and most cherished fantasy": a dream of the harmony between humankind and nature, a dream repeatedly betrayed as the land is exploited (4). This pastoral vision forms part of the historical quest by Americans for unity, for wholeness, for a sense of the sacred in a secular existence. Students should be made aware of this historical vision, this Romantic impulse in our literature, and they should come to perceive how both mainstream and modern ethnic writers have responded to this dream.

The class can begin by reviewing examples from mainstream American literature that reveal a reverence for the land, a pastoral vision that is often difficult for the protagonists of the works to achieve, and by discussing the success or failure of these pastoral quests. The instructor might get students started using some well-known works such as *The Octopus* by Frank Norris. In this novel the wheat symbolizes the vitalistic force moving everything, but this vision of cyclically renewed pastoral existence is unconvincing because it is overshadowed by the railroad's evil. A more recent work worth discussing is Ernest Hemingway's "Big Two-Hearted River," in which Nick ritualistically returns to the land, the meadow, and the river, carrying his too-heavy pack past the burnt-out wasteland. Because his return to pastoral existence is limited, he can only fish the river, healing and renewing himself, but he knows that fishing the swamp would be "tragic." Another comparison can be made to the "tragedy" found in "The Bear," by William Faulkner, a work discussed by Frank Papovich in the previous essay. Ike would repudiate ownership of the land in the hope of escaping his ancestor's sin; nevertheless, despite his repudiation, the wilderness does not remain sacred for Ike or others. In fact, as Annette Kolodny points out, like Cooper's Natty Bumppo, Ike incurs guilt from helping "to turn intimacy into violation" (143).

For a fuller understanding of this quest, the instructor should mention writings that explore the mythic world and its relation to literature. Works by Joseph Campbell (*Creative Mythology, Hero*), Mircea Eliade (*Rites and Symbols, Shamanism*), and others deal extensively with the sacred and the primitive, usually focusing on the beauty and everlasting quality of the land and a sense of the unity of life and time.

One point of view that students should discuss is that often the white, or mainstream, heroes fail or are unconvincing because their relation to the land is more fantasy than history and because they are conquerors and violators of both the land and the people who live on the land. Their pastoral vision must therefore remain either anomalous or forlorn and tragic. Such an assessment is even truer of recent mainstream writers who reflect modern America, a nation that, as Momaday says, has repudiated the pastoral ideal, uprooting human beings from the land and producing "psychic dislocation . . . in time and space" ("Man Made of Words" 166). These postmodern writers deny the validity of sacred or pastoral vision and create a literature described by Saul Bellow as "a dark literature, a literature of victimization, of old people sitting in ash cans waiting for the breath of life to depart" (219).

The instructor can now discuss the rejection of the pastoral vision in postmodern mainstream literature. This rejection can be found in works like Thomas Pynchon's *V*, in which Herbert Stencil's quest is undercut by a denial of form and meaning in the universe, or with *Gravity's Rainbow*, in which the hundreds of characters, appearing and disappearing, deny the possibility of individual, personal wholeness and vision. Other novels worth discussing include Saul Bellow's *Humboldt's Gift* and the once popular *Zen and the Art of Motorcycle Maintenance* by Robert M. Pirsig, which enable students to see the difference between secular and sacred transcendence, the difference between mythic wholeness that transcends time and society and a vision that is part of time and society.

As students move on to consider Momaday's writings, it is important to remind them that they will be comparing his works to those of other ethnic writers who have not betrayed the dream, who have watched outsiders intrude on their land and on their religious beliefs, and who desire to recapture and restate the sacred and pastoral vision. This desire often becomes a quest to recover a worldview held by ancient peoples, a view that offers modern America a mythic vision of the sanctity of all life, a vision of the beauty and everlasting quality of the land, and a sense of the unity of life and time that transcends the lineal, judgmental, and historical view accepted by the modern Western world. In works in which the quest ends in racial and mythic unity, the fictional narrative itself becomes myth, thus truth; the secular novel becomes a sacred form, part of the living myth, part of the sacred history of the people.

Momaday's *Way to Rainy Mountain* and *House Made of Dawn* exemplify the theme of the pastoral, mythic quest as defined by Campbell and Eliade. Both these works are forms of rediscovery, attempts to return to the sacred through the art of storytelling and mythmaking that is part of the Indian oral tradition. They attempt to push the secular mode of modern fiction into the sacred mode, registering a faith in and a recognition of the power of the word that "comes from nothing into sound and meaning . . . [and] gives origin to all things" (*Rainy Mountain* 33). In the prologue to *Rainy Mountain* Momaday makes clear that his personal retracing of the Kiowas' long migration to the Wichita Mountains, his actual journey, and his telling of the story are one. "In one sense, then, the way to Rainy Mountain is preeminently the history of an idea, man's idea of himself, and it has old and essential being in language" (4).

The Way to Rainy Mountain reflects Momaday's early life, described by him in *The Names* as the "pastoral time of my growing up" (150). Thus his journey is an effort to recapture this innocent childhood and to reaffirm the sacred within the secular, to find his personal identity in the mythic identity of his people. To help students relate to this idea, I ask them to compare Tosamah's two sermons (in the middle of *House Made of Dawn*) entitled "The Gospel According to John" and "The Way to Rainy Mountain" with Momaday's actual and fictional journey in *The Way to Rainy Mountain*.

Many readers of *House Made of Dawn* have identified the Reverend J. B. B. Tosamah, pastor and priest of the sun, with the author N. Scott Momaday. Students will quickly point out that both Tosamah and Momaday in *The Way to Rainy Mountain* identify with their grandmothers and that the "same" grandmother in each work tells the story of how Tai-me came to be with the Kiowas. It was long ago when times were bad and children cried from hunger that Tai-me and the Sun Dance culture was discovered and the Kiowas found themselves as a people. " 'Take me with you,' the voice said, 'and I will give you whatever you want.' " This story, told in both works (*House* 90; *Rainy Mountain* 36), is a repetition of creation, much as is the first sound heard by the biblical John; in this sound was the beginning. Ultimately, as Tosamah says, "It represents the oldest and best idea that man has of himself" (*House* 90).

If, however, students explore this comparison, they will come to understand the difference between the journey of Momaday and the failed quest of Tosamah. At the same time, they will understand the difference between the visions of modern ethnic writers and modern mainstream American writers. Like the Kiowas, who at the beginning of their journey were uncertain of themselves as a "people," Momaday is confused about his personal identity and his relation to Kiowa culture. His grandmother Aho has died, and he has returned in the heat of July to visit her grave: it is a time and a return that reminds us of Campbell's descriptions of the monomythic hero's descent to hell. As Momaday describes the scene:

[I]n summer the prairie is an anvil's edge. The grass turns brittle and brown, and it cracks beneath your feet . . . the steaming foliage seems almost to writhe in fire. Great green and yellow grasshoppers are everywhere in the tall grass, popping up like corn to sting the flesh, and tortoises crawl about on the red earth, going nowhere in the plenty of time. (*Rainy Mountain* 5)

In visiting his grandmother's grave and then in retracing the history of his people, Momaday will find a unity of landscape and a unity of time and space. The first legend he remembers from his people's journey is of the Devil's Tower, a huge rock to which the Kiowas came two centuries ago and out of which they created a story of seven sisters who climbed a tree to escape a bear and were borne into the sky to become the Big Dipper: "From that moment, and so long as the legend lives, the Kiowas have kinsmen in the night sky. . . . However tenuous their well-being, however much they had suffered and would suffer again, they had found a way out of the wilderness" (8).

The Way to Rainy Mountain begins with questions of identity and ends with a sense of oneness and wholeness suggested by this legend of the Devil's Tower. Throughout the work Momaday fuses past and present, myth and history, his personal memories with the memories of his people, his memory of his grandmother Aho and her memories of the evolution of the Kiowa culture, ultimately fusing creation and death as part of one circle of existence. The thematic unity is reinforced by the tripartite structure of the work, with its three major divisions subdivided into twenty-four sections and its sections consisting of the mythic, the historical, and the personal voices. Kenneth Roemer explains how these three voices reveal the different types of reality that are frames of reference for white and nonwhite cultures:

[A]s students discover the gradual merging of the three voices near the conclusion and the links between the voices throughout, they begin to realize how inappropriate their concepts of time and reality are when confronted with the types of experiences presented by Momaday. Hence they are encouraged to experiment with dynamic interminglings of the past and the present, the cultural and the personal and the spiritual, objective, and subjective if they are going to understand what Momaday means by the "miracle" of the Kiowa culture: the collapse of that culture and the persistence, wholeness, and vitality of the same culture, which is renewed each time the imagination recreates the ancient and recent pasts to illuminate presents and futures. ("Survey Courses" 621–22)

This fusion of theme and structure results in a re-creation of the pastoral and mythic unity found in the quest theme; the gods and heaven are a part of the total landscape, and the journey is all these. The journey and the telling of the journey are one. It is the Word that allows human beings to complete their quests and find unity with their world, for "By means of words can a man deal with the world on equal terms. And the word is sacred" (33).

On students' first reading, Tosamah's lecture "The Gospel According to John" might seem to reveal the same truth as *The Way to Rainy Mountain* does. "In principio erat Verbum," quotes Tosamah as he starts his sermon to the Indians gathering inside the Holiness Pan-Indian Rescue Mission surrounded by white Los Angeles. Two forty-watt bulbs illuminate the cold and dreary basement where Tosamah speaks about the first sound that came from nothingness: "It was almost nothing in itself, a single sound, a word—a word broken off at the darkest center of the night and let go in the awful void, forever and forever. And it was almost nothing in itself. It scarcely was; but it *was*, and everything began" (85).

However much this may sound like Aho or Momaday, the reality is that Tosamah cannot maintain his vision, his understanding. He is a caricature of the visionary—if you like, he is a parody of Momaday or of other Native Americans who could easily become such a personage: a hollow shell, full of words with unrealized meanings, unlived truths. Perhaps he is N. Scott Momaday without the experience of *The Way to Rainy Mountain*. Tosamah represents the subtlest kind of religious confidence agent: he is both critic and supporter of the white way; he is both priest and medicine man; he is both friend and foe. Ultimately, he is a religious sham, speaking the truth but never the whole truth; he is John Big Bluff Tosamah. He is trapped between two selves, two realities: "Conviction, caricature, callousness: the remainder of his sermon was a going back and forth among these" (86).

Tosamah's sermon on John is about John's failure to accept the Word, the truth as given to him. John's problem was that he was a white man, and "the white man has his ways. . . . He talks about the Word. He talks through it and around it. He builds upon it with syllables, with prefixes and suffixes, and hyphens and accents. He adds and divides and multiplies the Word. And in all of this he subtracts the Truth" (87). John's approach is in contrast to that of the storyteller, Tosamah's grandmother, who had "learned that in words and in language, and there only, she could have whole and consummate being" (88). So when Tosamah remembers his grandmother's stories from childhood, he remembers an imaginative experience:

> I was a child, and that old woman was asking me to come directly into the presence of her mind and spirit; she was taking hold of my imagination, giving me to share in the great fortune of her wonder and delight. She was asking me to go with her to the confrontation of something that was sacred and eternal. It was a timeless, *timeless* thing; nothing of her old age or of my childhood came between us.   (88)

This same experience is related in *The Way to Rainy Mountain*, where Momaday listens to his memories of his grandmother's memories. She could tell of the Crows, whom she had never seen, and Momaday "wanted to see in reality what she had seen more perfectly in the mind's eye" (7). Unfortunately, Tosamah is a false prophet, whether he is lecturing on John or conducting the peyote ritual. Despite his attractiveness to the reader, Tosamah clearly never fully understands sacred things, good or evil: everything to him is just a "Jesus scheme" or a peyote scheme. Christianity is not real to him, and yet he cannot see fully his ancestors' mystic ways. He ends his religious play with the advice, "Good night, . . . and get yours" (91).

The main character of the novel, Abel, should also be contrasted to Tosamah. Abel, who throughout the book is lost in the white world of war and peace, can emerge with a sacred vision at the end. He returns home to the reservation, and through his grandfather and his racial memory he rediscovers himself and his place in the landscape. Abel's quest takes him back to a reverence for all existence and for the land that supports this existence. In "Man Made of Words" Momaday has written of modern Americans' need to come to accept the land, to develop an American land ethic, "not only as it is revealed to us immediately through our senses, but also as it is perceived more truly in the long turn of seasons and of years. And we must come to moral terms" (166). This theme is repeated in both *House Made of Dawn* and *The Way to Rainy Mountain*. In *House* the narrator speaks of a prehistoric civilization that

> had gone out among the hills for a little while and would return; and then everything would be restored to an older age, and time would have returned upon itself and a bad dream of invasion and change would have been dissolved in an hour before the dawn. For man, too, has tenure in the land; he dwelt upon the land twenty-five thousand years ago, and his gods before him.   (56)

This is the pastoral dream not only of Momaday but of many other modern ethnic writers.

Reflecting this pastoral dream, two Native American writers the students should come to know are Leslie Marmon Silko and James Welch. James Welch's novel *Winter in the Blood* tells of a modern alienated hero whose world seems void of the sacred. At the beginning of the story, the narrator returns home to the reservation to find a land burnt and empty, a house full of women who mean nothing to him. The distance he feels from himself, "as a hawk from the moon" (2), is so great that it can be filled only with a search that will take him spiritually back to the beginning of his racial and religious self.

The narrator's rediscovery, as in many other Native American and Chicano novels, includes a rejection of Christianity—here represented by the Harlem priest Montana—and a return to a more ancient sacred center. Like Momaday, the narrator travels back in time and history through the stories of an old relative, this time a grandfather, the blind Yellow Calf. As a young brave the grandfather had helped the narrator's grandmother survive a winter of starvation. The tribe had been hunted by white men, and all the other Indians had died of hunger. But the narrator's grandparents had found each other and love; not only did they survive the winter in their blood, but they started a new generation. Even now, when all seems desolate, the old man continues to talk to the deer and the magpie, understanding his place in the land.

Returning home, the narrator sees a cow drowning in a pool of sucking mud, and, risking his life, he wades into the muddy earth to save the animal. Momentarily becoming entombed, he sees the greed and hate surrounding his life, and he frees himself. The novel ends at his grandmother's funeral, with the narrator symbolically affirming the sacred in the secular modern world and embracing the native vision of the continuity of existence.

Silko's *Ceremony* also links the human and the natural. Tayo, the central character, suffers severe emotional problems resulting from years of abuse and trauma. Doctors cannot cure him, but a Navajo medicine man succeeds. Moreover, Tayo's recovery occurs at the end of a six-year drought on the Laguna reservation, thus uniting the health of the central character and the well-being of the land and tribe.

Two Chicano novels that can be discussed in relation to *The Way to Rainy Mountain* are Ron Arias's *Road to Tamazunchale* and Rudolfo Anaya's *Bless Me, Ultima* (see Lattin, "Quest"). In *The Road to Tamazunchale*, the quest of the protagonist, Fausto Tejada, ends with a rediscovery of his Indian past through the Peruvian shepherd Marcelino Huanca. Fausto moves from feelings of self-pity and fear of dying to a sense of pastoral wholeness and of the continuity of past and present. At the end of the novel Fausto dies, but the book continues, the logic of the world and the dichotomy of life and earth having been transcended.

In *Bless Me, Ultima* we have the story of Antonio Marez growing up in a small new Mexican village. He learns from the old curandera Ultima about an existence older than Christianity. Ultima teaches Antonio about the everlasting power of the land, about the ancient understanding of the oneness of all life, and about the acceptance of all living things. She also teaches him that the battle against evil is real and eternal. Her battles against witches and curses are similar to Abel's battle against the albino in *House Made of Dawn*. The Anglo world cannot accept or understand this form of evil, and so it imprisons Abel for killing the albino. Likewise, the villagers think that Ultima is a witch and want to kill her. By the end of the novel, however, Antonio understands that Ultima's ability to enter what Eliade describes as sacred time represents an escape from profane existence in order to perform a variety of spiritual deeds. Thus out of destruction and even death, Antonio comes to accept the "great cycle that binds us all" and to see the cycle of the seasons as part of this greater cycle (113).

By now students should see that writers like Momaday, Welch, Silko, Arias, and Anaya have created a new romanticism, reflecting a pastoral vision, a reverence for the land, and a transcendent optimism. This perspective, with its celebration of the land and of mythic vision, contrasts with that of most mainstream literature and with that of Americans throughout the nation's history. By recognizing these different attitudes toward nature, students should be better able to understand both the American literature they have read all their lives and their own history as it relates to America's failure to see the land as anything more than a false dream of harmony or as an asset to be exploited. If students develop this understanding, they will have achieved a great deal.

The Indian as Purveyor of the Sacred Earth: Avoiding Nostalgic Readings of *The Way to Rainy Mountain*

Kathryn S. Vangen

N. Scott Momaday ends the prose section of *The Way to Rainy Mountain* with an epilogue about Ko-sahn, his ancestor and inspiration. As he muses over the meanings of her life, he implies the philosophical scope of his text and, perhaps, of his life as a writer:

> Probably Ko-sahn too is dead now. At times, in the quiet of evening, I think she must have wondered, dreaming, who she was. Was she become in her sleep that old purveyor of the sacred earth, perhaps, the ancient one who, old as she was, still had the feeling of play? And in her mind, at times, did she see the falling stars?   (88)

The individual and collective aspects of memory and imagination that inform Momaday's work are delineated here — Ko-sahn's (and Momaday's) evolving, changing dream of the self coupled with an inheritance of stories like that of the falling stars; a sense of play coupled with an inherited sense of duty to be a purveyor of the sacred earth.

Herein also lies a challenge in teaching *The Way to Rainy Mountain* in a course that takes American Indian literature as its subject. The image of Indians as purveyors of the sacred earth, however accurate as a historical portrayal, can evoke a sort of romantic response in the reader, a nostalgia that must be addressed, disassembled, and reassembled in the light of Indian religious philosophies, history, and contemporary life. Momaday's individual literary voice, too, must be set against the collective voice rising up from contemporary Pan-American Indian movements — literary and extraliterary — which struggle to promote the cultural survival of Indian peoples. Because I want the students themselves to raise the questions that are crucial to their understanding Indian literature, I prepare them for reading Momaday's text in three ways: (1) by acquainting them early on with relevant concepts and issues related to Indian history and cultures, as well as with stereotypes of Indians; (2) by offering the students a comparative context (i.e., the study of Lakota culture, which raises several issues pertinent to the discussion of *Rainy Mountain*); and (3) by emphasizing parts of *Rainy Mountain* that reveal fascinating combinations of loss, change, and continuity.

Exploring the meanings of the verb *to purvey* provides a way to open a discussion of Indians' relation to nature that will help the student to understand the complexity of Indian philosophical belief systems. *To purvey* comes from the Latin *providere* 'to foresee, provide.' In mainstream Euramerican consciousness, Indians were peoples who both lived off the land and provided for the continuance of natural cycles of life; in fact, Indian philosophies and ecological patterns are the basis for the present-day American conservation ethic, although it is more frequently seen as arising from "the diversification of western thought and . . . [from] transcendental writers" (Cornell 1). The visionary aspect of purveying (foreseeing) has its genesis in the material aspects of Indian existence (providing). Living in accordance with nature's laws, finding sustenance through its cycles of fat and lean, and "reading" nature's signs have enabled Indian peoples to survive, despite the many portents of cataclysmic disaster throughout the years. Momaday's book is itself a testimony to Kiowa survival and change, but his assertion of individual consciousness and imagination, though intended more accurately to represent the place of the individual within a tribal society, can easily be misconstrued as the voice of a single survivor.

Momaday's assertion of individual consciousness is, at least in part, a response to stereotypes of Indians. As he argues in "The Morality of Indian Hating,"

> The Indian has been for a long time generalized in the imagination of the white man. Denied the acknowledgement of individuality and change, he has been made to become in theory what he could not become in fact, a synthesis of himself. (30)

That synthesis—"the Indian," "the Kiowa," and so on—as Kenneth Lincoln notes, results when "we predispose to noble savages, academic methodologies reflexive of our own epistemologies, or disciplinary blinders" ("Tai-me" 116). Yet Momaday's text, as innovative as it is in form, is curiously lacking in an anticipated anger, an anger necessary to offset the image of a people in dignified defeat, an anger indicative of a stubborn refusal to disappear. Thus, the work can evoke the sort of age-old moral flagellation for past "sins" that eclipses "contemporary 'Indi'ns' in evolution within older cultural traditions" (Lincoln, "Tai-me" 116).

In fact, when Momaday's book was first published, reviewers remarked on how it "nags eloquently at the white conscience" and "is in its own way a conscience stabber" (Adams; Stevenson). For teachers of Native American literature, taking into account the way "white conscience" affects the reader's response to the material being taught ought to be an essential aspect of course design. Except for the handful of universities with relatively large American Indian student populations, American Indian literature is taught primarily to non-Indians. Those students may bring to the course some background in Indian history or personal knowledge of contemporary Indian life; they may simply be taking the course to fulfill a humanities requirement; or they may want to know more about Indians. Whatever their preparation or motivation, they generally come to a course in Indian literature from the segment of mainstream Euramerican population which feels that the US government has dealt unjustly with Indians throughout American history. In other words, they tend to be positively biased toward Indians from the start. From my experiences teaching at two large universities where the American Indian literature course is the only one offered as a literature course (as opposed to an anthropology or history course), I have designed a course in which I encourage students to explore their responses as readers to the form and content of the material in relation to the underlying American ideologies that have historically shaped attitudes toward Indians. *The Way to Rainy Mountain* functions, in the class, both as a transition piece between oral and written works and as a medium through which we can examine how differing epistemological approaches can affect the ultimate shape of the meanings derived from reading Indian texts.

To provide the students with a critical framework, I assign a number of articles related to "ways of seeing" to accompany the first several weeks of literary readings. The articles include W. Richard Comstock's "On Seeing with the Eye of a Native European," Arnold Krupat's "Native American Literature and the Canon," Simon J. Ortiz's "Towards a National Indian Literature," and Momaday's "Man Made of Words." The students keep a journal that includes their responses to key terms in their lexicon: *culture, myth, stereotype, archetype, symbol, image, civilization,* and *primitivism*. The course opens with definitions of culture taken from history, literature, anthropology, and folklore that help us make our first attempts to answer tentatively questions like What is an Indian? What makes Indian literature Indian? What makes it literature? I require little evaluated work of the students at the beginning of the course, since most students are unfamiliar with the subject matter and often fear making politically "incorrect" or even racist judgments. Class discussions are guided by the issues and questions raised in their journal entries on the works — assignments due before the discussion of the material begins. I stress my philosophy that the best education involves learning to ask the right questions, not necessarily knowing the "right" answers, and that all is process; we expand, grow, and change in relation to our acquisition of knowledge and experience.

Thereafter, we focus for two weeks on Lakota culture — its music, religious beliefs, and traditions; the history of government policy toward the Sioux people; and the people's own ways of defining history and literature. My efforts to provide students with a broad context for studying the literature of this particular tribe enables them to envision, however dimly, the complexity of other Indian cultures that have been eclipsed or condensed in the other literary works we will read, particularly *The Way to Rainy Mountain*. This historical-cultural approach seems to work; students often tell me at the end of the term that Indian literature should be blessed with the same sort of complex historical-cultural attention that is paid to works by writers like Chaucer, Shakespeare, and T. S. Eliot.

During our examination of Lakota culture and literature, we read John G. Neihardt's and (Nicolaus) Black Elk's *Black Elk Speaks*, comparing the text to passages in *The Sixth Grandfather* (DeMallie); we discuss the role of collaborators in autobiography and the differing images of Indians in popular culture at different times in American history. As Joseph Epes Brown wrote in his 1971 preface to *The Sacred Pipe*, the reading public for Indian texts during the 1970s was beginning to change:

> [T]he inescapable reality of the ecological crisis has for many people shattered a kind of dream world. It has forced us not only to seek immediate solutions to the kinds of problems fostered by a highly developed technology, but also and above all to look to our basic values concerning life and the nature and destiny of man. (xvi)

"Dream world" has a broader connotation here for Brown than it did in the earlier quotation by Momaday. In other words, the historical moment (the late 1960s and early 1970s), when both Black Elk's and Momaday's texts became popular, was a time when mainstream Euramerica focused not only on its specific problems but also on its problematic expansionist philosophy. Although popular images of Indians changed considerably between the publication of the two works, the association of Indians with ecological concerns represented, in 1971, yet another "creation" of Indians by Euramerican image-makers. Only recently have the difficulties associated with Indian "authorship" and "the tyranny of expectations" faced by Indian writers begun to come to academic light (Krupat, *For Those Who Came After* 9–16; Jahner 343).

From *Black Elk Speaks* we move to a discussion of *Lame Deer Seeker of Visions*, by Lame Deer (John Fire) and Richard Erdoes, emphasizing the continuity and change in cultural perspectives, the literary voice, and the author's knowledge and manipulation of the reader—issues that will be relevant to our examination of *The Way to Rainy Mountain*. Discussion focuses on the questions of "authenticity" and on the evidence of resistance by Indian authors to Euramerican definitions of them. The relation between the individual "authorial" voice and the community the author represents becomes crucial to understanding both Black Elk's and Lame Deer's texts. We consider how the "Indianism" created by academic institutions, by government and corporate institutions, and by popular culture media compares with Indians' accounts of their lives as expressed in their literatures and histories. Edward Said's discussion of the historical creation of "Orientalism," in which Said delineates the multifaceted process of co-opting Asian identity, can be useful to the teacher in examining the creation of "Indianism" in the imaginations of Euramericans (*Orientalism*).

From there we begin discussion of *The Way to Rainy Mountain*. After the assault on white sensibilities and values that *Lame Deer* often represents to the students, Momaday's book is a welcome relief. Momaday's lyricism is familiar to most contemporary readers; his solitary narrative voice also rings a bell, although the structure of the narrative uniquely unites historical and legendary points of view into a single interpreting voice. Like Black Elk, Momaday mourns the loss of a way of life, roots his vision in relation to land scape, and believes in the power of dream and in the sacredness of the word. In a general sense, those aspects of Indian ways are "familiar" to most readers—familiar to the point of being stereotypes. Reflecting back to *Black Elk Speaks* and other Lakota materials, however, enables students to recognize the deeper meanings in Momaday's text.

In *The Way to Rainy Mountain*, Momaday implicitly plays on both connotations of the verb *to purvey*. Although he begins his narrative with an elegiac statement—a statement that might mistakenly reinforce a Euramerican stereotype of Plains cultures, the passage should not be seen as "familiar" in a simplistic or overly romantic way:

> There came a day like destiny; in every direction, as far as the eye could see, carrion lay out in the land. The buffalo was the animal representation of the sun, the essential and sacrificial victim of the Sun Dance. When the wild herds were destroyed, so too was the will of the Kiowa people; there was nothing to sustain them in spirit. But these are idle recollections, the mean and ordinary agonies of human history. The interim was a time of great adventure and nobility and fulfillment. (3)

Through memory and imagination, Momaday blends his awareness of "a landscape that is incomparable," his knowledge of "a time that is gone forever," and his appreciation for "the human spirit, which endures," creating a holistic vision of cultural loss, change, and continuance (4). But given the solitary tone of the narrative and Momaday's use of words like "destroyed" and phrases like "the mean and ordinary agonies of human history," the actuality of cultural survival and renewal can be easily missed in the author's "idle recollections."

The journey to Rainy Mountain takes place in the past tense—the author's personal past and the past of the Kiowa people. He stops short of imagining himself as being within a present or a future Kiowa culture. Cultural continuance is implied and theorized but not illustrated as present, except in the private vision of the author himself; his children, for example, are never mentioned. Therefore, it is crucial to place *Rainy Mountain* in the context of other works of Indian literature and to highlight the elements within it that mitigate against belief in the irreversible demise of Indian cultures. Otherwise, the reader might be left believing that the only real Indians are dead Indians—or, worse, that the only good Indian is a singing one. In this new cycle of appreciation for American Indian literatures, we as critics and teachers must carry forth the things we have learned from past generations (Evers, "Cycles"). The weight of grief rightly associated with a past time and with the treatment of Indians in general must not overshadow present concerns and an awareness of Indian diversity; American Indian literature reflects a politics, and we must teach the politics as well as the poetics of the work.

I focus on two sections of *Way to Rainy Mountain*, 15 and 18, that relate to these general issues and to more specific questions about individual versus communal choice and cultural attitudes toward change. In section 15, Quoetotai and Many Bears's wife choose to run away together; being together apparently means more to them than do their places among the Kiowas or within their families. The telling of that tale is evidence of the power and consequence of individual choice. On returning after fifteen years, they are greeted as kin; in the interim they have lived among Comanches. The cultural mores that made them feel they must leave in order to live within their love have changed or been adapted so that they may now return.

In section 18 Kiowa warriors decide to seek an answer to the question "Where does the sun go?"; they head south, apparently to Central America. "The small men with tails" convince them that they have achieved their goal (60); the tale of their adventure lives on in Kiowa lore. The historical sketch that follows indicates that the horse represented the acquisition of a new "technology," enabling the Kiowas to expand their known world and their mythologies. In contrast, when "the animal representation of the sun" (3) — the bison — was destroyed, the Plains Indian cultures experienced a great crisis in belief; yet, when Indians from far-reaching places caught news of Wovoka, the prophet of the Ghost Dance, and his vision, they availed themselves of the railroads to go to hear firsthand of Wovoka's vision. Gods do not die easily.

A language, reflective of a people's worldview, adapts to change as well. For example, white people — "wasicus," as Lakotas call them — were originally associated with "special powers resident in the universe"; today they use the term to connote greed and to designate "the fat-takers" in the history of United States government policies toward Indians (Buechel 551; Johansen and Maestas 17). The language, worldview, and religious beliefs of the Lakotas reflect the significant change wrought by the tribe's encounter with "wasicus." Momaday's physical and symbolic journey to Rainy Mountain reflects loss, change, and continuance, although its occasion is contemporary and its language modern English.

Ko-sahn's dream of herself had a place in it for the portents of falling stars, as well as a place for play. Culture is created through imaginative play, material realities, and historical events, but most of all through stories. In his narrative, Momaday both provides for and foresees the need for the interplay of imagination and memory, individual consciousness and history. We must present his work in ways that will avoid tendencies to see only the romance, nostalgia, and guilt of the past. As teachers we must be purveyors of his words, rooting them in a holistic vision of our times, a legacy Momaday both helped to spawn and continues.

The Way to Rainy Mountain in a Community-Based Oral Narratives Course for Cree and Ojibway Students

Agnes Grant

Native American literature is a relatively new genre in Canadian schools and universities; Canadian Native American literature is even rarer. High school programs generally do not teach literature by Native Americans, and the only opportunity to study Native American literature in many universities is under the native studies umbrella. Thus it is not surprising that students enter the field of Native American literature with much skepticism, asking, "Is there such a thing as Native American literature?"

Brandon University offers a major and a minor in native studies within the faculty of arts; a native studies minor can also be taken as part of a bachelor of education degree. In the native studies program, I teach Indian and Métis students almost exclusively, both on and off campus. Most of my time is spent teaching in an off-campus program called Brandon University Northern Teacher Education Program (BUNTEP). The primary difference between our program and on-campus programs is that the students need not relocate; rather, university staff members travel to the communities to deliver courses. If a sufficiently large group of students wishes to take teacher training and if the community has acceptable facilities and supports the program, a center can be established. Although course requirements are the same as for on-campus students, it is hoped that the teaching staff in BUNTEP will make some modifications in course content and style of delivery while still maintaining university standards. Most of the communities are remote. Many are accessible only by small aircraft, and in most, English is a second language.

This is the ideal setting in which to teach the university's course Oral Narratives. Although those who enroll have to make considerable adjustments, their life-styles are not greatly disrupted; rather, they reflect a blend of modern technologies and old traditions. The intention of the program is not to upset and change the way students live but to teach them the skills they will need to deliver education programs that meet provincial standards. Students must fulfill university requirements, and they graduate with a bachelor of education degree. Naturally, their decision to attend a university affects their lives, but they themselves decide how the old order will adapt to the new.

Oral Narratives is one of the few courses where traditional Native American teachings can come into the classroom. Most of the off-campus students have at least some knowledge of their myths and legends and can tell the stories with competence and enjoyment. Nevertheless, students often start the Oral Narratives course with three deeply held convictions: (1) their folklore is unique, and only they themselves are interested in it; (2) their folklore will not be respected by outsiders and therefore should not be shared; and

(3) there is no relation between their folklore and written literature.

During the first third of the course—on the folklore of the community—I begin to challenge the first two convictions. If possible, I introduce the course using a local storyteller. In northern communities older people are quite reluctant to participate at the center. I have more success with Native American storytellers in the on-campus program, since more assimilation has taken place. If no storyteller is available, I use a cassette tape, *Native Storytelling*, produced by the Manitoba Department of Education. This tape would be useful to any teacher introducing oral narratives to Indian or non-Indian students. It features Ron Roulette, a Canadian Native American storyteller from Northern Saskatchewan; a narrator; and the Cree singer Winston Wuttunee. Roulette explains the role of myths and legends in traditional cultures, speaks about his experiences learning to become a storyteller, and relates some highly entertaining Wee-sak-ee-chak (trickster) adventures. (The tape is somewhat marred by the inclusion of excerpts from Longfellow's *Hiawatha*, an unlikely mixture of Iroquois and Ojibway materials.)

Problems arise with local storytellers because traditionally stories were not told in the summertime. Alex Grisdale, a Saulteaux from the Brokenhead Reserve in Manitoba, explains it this way:

> Legends must not be told in summertime for two reasons. First because so many people would listen to storytellers all day and never hunt or work. The other reason is that all legends are so interesting that even the mice and lizards and toads enter the tepee to listen.   (Qtd. in Shipley 3)

Once, in 1973, I discussed using legends in a university course with an elder from a southern reservation. He warned me that some students would be reluctant to tell legends because they did not know them "right," but he thought the young should try telling stories, always remembering that the trickster was the "biggest liar of them all." He emphasized that there is not necessarily a "right" way of telling many legends. If the details cannot be recalled precisely, the storyteller improvises. The elder was pleased to hear that universities are showing an interest in Indian folklore because in some areas the art of oral storytelling has all but died out among the young people.

We also discussed taboos surrounding the telling of stories in summer. He suggested that students could tell stories in summer because the original reasons for not telling them are now invalid, especially for young people who are training to become teachers. Storytelling should not be mandatory, however, since some students might have strong convictions. "And," he added, "don't come complaining to me if there are frogs and toads in your beds!" Students who do not wish to tell legends in summer usually substitute historical incidents.

Students tell their stories in English, for my benefit and for that of the few who are not proficient in a Native American language. Many students choose to present their legends first in the Native American language and then in English, often adding, "But it is so much more interesting in our languages!" I do not give students any particular guidelines, but usually no two tell the same story. If they do, their versions differ. Trickster tales predominate. Cree communities refer to the trickster as Wee-sak-ee-chak (or variations thereof), whereas Ojibway (Saulteaux) call him Nanabush. Jak-a-pes features predominantly in stories around Cross Lake, and tales of the dread Windigo, a cannibalistic being common to northern hunting cultures, are widespread. Though I provide books for students who insist they do not have a personal repertoire of legends, the materials are rarely used.

The primary source of stories is the students themselves; most of them are parents who are passing stories on to their children. They have an opportunity to consult with elders and one another and to reflect on the role of oral tradition in their lives. They not only tell their own stories but often tape their elders' stories and play the tapes in class. Evening legend-telling sessions take place in their homes as they collect or practice their stories.

Humor plays a prominent role in the storytelling sessions, especially when the stories are told in Cree or Saulteaux. Considerable humor also results from translations of forbidden topics into English. Students are unembarrassed as they tell of the trickster's pursuit of women and his unprecedented sexual feats. Nor do they hesitate to tell hilarious stories about bodily functions.

Many stories have been modernized; in one instance the trickster's "song bag" became a tape recorder. Country and western music is very popular in the north. Hank Snow's song "Your Cheating Heart" is heard on every radio station. I have heard various versions of a story where a Windigo bested Wee-sak-ee-chak in a contest. The trickster, always a poor loser, is still complaining about the unfair tactics of the Windigo, and his wailing of "Your Cheating Heart" can be heard across the north.

My obvious delight in these storytelling sessions helps the students to begin to overcome their conviction that only they can have interest in and respect for their tribal folklore. In the first part of the course I also introduce comparative mythology to convince students that scholars have respected their oral traditions. We study trickster cycles in some detail and read *The Trickster* by Paul Radin and *The Wishing Bone Cycle* by Howard Norman. Students enjoy these cycles because the stories are familiar, but several have pointed out that the Winnebago cycle is incomplete. One student is currently engaged in recording and translating the missing episodes as told in her community.

In the second part of the course students continue to see that their stories are not unrelated to other community and tribal stories as we compare folklore from different neighboring bands. Little of this folklore is recorded, but the stories have become known because of considerable intermarriage. My movement from community to community makes it possible to compare oral narratives within the context of a university course. The course then samples folklore from across Canada — stories from Plains Cree, Blackfeet, Iroquois, Micmac, and others. Students are given a written assignment, which asks them to find three myths or legends with a common theme from three cultures and to discuss how this theme is interpreted, noting similarities and differences.

Traditional poetry is also introduced but not studied in-depth. The emphasis is on songs, and an assignment consists of collecting five songs from five cultures and presenting them orally to the class with commentary. Usually students discuss reasons for differences in interpretation of theme and point out similarities to songs of their own culture, though they know few. Students have contributed insights, however, based on their own experiences. For example, Frances Densmore recorded the following Chippewa lullaby: "We we / We we / We / We we / We we / We / We we / We we / We." She explained that *wewe* is a root and *We we* implies a swinging motion that rocks a baby to sleep (qtd. in Colombo 44, 114). My students tell me the lullaby was not meant to be sung; it has no "words" and was meant to be whistled. These softly whistled lullabies can frequently be heard in northern airports, especially among older parents and grandparents. (False teeth have added a dimension to these lullabies that did not exist in earlier times.)

The final third of the course concerns the transition from oral to written literature and seeks to correct the misconception that the two are unrelated. Particularly useful for this topic are: Markoosie's *Harpoon of the Hunter* and N. Scott Momaday's *Way to Rainy Mountain*. Though written fiction is not a traditional Indian genre, *Harpoon of the Hunter* is readily accepted, probably for its realism. Though life in northern Manitoba is not as harsh as the life of the Inuit, there are many similarities. The students relate readily to the cold, the danger, the strong family ties, the optimism. Most of all, they relate to the style, which is truly that of oral narrative. Nevertheless, they still find it hard to believe that the "world out there" would accept *Harpoon of the Hunter* as literature.

The Way to Rainy Mountain convinces them, once and for all, that Indian experiences, beliefs, myths, legends, and stories can and do form the basis for written literature. Momaday is seen as a role model who has successfully committed to writing the experience of what it is to be an Indian. Like many other readers, Canadian Native American students romanticize Plains Indians; hence they are eager to read Momaday's book. By way of introduction, I trace on a map the historic journey of the Kiowas. Students recall from their introductory courses what life was like for mountain-dwelling Indians—cramped underground homes or crude shelters, long dark winters, difficult land travel, and dangerous waterways. Environmental factors explain why Momaday would say, "The Kiowas reckoned their stature by the distance they could see, and they were bent and blind in the wilderness" (7).

Students understand that a journey like that made by the Kiowas would entail considerable cultural adaptation, for they themselves have been part of dramatic cultural change. They have seen the limited vision of isolated communities broadened, almost overnight as it were, by modern technology. They have inherited a hunting and trapping culture, but that culture no longer exists. The students also identify with the freedom of the Kiowas. They do not know of the freedom in the sense that it was experienced by the lords of the Plains, but they know elders who tell of the free life of the bush Indians, who were restricted only by their physical limitations.

The poignancy of the religious experience is shared. The religion of the Plains Indians holds fascination for many students, and the "shared . . . divinity of the sun" (*Rainy Mountain* 6) is a familiar concept. These students, too, have memories of their elders adopting a new religion, while essentially retaining the old. Momaday's grandmother could well be considered a prototype: "There was a wariness in her, and an ancient awe. She was a Christian in her later years, but she had come a long way about, and she never forgot her birthright" (8). She never forgot despite the forceful encroachments on her religion, especially on the Kiowa Sun Dance, which was forbidden during her childhood: "Without bitterness, and for as long as she lived, she bore a vision of deicide" (10). Her experiences were the experiences of most North American Indians and the students can identify with her.

When I first planned to use *The Way to Rainy Mountain*, I mulled over different ways of presenting it, but I have found that little teaching is necessary if students have an adequate native studies background. Once they understand the organization of the book, it is not intimidating, because they, too, live in the world of three voices. Myths and legends are an integral part of their lives. There is no conflict between mythical knowledge and rational scientific knowledge. Like some persons today, Mammedaty "saw things other men do not see" (39). The legend of Devil's Tower is as logical as the legend of Jak-a-pes and his home in the moon. The factual information of the second voice parallels much of what students have learned at school—information imposed by an alien power and often quite irrelevant to their lives. The literary expression of the third voice comes as a delightful revelation to many, and the pleasure increases as the voices merge at the end of the book. A written assignment on the book consists of discussion of any episode. The episodes most often chosen are those dealing with Mammedaty's unusual powers or else section 24, in which students seem especially fascinated by the beautiful dress.

For most students, acceptance of Mammedaty's powers does not require suspension of rational belief, because they have been raised with respect for the supernatural. Medicine men are still actively involved in healing ceremonies in many communities; Christian burials are only one part of funeral rites. Whether or not Mammedaty had these powers is never questioned. Therefore, the discussion of section 11 is fairly predictable. The "water beast with little short legs and a long heavy tail" lives on. It is only natural that Mammedaty should have the power to see it move the water and create an "awful commotion." Though he did not actually see this prehistoric creature, it is enough that he saw the marks left on the river bank. Similarly, no one to my knowledge has ever seen a Windigo, yet there is little doubt that they exist, and proof is found in the accounts of many a fearful hunter.

The beautiful dress in section 24 lives on as a memorial to the richness of a disappearing heritage. The "cabinet" ensures that it is still there, as carefully preserved as an Egyptian mummy. The whereabouts of the grave is vague; that only Mammedaty had exact knowledge is the best possible protection against inquisitive anthropologists. Yet for my students it is not a disappearing heritage; Aho's carefully described moccasins vary only in small details from the moccasins of every Kokum in the north. These northern grandmothers are crucial to the heritage that lives on, a heritage that celebrates the sacredness of the earth and woman as the earth mother. Hence this last section acts as balm to contemporary Indians. Technology has brought many changes, but basic to all survival is the "remembered earth," essentially unchanged.

In their papers and class discussions students draw on many parallels between their lives and the lives of the Kiowas—the feasts in summer because in winter the people were "cold and kept to themselves," the "aged" visitors with "bright shirts" and "scars of old cherished enmities," the chattering women and the "meals that were banquets" (11). They also see parallels between *Rainy Mountain* and another book, Maria Campbell's autobiography, *Halfbreed*, with which most of the students are familiar. Momaday's Ko-sahn fascinates students because of her similarity to Campbell's Cheechum. Momaday describes Ko-sahn:

> Her thin white hair was held in place by a cap of black netting, though she wore braids as well. . . . She was dressed in the manner of the Kiowa matron, a dark, full-cut dress that reached nearly to her ankles, full, flowing sleeves, and a wide, apron-like sash. She sat on a bench in the arbor so concentrated in her great age that she seemed extraordinarily small.   (86)

Maria Campbell describes Cheechum:

> I remember her as a small woman, with white hair always neatly braided and tied with black thread. She wore black ankle-length full skirts and black blouses with full sleeves and high collars. Around her neck were four or five strings of bright beads and a chain made of copper wire. . . . She wore moccasins and tight leggings to emphasize her tiny ankles.   (15)

The physical similarity between the two women acts as a final reinforcement of shared experience.

The class's closing activity consists of oral readings of *The Way to Rainy Mountain* by the students. Though I expect no great dramatic production, the voices of the readers tell much about the students' involvement with the book. Each group is different; each reading further enhances the book for me. For example, one group darkened the room and had participants sitting in a circle around a dancing "fire" made of electric fireplace logs. The three voices moved in and out of the circle while seated narrators read the descriptive parts. Another group rearranged the room so that the reading was done from the four cardinal directions — three voices and the narrators. Yet another group very effectively had a low, steady drumbeat coming from the fourth direction; the drummer and the three voices were hidden behind screens with only the narrators in view. Each "production" takes on the personality of the group, but the three voices are always very well done and the character of Ko-sahn dominates.

Rainy Mountain opens up a new avenue of expression to my Indian, Métis, and non–Native American students. They see that fine written literature can spring from myth and legend and that this facet of literature can involve all cultures, not only the predominantly Western cultures represented in existing literature courses. They see that their experiences, big or small, can become subjects of literary works. Kenneth Roemer has demonstrated that *The Way to Rainy Mountain* can be used successfully as a writing model for both American and Japanese students ("Inventive Modeling"). They can experiment with their experiences to determine how myth and legend, fact and fancy, historic and contemporary occurrences can all combine to make a work of art.

The book lends itself particularly well to oral performances. Although the author's own voice is preferable, student renditions can enhance an appreciation of the book immeasurably. Richard Fleck of the University of Wyoming has even used outdoor readings situated around an ancient medicine wheel overlooking the prairie and in a traditional tipi with the flap opening to the east ("Outdoor Teaching"). Though I have not experimented with outdoor readings, I have had unexpected responses from students who have come on campus for the summer. Desperately homesick, they choke with emotion as Momaday reminds the reader to "give himself up to a particular landscape in his experience," to look, wonder, touch, listen, recollect and dwell on the "remembered earth" (83). This sense of place is by no means unique to Native American students.

Momaday created an unusual combination of oral and written styles to convey truths about myth and legend, tribal history, and personal experience — truths that can help Indian and Métis students in remote Canadian communities as well as non-Indian students in cities in the southern areas to understand that uniquely Indian literature has a valued position in contemporary society.

EPILOGUE

An Interview with Gary Kodaseet

Conducted by Kenneth M. Roemer

No one Kiowa can "represent" Kiowa views, and certainly Gary Kodaseet does
not pretend any such representation. His responses to *The Way to Rainy Mountain* are, nonetheless, particularly interesting because his background allows
for both distance from and empathy with Momaday's feelings about the landscapes, stories, and history presented in the book. Unlike Momaday, Kodaseet
spent his precollege years entirely in Oklahoma, Kiowa country, surrounded
by Kiowa relatives who taught him the Kiowa language. He attended Haskell
Institute, a Bureau of Indian Affairs boarding school in Kansas, where his father, Frank Kodaseet, and Momaday's mother had studied. He served in the
US Marines and now works for the Dallas Regional Office of Health and Human Services, where he focuses on tribal conditions. These differences between Momaday's and Kodaseet's backgrounds are significant but no more
so than are the striking similarities. Both men are of the same generation.
Momaday was born in 1934; Kodaseet in 1936. They were even born in the
same hospital, the Kiowa Indian Hospital in Lawton, Oklahoma. As children
they experienced the same landscape. Momaday's family lived in Mountain
View; Kodaseet's in the Sugar Creek community. Rainy Mountain is within
a few miles of both places. (During his kindergarten and part of his first-grade
years, Kodaseet lived in Mountain View.) Both have strong attachments to their
grandparents. Aho and Mammedaty are central to *Rainy Mountain*. While
Kodaseet was in his preschool years and his father was traveling to remote
areas with the Civilian Conservation Corps, he was raised by his grandmother
Abbie To-dome (Pau-daw) and his great-grandfather James To-dome, who had
been a sergeant and a scout for the Seventh Cavalry. (For an account of
Kodaseet's family background, see Boyd 2: 167–72.) They became his parents,

teachers, and playmates. Kodaseet has clear memories of his grandmother driving a wagon and team of horses (she never drove a car) and dreamlike memories of himself trying to teach his great-grandfather a few English words and of his great-grandfather's dying, when Kodaseet was three years old. When he began school, he lived with his parents and his grandmother. Like Momaday's parents, his parents had a strong sense of their Indian identity. (Kodaseet's mother, Lilly Botone Kodaseet, also known as Nina, is one of the tribe's Taime keepers.) Another significant similarity: while Kodaseet has succeeded in a career outside his tribal context, he has maintained strong commitments to his tribal identity. While he was a marine stationed in San Diego, he helped found an Indian club that revived interest in traditional dance among California Indians in the area; he has served as vice president and president of the Texas Indian Heritage Society; he is a member of the Kiowa Black Leggings Organization (a veteran's group with tribal historical roots); and, like Momaday, he is a member of the Kiowa Gourd Clan or Tiapiah Society.

The following interview was made on 5 November 1986, in Arlington, Texas, and subsequently edited jointly by Kodaseet and me. I would like to thank two Kiowa artists, Roland N. Whitehorse and Sherman Chaddlesone, for offering their suggestions to us about the types of questions that should be covered in this interview. I would also like to acknowledge the hospitality of the Kiowas who were assembled during the 12 October 1986 Black Leggings ceremonial dances, when Kodaseet introduced me to the artists and to several other Kiowas interested in their tribal heritage.

Kenneth M. Roemer: One question my students often ask when they begin to discuss *The Way to Rainy Mountain* is, "How did Rainy Mountain get its name?" The written sources I've examined don't answer this question very well. Are there any Kiowa stories that explain the name?

Gary Kodaseet: I asked my mother after you contacted me. She grew up in that area, so I asked her, "What was the meaning of Rainy Mountain?" Her story was a little different from the one Sherman [Chaddlesone] told us. [On 12 October Chaddlesone said that the long journey of the Kiowas from the headwaters of the Yellowstone had ended at Rainy Mountain. When they arrived, it was raining, and it kept raining so hard for three days that the Kiowas could not set up camp. Most of the time they stayed on their horses.] She said that whenever the Kiowas camped near this mountain, it always rained. And that was her story. I asked her if there was a Kiowa name for the area. She said it was *Sape yal-daw*. [For an alternative spelling, see Lawana Trout's essay in pt. 2.]

KMR: You grew up near Rainy Mountain. Would you like to comment on any of Momaday's descriptions of the area? How do they compare with your memories of the landscape?

GK: Well, in the beginning of the book, he speaks of Rainy Mountain as being a "single knoll." It is a knoll. It's single in that it's not in the same line with the other hills. But there are other hills in that area. It's not flat, and Rainy Mountain's not the only landmark. Directly south and southwest and southeast of Rainy Mountain there are hills, the same type of hills. But Rainy Mountain is separate — in other words, away from the groupings of the hills.

I think that his descriptions are fairly accurate. I mean, I can see those things he's talking about. He talks about the landscape being very harsh. There's a lot of mesquite trees there. The streams are real small; they're not very wide. You wouldn't even know there were streams there until you see the little clumps of trees. In one of the sentences he talks about the grass crackling as you step on it. In the summertime I've seen it get that dry. The grass does crack as you walk.

He spoke of the grasshoppers. I know them. We used to find the big green grasshoppers. The yellow ones are all over, but the big green ones, they were unusual in that they didn't seem to be able to fly like the other grasshoppers. They were just huge green grasshoppers. He talks about tarantulas. I know that we used to find tarantulas in the area, too, and the land turtles, the terrapins. We called them land turtles. They're a kind of delicacy to the Kiowas. They cook those land terrapins. They say that if a man loses his appetite, then you should cook a turtle for him. There're different flavors of meat that you taste in the turtle. That brings his appetite back.

KMR: Another aspect of the book that interests college students is the traditional Kiowa storytelling. How do the tribal stories in *The Way to Rainy Mountain* compare with the stories you were told by your grandmother and other relatives and friends?

GK: Of all the stories that I read in *The Way to Rainy Mountain* there are several that stand out. I've heard the stories. The endings are the same, but the stories are different — little differences.

He talks about the tornado [sec. 14]. The Kiowas created the tornado. In the story that Momaday tells, the tornado was created because a Kiowa made the figure of a horse. The way I heard the story was that a Kiowa was making the figure of a horse out of clay or mud, just as Momaday says. But there was another part to the story. Once the Kiowa made this horse, it spoke to him and said, "You forgot one thing on the figure of the horse." Because of this, the horse would become a whirlwind. The one thing he forgot was that on the inside of a horse's leg, usually the back leg, there's always a wart, a hard growth that comes out. This clay horse said, "That's the reason: because you forgot that one thing when you made me. Now I'll be this terrible wind."

In this story Momaday talks about how the Kiowas speak to the wind; they do. The old-timers did when there was a tornado. I've been in several tornadoes when the old people would talk to the wind. I remember this one old woman. She lived with a family called Bear Track, but I don't think her name was Bear Track. I think she was Kiowa. In the Kiowa language, she told the storm to attack Germany and Japan. The grandchildren were teasing her, "Grandma we're not at war with them anymore." They do that; the old people talk to the storm and tell it to pass them by.

The other story is about the Devil's Tower [8]. In the book Momaday talks about the bear being a boy. In the story I heard it's a girl that becomes the bear. The older sister becomes the bear. The younger sister is warned by her older sister before this thing takes place, before she changes into the bear. She tells the younger sister to go to this place where the dogs stay, to stay there no matter what happens. The older sister does turn into a bear, and she kills everyone — the whole village. Then she goes back to her younger sister and tells her to come out, says she's not going to harm her. She wants her to be her slave for the rest of her life. The young girl does come out, and she is doing this for this bear. Then she's rescued. Some young men come. They have horses, so this would have to be after the Spaniards had arrived and the Kiowas had horses. Momaday tells of it being a stump that grew and saved the young people. In the story I heard, it's a stone that grew, and the sister and the young men become stars. That's the same ending that he tells in his book — just a few little changes in the story. The changes could be because the story is oral history, and things change. You know, when you tell people, you either add to the story or maybe you take something away. But it comes out to the same ending.

KMR: Do Kiowas still tell stories like the ones you heard and the ones Momaday presents in *Rainy Mountain*?

GK: I can only speak from my own experience. I tell the stories. I told the stories to my children, not only my children but my nephews and nieces. Now they are telling these stories the way I heard them. . . . These stories, I don't know, I guess they were just told in our families by someone who took up that responsibility to tell us. My stories came from my grandmother, Abbie. She's the one who told us those stories. We would all gather around in her lap or bed, and she would start telling stories. I think that at one time, you know, we were talking to Roland [Whitehorse], we were saying that there was a time when the Kiowas would gather, and there were people who told stories. The stories of our beginning, the stories of the ten bundles. Now it's kind of an individual thing. You tell them to your children and grandsons and granddaughters. They're sentiments that you pass on to young children. When they're that age, they don't want to watch tv. They'd rather sit and listen to stories.

And we were not only entertained by these stories when we were children, we were also told family histories — where we came from, who our ancestors were. At the Kiowa agency, the Bureau of Indian Affairs, I'm listed as full-blood Kiowa. But the stories told me I'm not. I've Mescalero Apache blood, Mexican blood, Scotch-Irish blood. We've always said French Canadian, but we think it might have been English or Irish, we also have their blood, you know, in our family. At the BIA level I'm full-blooded Kiowa. All these other bloods I've learned about from the family stories.

KMR: This description of your story-listening experience is very interesting. Students often assume that the unusual form, the mixing of voices in *The Way to Rainy Mountain*, is related to experiments in twentieth-century written literature, which to some degree it is. Your situation demonstrates, however, that the family storytelling situation naturally mixed traditional tribal stories and family and tribal histories, and, since the whole situation was very intimate, you obviously also had the presence of the personal voice. We've begun to move toward another topic college students find interesting, the family and tribal historical information, especially the migration of the Kiowas. Do you have any comments about this type of historical material in Momaday's book?

GK: Well, one of the things that he talks about is that his grandmother, Aho, although she never saw the places that we came from—the Black Hills and further north—the stories made her feel that these places were in her memory. We feel they are in our memory. I've never seen Devil's Tower, but I've heard about it all my life, since I was very small. Devil's Tower grew because of these Kiowa children. And it's there. I want to see it. And I plan to go up there sometime, because I think that probably somewhere in our genetic makeup something says, "You know, you're home. This is where you're from."

KMR: You've given me a good idea of how you've responded to *The Way to Rainy Mountain*. Do you have any notion of how other Kiowas, storytellers or others, responded to the book?

GK: I know I enjoyed the book. . . . A lot of the writing about Indians is historical. Momaday talks about history, but he also writes about more recent times in this book and in *House Made of Dawn*. Most of what you read about Indians is set back when they fought the cavalry, those kinds of things. I think most of the people, the Kiowas who have read *The Way to Rainy Mountain*, probably support Momaday's different way of writing about Indians.

I think I do. But I remember having feelings about the book when I read it the first time. It's kind of sad, the ending. This is all gone. This is what we had or they had. I remember getting that feeling before when I first read it and again when I read it this time.

KMR: Earlier you also said that the book gave you other types of feelings—a desire to see places where the Kiowas came from, to write or tell stories about your own family—in a sense a desire to tell what it is for you to be a Kiowa. One way that many scholars and students read *The Way to Rainy Mountain* is as an attempt by a Kiowa—in this case one who has spent much of his life away from traditional Kiowa areas—to define what it means for him to be a Kiowa. Have you seen evidence of other Kiowas who have been away from their homeland trying to answer this question? If so, how are they doing this?

GK: Well, I've seen Scott come home and take part in some of the dances we do. The year he won the Pulitzer there was a family reunion, and we were invited to attend. Most of the Kiowa tribe was invited to attend. It was in Mountain View. Some of the people representing the state of Oklahoma came to honor Scott. I've got a recording of that gathering. Scott gave a poem dedicated to his grandfather. It's called "The Gourd Dancer." Scott comes home to the celebrations in the summer. He takes part in the gourd dancing, and he's been to the Kiowa Black Leggings dances.

I think that there are a lot of Kiowas who do that, who just come home in the summertime. I have one friend who's half Comanche and half Kiowa. Even though he has a Kiowa last name, the culture he learned from his mother was Comanche. Well, this was fine until five or six years ago when he found out that he was on the Kiowa tribal rolls. He's not on the Comanche rolls. So, he came to me and said, "What do I do? What do I have to do to become a Kiowa? What do Kiowas do?" You know, he didn't understand the language. He knows some of the songs—a lot of the songs. But he always thought he was Comanche.

I think that people who are never able to come back home, who can't visit with the Kiowa people, would have problems. But I can't think of very many that don't come. I've seen other Indians from other tribes who have identity problems. They're not sure how to act. In a lot of cases they overact. They're the ones that you see wearing the chokers, the feathers, the braids, and the ribbon shirts because they think that is what being an Indian is. The Indians who don't have a problem accept the fact that they're Kiowa or Comanche or other tribes.

I don't think Momaday has the problem. He remembers his grandmother, remembers certain things about how she was, and his grandfather. And, as I said, he comes to the dances, and he takes part. It may just be once a year, but it means a lot to him and to the family.

KMR: Do you know of any other Kiowas or other Indians who use writing to help them define or imagine who they are?

GK: There are a number of Indian poets—they don't have the status of Momaday. I see their work in Indian newsletters. One friend, he's Kiowa, he's Harlan Hall, lives in Los Angeles; he writes a lot of poetry. When I was in the Los Angeles area and was a director of an Indian center, we put out a little newsletter. I said to [Harlan], "Poems are something we use as fillers. We'd be glad to use some of yours." He sent me about a pound of paper with nothing but poetry on it. His poetry is about places in Oklahoma, around Rainy Mountain. He speaks of Sugar Creek. He's been published in little local Indian newsletters. He's not known nationally, but he likes to write poems. I see a lot of that.

I think that the Kiowas needed something like this—writing the English language. It's going to help preserve the history of the people to write things down. You know, we're losing the storytellers. During the age when I grew up, we were very close-knit families. I lived with my grandmother. We walked or took the wagon to her brother's and visited. There was no tv. We had a few radios, but there was more of a storytelling atmosphere. Now anyone who tells a story has to compete with television or MTV or tapes or rock music or whatever the kids are into. During the time that I grew up, we were more into storytelling, listening for hours to the grandparents tell stories.

I'm not sure how old Scott is, but I think he's probably a year or two older than I am. He probably came through the same period. He was told these stories. He is able to write them down, to preserve them for other Kiowa generations or non-Kiowa generations. So I think that writing is just now starting to be used by Kiowas. I think they were always artistic, always able to draw, to paint, because they kept calendars before writing. Writing is something that's still fairly new to us; it probably started during our—Momaday's—generation. It's a new tool. It's the new Kiowa calendar. We have a few artists that use it, and Scott is one of them. Hopefully, we can have more who will come up and do these things. It's always been that the Kiowas have had to tell their stories to the non-Indian, and the non-Indian wrote them. Scott was probably the first who was an Indian and was able to write the stories that he knew as a Kiowa—written by a Kiowa. We have a lot of Kiowa stories, but they're written by [Alice] Marriott, Wilbur Nye, Maurice Boyd, and other non-Kiowas, non-Indians. Scott is a Kiowa writing about Kiowa experiences. Hopefully, there will be more Kiowas who do that.

KMR: You've been talking about how Kiowas respond to Momaday's book and how Kiowas respond to being Kiowas. Now I'd like to switch the viewpoint a bit to non-Kiowas, non-Indians. Much of *The Way to Rainy Mountain* is about places, people, and stories that are unfamiliar to most college students. They might even think that the subject matter is irrelevant to their lives. I'm wondering, why should a non-Indian student in South Philadelphia read a book like Momaday's?

GK: I think that question could be asked about any history of a people. When I was in Saint Patrick's Mission parochial school, I had to take Latin for two years. A lot of the Latin we read was history. We had to study about Romulus and Remus, who nursed off a she-wolf to keep them going. I could ask the same question. How was that relevant to me?

I think that *The Way to Rainy Mountain* is relevant in that it gives you a historical view of a people who are still there. You're able to see a tribe of Indians who came, within the last hundred years or so, from the Stone Age into the present. It's very recent, and it's a history of America. The student in Philadelphia needs to see that this is American history; the Kiowas are very much a part of American history. They were here—we always say, "We were here when you came, and we're still here." And that history, to me, is more relevant than Romulus and Remus, because you're studying about people who are in your own country.

And *The Way to Rainy Mountain* is relevant because of its unique style of writing; to me it's almost poetic, the way that he explains certain things and feelings that he has. The descriptions are very good, very clear. I think that students who are learning writing can use a lot of the style he's presenting in his book. You can read it in a day or less if you're a fast reader.

He also gives the myths of the Kiowa people, and how are we to know if that isn't history too? The myth may have at one time really happened. But, you know, through the years it comes down to us as a fairy tale. But it may have happened, and probably did. It's hard for me to imagine it raining forty days and forty nights and flooding the earth. I can't imagine that. To me that's a myth. But it's in the Bible. It happened sometime. It's important for students to see that sort of thing in Kiowa myths, too.

KMR: Now let's conclude by switching from the students to the teachers. Do you have any general advice you'd like to offer to college instructors who are introducing *The Way to Rainy Mountain* to their students?

GK: This book was written by a man whose Kiowa grandparents couldn't even read or write English. But in one or two generations he's come to a point where he's won a Pulitzer. How many writers, how many professors can say, "I have a Pulitzer." I think that he should be taught because of his writing style and because in some of his descriptions in *House Made of Dawn* and *The Way to Rainy Mountain* you can almost feel that you're part of the story and that this is not just happening to him; it's happening to you, too.

For me, his description of when he went with his father and grandmother to see the Tai-me bundle is like that (sec. 10). I too visited the bundle. I was a marine on leave with my friend who was a Kickapoo-Potawatomi. My father and mother took us to see my grandfather, Moses Botone, who was a keeper of the Tai-me bundle. They wanted us to be blessed. My grandfather kept the bundle down in his cellar. He went down first—I guess to make some preparations. Then I went down. He prayed in Kiowa that no danger would come to us while we were in the service. I served for four years between the Korean and Vietnam wars. I was always stationed in the US and was always safe. My friend served for twenty years and went to Vietnam. He was never hurt. I used to say that the bundle was so powerful that it protected us both. You know, when you're near the Tai-me bundle, you have the sense of being in the presence of something holy and very powerful and very old. It's tangible. It's not like Christianity; we're not asked to depend on faith. We see it—the bundle. I picked it up. I've been blessed with it. Scott felt that when he went to the Tai-me. It's old and it's still with us.

Another description that made me feel like I was part of the story comes near the end of the book when the old woman Ko-sahn remembers the Sun Dance and imagines an even older woman who sang, "As old as I am, I still have the feeling of play" [88]. A lot of old Kiowa people are like that. They're always teasing you. They laugh a lot. They may have arthritis or may have lost a leg. They look like they shouldn't be laughing. But they do. For at least ten years my grandmother was in great pain with arthritis, but we could always get her to laugh. Sometimes she'd try to keep from laughing, but she'd break into a laugh. These old people and the old woman in *Rainy Mountain* are like that; they have a sense of play. They're not silent, stoic Indians. Teachers need to show students the old Sun Dance woman so that they will know that the stereotypes are wrong.

PARTICIPANTS IN THE SURVEY OF *THE WAY TO RAINY MOUNTAIN* INSTRUCTORS

All the following scholars responded to the questionnaire on teaching *The Way to Rainy Mountain*; most of them also submitted essay proposals for part 2. Without their help it would have been impossible to produce this volume. The list indicates colleges where the participants taught when they submitted their survey responses.

Julia Alvarez, University of Illinois; Lauri Anderson, Suomi College; Sonja Bahn, Universität Innsbruck, Austria; Carole Barrett, Mary College; Ruth Barton, Colorado College; Gretchen M. Bataille, Iowa State University; Robert L. Berner, University of Wisconsin, Oshkosh; Helmbrecht Breinig, Universität Bamberg, West Germany; H. David Brumble III, University of Pittsburgh; Lawrence Clayton, Hardin-Simmons University; Laura Coltelli, University of Pisa, Italy; Elizabeth Cook-Lynn, Eastern Washington University; Roger Dunsmore, University of Montana; Larry Evers, University of Arizona; Ruth Feldman, Chabot College; Richard F. Fleck, University of Wyoming; Agnes Grant, Brandon University, Canada; Regina Harrison, Bates College; Joan Henley, University of Baltimore; David Hoehner, University of Utah; Carol Hunter, University of Oklahoma; Elaine A. Jahner, Dartmouth College; Helen Jaskoski, California State University, Fullerton; Arnold Krupat, Sarah Lawrence College; Mervin Lane, Santa Barbara City College; Charles R. Larson, American University; Vernon E. Lattin, University of Wisconsin, Madison; Charles Link, East Texas State University; John Lowe, Harvard University; Suzanne Evertsen Lundquist, Brigham Young University; Beatrice Medicine, University of Calgary, Canada; William Oandasan, University of California, Los Angeles; Delilah Orr, Navajo Community College; J. Frank Papovich, University of Virginia; Bernd C. Peyer, J. W. Goethe–Universität Frankfurt, West Germany; Richard C. Poulsen, Brigham Young University; K. S. Ramamurti, Bharathidasan University, India; Jarold Ramsey, University of Rochester; Stephen Ratcliffe, Mills College; Charles Roberts, California State University, Sacramento; Gretchen Ronnow, University of Arizona; A. LaVonne Brown Ruoff, University of Illinois, Chicago; James Ruppert, University of New Mexico, Valencia Campus; Susan Scarberry-García, Colorado College; Matthias Schubnell, Bucknell University; Janet Sutherland, Universität Regensburg, West Germany; Yuri Tambovtsev, University of Novosibirsk, USSR; Lawana Trout, Newberry Library; Clara Lee Turner, University of Arizona; Kathryn S. Vangen, University of Washington; Ann Waggoman, Cooke County College; Floyd C. Watkins, Emory University; Roger Weaver, Oregon State University; Bette S. Weidman, Queens College, City University of New York; Andrew Wiget, New Mexico State University, Las Cruces; Norma C. Wilson, University of South Dakota; James C. Work, Colorado State University; Ona Wright, Cooke County College.

APPENDIX A
Selected Comparative Possibilities

I have based the organization of the following list of comparative possibilities on the structure of *The Way to Rainy Mountain*. Momaday organized the body of his text into twenty-four numbered sections, which he grouped together into three major divisions ("The Setting Out," "The Going On," and "The Closing In"). Each of the numbered sections is further divided into three voices. This appendix is not a list of "sources"; it is a selected list of possible comparisons between parallel passages in Momaday's text and in works published before and after *Rainy Mountain*. Analyses of the similarities and differences between Momaday's and other parallel texts illuminate processes that transform personal reflections and family and tribal oral narratives into multigenre, written literature for a "general" readership.

Key to Abbreviations

[B, 1]	Boyd, *Kiowa Voices*, vol. 1
[B, 2]	Boyd, *Kiowa Voices*, vol. 2
[H]	Highwater, *Anpao*
HA	Harrington, *Vocabulary of the Kiowa Language*
MA	Mayhall, *The Kiowas*
MO	Mooney, *Calendar History*
MT	Marriott, *Ten Grandmothers*
[MT & R-A]	Marriott and Rachlin, *American Indian Mythology*
[MT & R-P]	Marriott and Rachlin, *Plains Indian Mythology*
NB	Nye, *Bad Medicine and Good*
NC	Nye, *Carbine and Lance*
P	Parsons, *Kiowa Tales*

See "Works Cited" for bibliographical information. Brackets indicate a work published after *The Way to Rainy Mountain*.

Division of *WTRM*	Possible Comparisons
Prologue, introd. (3–14)	[B, 1: 10–11]; [B, 2: 87–93]; MA: ix–xi, 3, 106, 205–06, 331–32; MO: 151, 152–57, 221, 355, 389; MT: 151; P: 9–11
"Setting Out" (15–42)	
1, 1	[B, 1: 1]; [B, 2: 14]; MA: 6; MO: 152–53; [MT & R–P: 36–37]
1, 2	MA: 21; MO: 148–52
2, 1	[B, 1: 9–10]; [B, 2: 61–62]; HA: 252–55 (bilingual); MA: 11; MO: 153–54; MT: viii; [MT & R–P: 38]; P: 89
2, 2	MA: 177; MO: 152, 154, 287–89
3, 2	[B, 1: 6]; MA: 12–13, 138–39, 176; MO: 153, 161, 230, 284–285; MT: 7, 41; NB: viii

4, 1	[B, 1: 7]; [B, 2: 3]; [H: 61]; MO: 238; [MT & R–A: 103]; P: 4–5
5, 1	[B, 1: 7]; [B, 2: 3–4]; [H: 62–70]; MO: 238; [MT & R–A: 104–10]; P: 1–2, 5
5, 2	MA: 7; MO: 153; MT: viii, 206
6, 1	[B, 2: 4]; [H: 70–73]; MO: 238–39; [MT & R–A: 110–12]; P: 2, 5–7
6, 2	MA: 198; MO: 339; NB: 198; NC: 220–21
7, 1	[B, 1: 7]; [B, 2: 5]; [H: 75–77]; MO: 239; [MT & R–A: 113–15]; P: 2, 7
8, 1	[B, 2: 7]; P: 2–3, 8
8, 2	MO: 152, 231
9, 1	[B, 1: 7–8]; [B, 2: 6]; P: 4, 7
9, 2	[B, 1: 8]; [B, 2: 11–12]; MA: 7; MO: 238–39; P: 1
10, 1	[B, 2: 47–50]; MO: 304–05; NB: 42
10, 2	[B, 2: 48]; MA: 147, 149; MO: 240
11, 1	[B, 2: 131–33]
11, 2	[B, 1: 103–11]; MT: 169–72
"Going On" (43–64)	
12, 2	MA: 194, 197, 282; MO: insert between 336 and 337
14, 1	NB: 155–56; P: 15, 16–17, 109
14, 2	MA: ix
15, 2	MA: 78–79; MO: 171, 261–69
15, 3	[B, 1: 12]; MA: 79; MO: facing 268
16, 1	[B, 2: 70–73]
17, 2	MA: 141, 152, 163, 174, 178; MO: 233, 280–81, 294; NB: 82
17, 3	MA: 163; NB: xiv
18, 1	MT: 103; NB: ix
18, 2	MA: 13; MO: 161
"Closing In" (65–84)	
19, 2	MA: 126, 200, 296–97, 304; MO: 214, 339–40, 344–45; NB: 198–201; NC: 222–23, 228, 229–30
20, 2	MA: 126, 150, 185; MO: 310
22, 2	MA: 178; MO: 295
23, 1	P: 109
Epilogue (85–88)	[B, 1: 47]; MA: 81, 113, 169; MO: 169–70, 241, 243, 257–59, 260–61, 269; [MT & R–P: 115–17]; NB: ix, x, 70; [Moma-day, *The Names*: 48 (Pohd-lohk's ledgerbook)]; Sullivan

APPENDIX B
Basic Chronology Relating to
The Way to Rainy Mountain

The following basic chronology, which begins with the Kiowa migration and ends with Momaday's retracing of the migration, his pilgrimage to his grandmother's grave, and his visits to Kiowa elders to collect stories, should help students "place" *The Way to Rainy Mountain* within the contexts of tribal and family histories. More important, it should encourage them to examine how Momaday selected and used Kiowa events and dates as he composed the exchanges among the three voices in the twenty-four sections of the book. My main sources are *The Way to Rainy Mountain, The Names,* James Mooney's "Summary of Principal Events" (226) and his descriptions of Kiowa calendar entries (254–364) in *Calendar History,* Lawana Trout's essay in this collection, and the gravestones in the old cemetery at Rainy Mountain Kiowa Indian Baptist Church, near Mountain View, Oklahoma. The third volume of Maurice Boyd's *Kiowa Voices* (forthcoming) will provide extensive historical contexts for *Rainy Mountain.* (I would like to thank A. LaVonne Brown Ruoff for suggesting the inclusion of a chronology and for sending me the dates she uses in her classes. I would also like to thank N. Scott Momaday and Matthias Schubnell for examining a draft of the chronology.)

Note: An asterisk indicates a date not mentioned in *Rainy Mountain;* "epilogue," "pro.," "introd.," and "sec." refer to parts of *Rainy Mountain.*

1700* (approx.) Migration of the Kiowas from the Yellowstone region (pro. 4; introd. 6–8; Mooney 226)

1732*   Kiowas mentioned in Spanish description of New Mexico (Mooney 226)

1740   Beginning of the golden era of the Kiowa Plains culture (epilogue 85; Mayhall 112)

1770* (approx.) Expulsion of the Kiowas from the Black Hills (Mooney 226)

1790* (approx.) Peace and alliance with Comanche (pro. 4; Mooney 226)

1805*   First "American" mention of Kiowas in North Platte region (Mooney 226)

1833   Osage massacre of Kiowas; Tai-me stolen; falling stars (epilogue suggests that the massacre was in 1832; Mooney 257–61)

1834   Kau-au-ointy (Mammedaty's grandmother) born (sec. 17); Catlin travels among and paints the Kiowas (sec. 15; Mooney 264–69); first official contacts with United States government (Mooney 226)

1837   First Kiowa treaty with the United States government signed at Fort Gibson (epilogue 85; Mooney 226)

1839*   Smallpox epidemic (Mooney 226)

1843   Woman stabbed by a jealous husband for riding with Chief Dohasan (sec. 17; Mooney 280–81)

1848–49   Buffalo scarce; antelope drive held (sec. 2; Mooney 287–89)

1849*   Cholera epidemic (Mooney 226)

1851–52   Big Bow held in conversation with his father while the woman he "stole" waits outside; her feet freeze (sec. 17; Mooney 294)

1852–53   A Pawnee steals a fine Kiowa horse (sec. 22; Mooney 295)

1861   Spotted horse sacrificed at Sun Dance; smallpox epidemic; Gaapiatan sacrifices a fine horse (sec. 20; Mooney 310)

1864*   General outbreak of Plains tribes (Mooney 226)

1866*   Death of Chief Dohasan (Mooney 226)

1867*   Medicine Lodge treaty; Kiowas agree to move to reservation (Mooney 226)

1868*   Battle of Washita; Utes steal Tai-me (Mooney 226)

1869*   Kiowas move to reservation (Mooney 226)

1871*   Setangya killed (Mooney 226)

1872*   First attempts to establish reservation schools (Mooney 226)

1872–73   Do-giagya guat (a heraldic tipi) burns (sec. 12; Mooney 336)

1874–75   Confrontation with troops at Palo Duro Canyon, Texas; Kiowas surrender; end of golden age (introd. 8; sec. 6; sec. 19; epilogue 85; Mooney 339)

1879   Buffalo scarce; Kiowas forced to eat their ponies (sec. 19; Mooney 344–45)

1880*   Aho and Mammedaty born (introd. 8, 10; Names 26; gravestones)

1881*   Datekan's prophecy about bringing back the buffalo (Mooney 226, 349–50)

1886*   First payment for "grass money" from cattlemen using Kiowa lands (Mooney 354)

1887   Last Kiowa Sun Dance held near the mouth of a small tributary of the Washita north of Rainy Mountain Creek (introd. 10; Mooney 355)

1890*   Sun Dance stopped by agent (Mooney 358–59)

1913*   Mayme Natachee Scott (Momaday's mother) born (Names 20); Alfred Morris Mammedaty (Momaday's father) born (Names 33)

1929   Kau-au-ointy dies (sec. 17)

1932*   Mammedaty dies (gravestone)

1934*   Novarro Scott Mammedaty born; Pohd-lohk names him Tsoai-talee (Names 42, 57)

1939   Pohd-lohk dies (gravestone)

1963*   With his father and Aho, Momaday visits the Tai-me bundle (sec. 10; Schubnell 142)

1965*   Aho dies; Momaday traces the migration route of the Kiowas and visits her grave (introd. 5–6, 7, 12); with the assistance of his father, Momaday collects stories from Kiowa elders.

WORKS CITED

Those primarily interested in introductions to Momaday and American literary genres should examine the "Background Studies" section of part 1 before consulting this listing.

Adams, Phoebe. Rev. of *The Way to Rainy Mountain*, by N. Scott Momaday. *Atlantic* June 1969: 117.

Allen, Paula Gunn, ed. *The Sacred Hoop: Recovering the Feminine in American Indian Traditions*. Boston: Beacon, 1986.

——, ed. *Studies in American Indian Literature: Critical Essays and Course Designs*. New York: MLA, 1983.

——. *The Woman Who Owned the Shadows*. San Francisco: Spinsters, 1983.

American Indian Literature. Filmstrip 2. Films for the Humanities, 323D, 1980.

Anaya, Rudolfo A. *Bless Me, Ultima*. Berkeley: Quinto Sol, 1972.

Andrist, Ralph K. *The Long Death: The Last Days of the Plains Indian*. New York: Macmillan, 1964.

Arguelles, Jose, and Miriam Arguelles. *Mandala*. Berkeley: Shambala, 1972.

Arias, Ron. *The Road to Tamazunchale*. Reno: West Coast Poetry Review, 1975.

Azcuy, Eduardo A. *Arquetipos y simbolos celestes*. Buenos Aires: Garcia Cambeiro, 1976.

Ballinger, Franchot. "A Matter of Emphasis: Teaching the 'Literature' in Native American Literature Courses." *American Indian Culture and Research Journal* 8.2 (1984): 1–12.

Bartlett, Mary Dougherty, ed. *The New Native American Novel: Works in Progress*. Albuquerque: U of New Mexico P, 1986.

Bataille, Gretchen M. *Inside the Cigar Store: Images of the American Indian*. Slide and audiocassette program. Iowa State U Medias Resources Ctr., 1979. 140 slides.

Bataille, Gretchen M., and Charles P. Silet. *The Make-Believe Indian: Native Americans in the Movies*. Slide and audiocassette program. Iowa State U Research Foundation, 1981. 140 slides.

Beck, Peggy V., and A. L. Walters. *The Sacred: Ways of Knowledge, Sources of Life*. Tsaile: Navajo Community Coll., 1977.

Beidler, Peter G. Rev. of *Studies in American Indian Literature*, ed. Paula Gunn Allen. *American Indian Quarterly* 9 (1985): 468–71.

Bellah, Robert N. "The New Religious Consciousness and the Secular University." *Daedalus* 103.4 (1974): 110–15.

Bellah, Robert N., et al. *Habits of the Heart*. New York: Harper, 1985.

Bellow, Saul. *Saul Bellow and the Critics*. Ed. Irving Malin. New York: New York UP, 1967.

Berner, Robert L. "N. Scott Momaday: Beyond Rainy Mountain." *American Indian Culture and Research Journal* 3.1 (1979): 57–67.

Berry, Wendell. *A Continuous Harmony*. New York: Harcourt, 1972.

——. "A Secular Pilgrimage." *Hudson Review* 23 (1970): 401–24.

Bloodworth, William. "Neihardt, Momaday, and the Art of Indian Autobiography." *Where the West Begins: Essays on Middle Border and Siouxland Writing, in Honor of Herbert Krause*. Ed. Arthur R. Huseboe and William Geyer. Sioux Falls: Center for Western Studies P, 1978. 152–160.

Blyth, R. H. *Haiku*. Vol. 1. N.p. [Japan]: Hokuseido, 1949.

Boas, Franz. *The Religion of the Kwakiutl Indians*. Columbia Univ. Contributions to Anthropology 10, pt. 2. New York: Columbia UP, 1930.

Bogan, Louise. "Henceforth, from the Mind." *The Blue Estuaries*. New York: Ecco, 1960. 64.

Booth, Wayne C. "The Rhetorical Stance." *The Writing Teacher's Source Book*. Ed. Barry Tate and Edward P. J. Corbett. New York: Oxford UP, 1981. 108–16.

Boyd, Maurice. *Kiowa Voices. Ceremonial Dance, Ritual and Song*. Vol. 1. *Myths, Legends and Folktales*. Vol. 2. Fort Worth: Texas Christian UP, 1981, 1983.

Brown, Dee. *Bury My Heart at Wounded Knee*. New York: Holt, 1971.

Brown, Joseph Epes. Preface. *The Sacred Pipe: Black Elk's Account of the Seven Rites of the Oglala Sioux*. Ed. Joseph Epes Brown. 1953. Baltimore: Penguin, 1971. xiii–xx.

Brumble, H. David III. *American Indian Autobiography*. Berkeley: U of California P, forthcoming.

——. *An Annotated Bibliography of American Indian and Eskimo Autobiographies*. Lincoln: U of Nebraska P, 1981.

——. "Indian Sacred Materials: Kroeber, Kroeber, Waters, and Momaday." *Smoothing the Ground: Essays on Native American Oral Literature*. Ed. Brian Swann. Berkeley: U of California P, 1983. 283–300.

Buechel, Eugene, SJ. *A Dictionary of the Teton Dakota Sioux Language*. Pine Ridge: Red Cloud Indian School, 1970.

Campbell, Joseph. *Creative Mythology: The Masks of God*. Vol. 4. New York: Compass-Viking, 1970.

——. *The Hero with a Thousand Faces*. Princeton: Princeton UP, 1968.

Campbell, Maria. *Halfbreed*. Toronto: McClelland, 1973.

Canetti, Elias. "The Writer's Profession." *The Conscience of Words*. Trans. Joachim Neugroschel. New York: Farrar, 1984. 236–46.

Carrasco, David. "A Context to Understand the Religious Claims of the Kootenai Indians." Working paper for Native American Rights Fund. 1980.

Chapman, Abraham, ed. *Literature of the American Indians: Views and Interpretations: A Gathering of Indian Memories, Symbolic Contexts, and Literary Criticism*. New York: Meridian-NAL, 1975.

A Chronicle of the Kiowa Indians (1832–1892). Berkeley: Lowie Museum of Anthropology, 1968.

Colombo, John Robert. *Songs of the Indians*. Vol. 1. Ottawa: Oberon, 1983.

Colonnese, Tom, and Louis Owens. *American Indian Novelists: An Annotated Critical Bibliography*. New York: Garland, 1985.

Comley, Nancy, et al., eds. *Fields of Writing: Reading across the Disciplines*. New York: St. Martin's, 1984.

Comstock, W. Richard. "On Seeing with the Eye of the Native European." *Seeing with a Native Eye: Essays on Native American Religion*. Ed. Walter Holden Capps. New York: Harper, 1976. 58–78.

Cooper, James Fenimore. *The Pathfinder.* Ed. Richard D. Rust. Albany: State U of New York P, 1981.

Cornell, George L. "Native American Contributions to the Formation of the Modern Conservation Ethic." Diss. Michigan State U, 1982.

Cushing, Frank Hamilton. *Zuni: Selected Writings*. Ed. Jesse Green. Lincoln: U of Nebraska P, 1979.

DeMallie, Raymond J., ed. *The Sixth Grandfather: Black Elk's Teachings Given to John G. Neihardt*. Lincoln: U of Nebraska P, 1984.

———. *Warpath: The True Story of the Fighting Sioux Told in a Biography of Chief White Bull*. Lincoln: U of Nebraska P, 1984.

Denig, E. T. *Indian Tribes of the Upper Missouri*. Annual Report of the Bureau of American Ethnology 46 (1928).

Denton, Joan Frederick. "Kiowa Murals: 'Behold I Stand in Good Relation to All Things.'" *Southwest Art* July 1987: 68–75.

Devil's Tower. Washington: US Dept. of Interior–Natl. Park Service Handbook 3, 1981.

Dickinson, Emily. No. 1068. "Further in summer than the birds." *The Complete Poems of Emily Dickinson*. Ed. Thomas H. Johnson. Boston: Little, 1960. 485–86.

Donaldson, Margaret. *Children's Minds*. New York: Norton, 1979.

Dorris, Michael. "Native American Literature in Ethnohistorical Context." *College English* 41 (1979): 1147–62.

Dundes, Alan. *Sacred Narrative: Readings in the Theory of Myth*. Berkeley: U of California P, 1984.

Eliade, Mircea. *Myth and Reality*. New York: Harper, 1963.

———. *The Myth of Eternal Return of Cosmos and History*. Princeton: Bolligen-Princeton UP, 1954.

———. *Rites and Symbols of Initiation*. New York: Harper, 1958.

———. *The Sacred and the Profane: The Nature of Religion*. New York: Harcourt, 1959.

———. *Shamanism: Archaic Techniques of Ecstasy*. New York: Pantheon, 1964.

Erdrich, Louise. *The Beet Queen*. New York: Holt, 1986.

———. *Love Medicine*. New York: Holt, 1984.

Eschholz, Paul, and Alfred F. Rosa, eds. *Outlooks and Insights: A Reader for Writers*. New York: St. Martin's, 1983.

Evers, Larry. "Continuity and Change in American Indian Oral Literature." *ADE Bulletin* 75 (1983): 43–46.

———. "Cycles of Appreciation." *Studies in American Indian Literature: Critical Essays and Course Designs*. Ed. Paula Gunn Allen. New York: MLA, 1983. 23–32.

————. "Native American Literature: Other Sources." *The South Corner of Time: Hopi, Navajo, Papago, Yaqui Tribal Literature.* Ed. Larry Evers et al. Tucson: U of Arizona P, 1980. 235–40.

————. "Native American Oral Literatures in the College English Classroom: An Omaha Example." *College English* 36 (1975): 649–62.

————. "Words and Place: A Reading of *House Made of Dawn.*" *Western American Literature* 11 (1977): 297–320.

Faulkner, William. "The Bear," "Delta Autumn." *Go Down, Moses.* New York: Vintage-Random, 1973. 191–331; 335–65.

Fields, Kenneth. "More than Language Means." Rev. of *The Way to Rainy Mountain,* by N. Scott Momaday. *Southern Review* ns 6 (1970): 196–204.

Fleck, Richard F. "Outdoor Teaching of Momaday's *Way to Rainy Mountain.*" *Ethnic Reporter* 11.2 (1986): 5–8.

Forbes, Jack. *The Indian in America's Past.* Englewood Cliffs: Prentice, 1964.

————. "Only Approved Indians Can Play: Made in USA." *Earth Power Coming.* Ed. Simon Ortiz. Tsaile: Navajo Community Coll. P, 1983. 262–75.

Frankl, Viktor. *Man's Search for Meaning.* New York: Pocket, 1963.

Freire, Paulo. *Education for Critical Consciousness.* New York: Continuum, 1983.

————. *Pedagogy of the Oppressed.* New York: Continuum, 1984.

Gardner, John. "A Brief History of Astronomy." *General Education Catalogue.* Provo: Brigham Young UP, 1983. Insert between 32 and 33.

Garrett, Roland. "The Notions of Language in Some Kiowa Folk Tales." *Indian Historian* 5.2 (1972): 32–37, 40.

Geertz, Clifford. *Local Knowledge.* New York: Basic, 1983.

Gill, Sam D. *Native American Religions: An Introduction.* Belmont: Wadsworth, 1982.

Goddard, Pliny Earle. "Notes on the Sun Dance of the Sarsi." *Anthropological Papers of the American Museum of Natural History* 16.4 (1919): 281–82.

Grant, Agnes. *Native Literature in the Curriculum.* Ed. Alexander Gregor and Keith Wilson. Winnipeg: U of Manitoba, 1986.

Gregg, Josiah. *Commerce of the Prairies: A Selection.* 1844. Indianapolis: Bobbs, 1970.

Grinnell, George Bird. "Coup and Scalp among the Plains Indians." *Selected Papers from the American Anthropologist 1888–1920.* Ed. Frederica de Laguna. Evanston: U of Illinois P, 1960. 650–64.

Harrington, John P. *Vocabulary of the Kiowa Language.* Smithsonian Inst. Bureau of American Ethnology Bull. 84. Washington: GPO, 1928.

Hayakawa, S. I. *Language in Thought and Action.* New York: Harcourt, 1964.

Hefferman, William A., ed. *The Harvest Reader.* New York: Harcourt, 1984.

Hemingway, Ernest. "Big Two-Hearted River," pts. 1 and 2. *The Short Stories of Ernest Hemingway.* New York: Scribner's, 1953. 207–32.

Herbert, Belle. *Shandaa: In My Lifetime.* Ed. Bill Pfisterer et al. Anchorage: U of Alaska Native Language Ctr., 1982.

Hesburgh, Theodore. "The Future of Liberal Education." *Change* Apr. 1981: 36–40.

Highwater, Jamake. *Anpao: An American Indian Odyssey.* 1977. New York: Colophon-Harper, 1980.

——. *Song from the Earth: American Indian Painting*. Boston: New York Graphic Soc., 1976.

Hobson, Geary, ed. *The Remembered Earth: An Anthology of Contemporary Native American Literature*. 1979. Albuquerque: U of New Mexico P, 1980.

Hodge, Frederick Webb, ed. *Handbook of American Indians North of Mexico*. Vol. 1. New York: Pageant, 1959.

Hoebel, E. Adamson. *The Cheyennes: Indians of the Great Plains*. New York: Holt, 1978.

Holm, G. "Sanimuinak's Account of How He Became an Angakok." *The Ammassalik Eskimo: Contributions to the Ethnology of the East Greenland Natives*. Pt. 1. Ed. William Thalbitzer. Copenhagen: Bianco Luno, 1914. 298–300.

House Made of Dawn. Dir. Richardson Morse. With Larry Littlebird and John Saxon. New Line Cinema, 1972. 16mm, 91 min.

Howard, James H. *The Warrior Who Killed Custer: The Personal Narrative of Chief Joseph White Bull*. Lincoln: U of Nebraska P, 1968.

Hunter, Carol. "American Indian Literature." *MELUS* 8.2 (1981): 82–85.

Hymes, Dell. "Discovering Oral Performance and Measured Verse in American Indian Narrative." *New Literary History* 8 (1977): 431–57.

——. *In Vain I Tried to Tell You*. Philadelphia: U of Pennsylvania P, 1981.

Jahner, Elaine. Introduction. *Book Forum* 5 (1981): 343–56.

Johansen, Bruce, and Roberto Maestas. *Wasi'chu: The Continuing Indian Wars*. New York: Monthly Review, 1979.

Jung, C. G. "A Psychological Approach to the Dogma of the Trinity." *Collected Works*. Vol. 2. 2nd ed. Trans. R. F. C. Hull. Princeton: Bollingen-Princeton UP, 1969. 107–200.

Kellman, Steven G., ed. *Approaches to Teaching Camus's* The Plague. New York: MLA, 1985.

Kluckhohn, Clyde, and Henry A. Murray. *Personality in Nature, Society and Culture*. 2nd ed. New York: Knopf, 1956.

Kolodny, Annette. *The Lay of the Land*. Chapel Hill: U of North Carolina P, 1975.

Kress, Gunther, and Robert Hodge. *Language and Ideology*. London: Routledge, 1979.

Krupat, Arnold. *For Those Who Came After: A Study of Native American Autobiography*. Berkeley: U of California P, 1985.

——. "Native American Literature and the Canon." *Critical Inquiry* 10 (1983): 145–71.

Lame Deer (John Fire) and Richard Erdoes. *Lame Deer Seeker of Visions*. 1972. New York: Pocket, 1976.

Land as Symbol: The American Indian. Audiotape. Natl. Public Radio, OP-79-01-23, 1981, 59 min.

Larson, Charles R. *American Indian Fiction*. Albuquerque: U of New Mexico P, 1978.

Lattin, Vernon. "The Quest for Mythic Vision in Contemporary Native American and Chicano Fiction." *American Literature* 50 (1979): 625–40.

Lauter, Paul, et al., eds. *The Heath Anthology of American Literature*. New York: Heath, forthcoming.

Le Guin, Ursula K. "Myth and Archetype in Science Fiction." *Parabola* 1.4 (1976): 42–47.

Lincoln, Kenneth. *Native American Renaissance.* Berkeley: U of California P, 1983.

———. "Tai-me to Rainy Mountain: The Makings of American Indian Literature." *American Indian Quarterly* 10 (1986): 101–17.

Litzinger, Boyd, ed. *The Heath Reader.* New York: Heath, 1983.

Mackie, Robert. Introduction. *Literacy and Revolution: The Pedagogy of Paulo Freire.* Ed. Robert Mackie. New York: Continuum, 1981. 1–11.

Madox, Melvin. "The Limitations of Language." *Insight: A Rhetoric Reader.* Ed. Emil Hartik. New York: Lippincott, 1973. 296–99.

Marken, Jack, comp. *The American Indian: Language and Literature.* Arlington Heights: AHM, 1978.

Markoosie. *Harpoon of the Hunter.* Toronto: McGill-Queen's UP, 1970.

Marriott, Alice. *Saynday's People: The Kiowa Indians and the Stories They Told.* Lincoln: U of Nebraska P, 1963.

———. *The Ten Grandmothers.* Norman: U of Oklahoma P, 1945.

Marriott, Alice, and Carol K. Rachlin. *American Indian Mythology.* New York: Mentor-NAL, 1968.

———. *Plains Indian Mythology.* 1975. New York: Meridian-NAL, 1985.

Marx, Leo. "Pastoral Ideals and City Troubles." *Western Man and Environmental Ethics.* Ed. Ian G. Barbour. Reading: Addison, 1973. 93–115.

Mayhall, Mildred P. *The Kiowas.* 2nd ed. Norman: U of Oklahoma P, 1971.

McAllister, Mick. "The Topology of Remembrance in *The Way to Rainy Mountain.*" *Denver Quarterly* 12.4 (1978): 19–31.

McQuade, Donald, et al., eds. *The Harper American Literature.* Vol. 2. *The Harper American Literature.* Compact ed. New York: Harper, 1987.

Momaday, N. Scott. Address. U of Lethbridge, Canada, 7 Apr. 1982.

———. "The American Indian in the Conflict of Tribalism and Modern Society." Lecture. Colorado State U, Fort Collins, 31 Jan. 1971.

———. "An American Land Ethic." *Ecotactics: The Sierra Club Handbook for Environmental Activists.* Ed. John G. Mitchell with Constance L. Stallings. New York: Simon, 1970. 97–105.

———. "Angle of Geese." *Southern Review* ns 1 (1965): 423.

———. "Cherish the Legend of Billy the Kid." *Viva* 29 Oct. 1972: 2.

———. "A First American Views His Land." *National Geographic* July 1976: 13–20.

———. *The Gourd Dancer.* New York: Harper, 1976.

———. "Growing Up at Jemez Pueblo." *Viva* 25 June 1972: 2.

———. *House Made of Dawn.* 1968. New York: Perennial Library–Harper, 1977.

———. "I Am Alive . . . ." *The World of the American Indian.* Ed. Jules B. Billard. Washington: National Geographic Soc., 1974. 11–26.

———. Interview. With Rich Mueller. Public tv film. South Dakota Committee on the Humanities. 18 Jan. 1986.

———. Interview. With students at the U of New Mexico, Las Cruces. Ts. New Mexico State U Library, Las Cruces, 1973.

———. "An Interview by Joseph Bruchac." *American Poetry Review* 13.4 (1984): 13–18. Rpt. in *Survival This Way: Interviews with American Indian Poets.* Ed. Joseph Bruchac. Tucson: U of Arizona P, 1987. 173–91.

———. "Interview with N. Scott Momaday." With Lee Abbott. *Puerto del Sol* 12.1 (1973): 21–38.

———. "An Interview with N. Scott Momaday." With Gretchen Bataille. *Iowa English Bulletin* 29.1 (1979): 28–32.

———. "Interview with N. Scott Momaday." With Gretchen Bataille. *Studies in American Indian Literatures* 4.1 (1980): 1–3.

———. *The Journey of Tai-me.* Santa Barbara: privately printed, 1967.

———. "Kiowa Legends from *The Journey of Tai-me.*" *Sun Tracks* 3.1 (1976): 6–9.

———. Letter to Whitney Blake. 5 Apr. 1965. Bancroft Library, U of California, Berkeley.

———. "The Man Made of Words." *Indian Voices: The First Convocation of American Indian Scholars.* San Francisco: Indian Historian, 1970. 49–84. Rpt. in Hobson 162–73.

———. "A *MELUS* Interview: N. Scott Momaday—A Slant of Light." With Bettye Givens. *MELUS* 12.1 (1985): 79–87.

———. "The Morality of Indian Hating." *Ramparts* 3.1 (1964): 29–40.

———. *N. Scott Momaday: Interview with Kay Bonetti.* Audiotape. American Audio Prose Library, 3092, 1983.

———. *N. Scott Momaday Reads "Tsoai and the Shieldmaker" and Excerpts from* House Made of Dawn. Audiotape. American Audio Prose Library, 3091, 1983.

———. *The Names: A Memoir by N. Scott Momaday.* New York: Harper, 1976. Tucson: U of Arizona, 1987.

———. "Native American Attitudes to the Environment." *Seeing with a Native Eye: Essays on Native American Religion.* Ed. Walter Holden Capps. New York: Harper, 1976. 79–85.

———. "The Native Voice." *Columbia Literary History of the United States.* Ed. Emory Elliott. New York: Columbia UP, 1988. 5–15.

———. "The Night the Stars Fell." *Viva* 14 May 1972: 2.

———. "Notes and Fragments [*The Way to Rainy Mountain*]." Bancroft Library, U of California, Berkeley.

———. Personal interview. With H. David Brumble III. 5 Apr. 1985.

———. Personal interview. With Matthias Schubnell. 21 Dec. 1981.

———. *Remember My Horse.* Cambridge, Credo Records, no. 4, 1976.

———. "The Story of the Arrowmaker." *New York Times Review of Books* 4 May 1969: 2.

———. "To Save a Great Vision." *A Sender of Words: Essays in Memory of John G. Neihardt.* Ed. Vine Deloria, Jr. Chicago: Howe, 1984. 30–38.

———. "Tsoai and the Shieldmaker." *Four Winds* 1.3 (1980): 38–43.

———. *Tsoai-talee: Interviews with N. Scott Momaday.* Ed. Charles Woodard. Lincoln: U of Nebraska P, forthcoming.

———. "A Vision beyond Time and Place." *Life* 21 July 1971: 66.

———. *The Way to Rainy Mountain.* 1969. Albuquerque: U of New Mexico P, 1976.

———. "The Way to Rainy Mountain." *Reporter* 26 Jan. 1967: 41–43.

Momaday, Natachee Scott, ed. *American Indian Authors.* Boston: Houghton, 1972.

Moneyhun, Clyde, and Jeff Huffman, eds. *The Rains of the Dragon: Stories from Japan.* Nagoya: Trident School of Languages, 1988.

Mooney, James. *Calendar History of the Kiowa Indians.* 1898. Introd. John C. Ewers. Washington: Smithsonian, 1979.

More than Bows and Arrows. Narr. N. Scott Momaday. Cinema Associates, 1978. 16mm, 56 min.

Muller, Gilbert H. *The McGraw-Hill Reader.* 2nd ed. New York: McGraw, 1985.

Muscatine, Charles, and Marlene Griffith. *The Borzoi College Reader.* 5th ed. New York: Knopf, 1984.

Nabokov, Peter. Biographical essay. Ts. in possession of Matthias Schubnell.

Native Storytelling. Audiotape. Manitoba Dept. of Ed., Native Education Branch, 1981.

Neihardt, John G., ed. *Black Elk Speaks: Being the Life Story of a Holy Man of the Oglala Sioux as Told through John G. Neihardt.* Introd. Vine Deloria, Jr. Lincoln: U of Nebraska P, 1979.

Niatum, Duane, ed. *Carriers of the Dream Wheel: Contemporary Native American Poetry.* New York: Harper, 1975.

———, ed. *Harper's Anthology of Twentieth Century Native American Poetry.* New York: Perennial Library–Harper, 1988.

Nicholas, Charles A. "*The Way to Rainy Mountain*: N. Scott Momaday's Hard Journey Back." *South Dakota Review* 13.4 (1975–76): 149–58.

Norman, Howard. *The Wishing Bone Cycle.* New York: Stonehill, 1976.

Nye, Wilbur Sturtevant. *Bad Medicine and Good: Tales of the Kiowa.* Norman: U of Oklahoma P, 1962.

———. *Carbine and Lance: The Story of Old Fort Sill.* Norman: U of Oklahoma P, 1942.

Ortiz, Simon J. "Literature." *American Indian Journal* 6 (1980): 32–35.

———. "Towards a National Indian Literature: Cultural Authenticity in Nationalism." *MELUS* 8.2 (1981): 7–12.

Oxenham, John. *Literacy: Writing, Reading and Social Organization.* London: Routledge, 1980.

Papovich, J. Frank. "Landscape, Tradition, and Identity in *The Way to Rainy Mountain*." *Perspectives on Contemporary Literature* 12 (1986): 13–19.

Parsons, Elsie Clews. *Kiowa Tales.* New York: American Folk-Lore Soc., 1929.

Petersen, Karen Daniels. *1877: Plains Indian Sketch Books of Zo-Tom and Howling Wolf.* Flagstaff: Northland, 1969.

———. *Plains Indian Art from Fort Marion.* Norman: U of Oklahoma P, 1971.

Radin, Paul. *The Trickster.* New York: Schocken, 1972.

Ramsey, Jarold. "American Indian Literatures and American Literature: An Overview." *ADE Bulletin* 75 (1983): 35–38.

———. "The Teacher of Modern American Indian Writing as Ethnographer and Critic." *College English* 41 (1979): 163–69.

Rasmussen, Knud Johan Victor. "Aua Is Consecrated to the Spirits." *Intellectual Culture of the Hudson Bay Eskimos. Report of the Fifth Thule Expedition, 1921–24* 7.2 (1930): 115–20.

Robinson, Jay. "Literacy in the Department of English." *College English* 47 (1985): 482–98.

Rodebaugh, Dale. "Indians Keep Identity in Cultural Migration." *San Jose News* 10 Mar. 1977: n. pag.

Roemer, Kenneth M. *American Indian Folklore.* Audiotape. Everett/Edwards, 1627, 1979.

———. "Inventive Modeling: *Rainy Mountain*'s Way to Composition." *College English* 46 (1984): 767–82.

———. "Japanese Ways to Rainy Mountain: An Approach to Teaching English Composition in Japan." *Memoirs of the Faculty of Law and Literature* [Shimane University] 6 (1983): 75–101.

———. "Survey Courses, Indian Literature, and *The Way to Rainy Mountain*." *College English* 37 (1976): 619–24.

Ruoff, A. LaVonne Brown. "American Indian Literatures: Introduction and Bibliography." *American Studies International* 24.2 (1986): 2–52.

———. "A Selected Bibliography of American Indian Literatures." *ADE Bulletin* 75 (1983): 47–48.

———. "Teaching American Indian Authors." *ADE Bulletin* 75 (1983): 39–42.

Said, Edward. *Orientalism.* New York: Vintage, 1979.

Sawyer, T. E. "Assimilation versus Self-Identity: A Modern Native American Perspective." *Contemporary Native American Address.* Ed. John R. Maestas. Provo: Brigham Young UP, 1976. 197–207.

Scarberry-García, Susan. "Sources of Healing in *House Made of Dawn*." Diss. U of Colorado, Boulder, 1986. To be published as *Landmarks of Healing.* Albuquerque: U of New Mexico P, forthcoming.

Schubnell, Matthias. Interview. With Kenneth M. Roemer. 15 July 1986.

———. *N. Scott Momaday: The Cultural and Literary Background.* Norman: U of Oklahoma P, 1985.

Scollon, Ronald, and Suzanne Scollon. *Linguistic Convergence: An Ethnography of Speaking at Fort Chipewyan, Alberta.* New York: Academic, 1979.

———. *Narrative, Literacy and Face in Interethnic Communication.* Norwood: ABLEX, 1981.

Scott, Hugh Lennox. "Notes on the Kado, or Sun Dance of the Kiowa." *American Anthropologist* ns 13 (1911): 345–79.

Shipley, Nan, ed. *Wild Drums.* Winnipeg: Peguis, 1972.

Silko, Leslie Marmon. *Ceremony.* New York: Seaver-Viking, 1977.

———. "An Old-Time Indian Attack Conducted in Two Parts. Part One: Imitation 'Indian' Poems; Part Two: Gary Snyder's *Turtle Island*." *The Remembered Earth.* Ed. Geary Hobson. Albuquerque: U of New Mexico P, 1980. 211–16.

———. *Storyteller.* New York: Seaver, 1981.

Smith, Marian W. "The War Complex of the Plains Indians." *Proceedings of the American Philosophical Society* 78.3 (1938): 425–64.

Smith, Marie. "Rainy Mountain, Legends and Students." *Arizona English Bulletin* 13 (1971): 41–44.

Snyder, Gary. *Myths and Texts*. New York: New Directions, 1978.

———. *The Old Ways*. San Francisco: City Lights, 1977.

———. *Riprap and Cold Mountain Poems*. San Francisco: Four Seasons, 1969.

Spier, Leslie. "Notes on the Kiowa Sun Dance." *Anthropological Papers of the American Museum of Natural History* 16, pt. 6. (1921): 433–50.

Stegner, Wallace. *The Sound of Mountain Water*. Garden City: Doubleday, 1969.

Stevenson, Joan W. Rev. of *The Way to Rainy Mountain*, by N. Scott Momaday. *Library Journal* 15 Sept. 1969: 3079.

Storm, Hyemeyohsts. *Seven Arrows*. New York: Harper, 1972.

Strelke, Barbara. "N. Scott Momaday: Racial Memory and Individual Imagination." *Literature of the American Indians*. Ed. Abraham Chapman. New York: Meridian-NAL, 1975. 348–57.

Sullivan, Walter. "Meteor Shower Is Due Tonight." *New York Times* 16 Nov. 1966: 49 + .

Tedlock, Dennis. *Finding the Center: Narrative Poetry of the Zuni Indians*. New York: Dial, 1972.

———. *The Spoken Word and the Work of Interpretation*. Philadelphia: U of Pennsylvania P, 1983.

———. "Toward an Oral Poetics." *New Literary History* 8 (1977): 507–19.

Terrell, John Upton. *The Plains Apache*. New York: Crowell, 1975.

Theisz, R. D. *Perspectives on Teaching American Indian Literature*. Rosebud: n.p.; Spearfish: Ctr. of Indian Studies, Black Hills State Coll., 1977.

Thoreau, Henry David. *The Journal of Henry David Thoreau*. Vol. 4. Ed. Bradford Torrey and Francis H. Allen. Boston: Houghton, 1949.

———. Walden *and* Civil Disobedience. Ed. Owen Thomas. New York: Norton, 1966.

Toelken, Barre. "Seeing with a Native Eye: How Many Sheep Will It Hold?" *Seeing with a Native Eye: Essays on Native American Religion*. Ed. Walter Holden Capps. New York: Harper, 1976. 9–24.

Toffelmier, Gertrude, and Katherine Luomola. "Dreams and Interpretations of Diegueño Indians." *Psychoanalytic Quarterly* 5 (1936): 195–225.

Trachtenberg, Alan, and Benjamin DeMott, eds. *America in Literature*. Vol. 2. New York: Wiley, 1978.

Trimble, Martha Scott. *N. Scott Momaday*. Boise State Coll. Western Writers Ser. Boise: Boise State Coll., 1973.

———. "N. Scott Momaday." *Fifty Western Writers: A Bio-Bibliographical Sourcebook*. Ed. Fred Erisman and Richard W. Etulain. Westport: Greenwood, 1982. 313–24.

Trimmer, Joseph, and Maxine Hairston. *The Riverside Reader*. New York: Houghton, 1981.

Velie, Alan R. *Four American Indian Literary Masters: N. Scott Momaday, James Welch, Leslie Marmon Silko, and Gerald Vizenor*. Norman: U of Oklahoma P, 1982.

Vizenor, Gerald. *Darkness in Saint Louis Bearheart*. St. Paul: Truck, 1978.

Waters, Frank. *Book of the Hopi*. New York: Viking, 1977.

Watkins, Floyd C. *In Time and Place: Some Origins of American Fiction.* Athens: U of Georgia P, 1977.

Wax, Murray L. *Indian Americans: Unity and Diversity.* Englewood Cliffs: Prentice, 1971.

Welch, James. *The Death of Jim Loney.* New York: Harper, 1979.

———. *Winter in the Blood.* New York: Harper, 1974.

Wiget, Andrew. "Identity and Direction: Reflections on the *ASAIL Notes* Survey." *ASAIL Notes* 3.1 (1986): 4.

———. *Native American Literature.* Boston: Twayne, 1985.

———. "Native American Literature: A Bibliographic Survey of American Indian Literary Traditions." *Choice* June 1986: 1503–12.

———, ed. *A World of Hope: Writing from SNMCF.* N.p.: n.p., n.d.

Wilson, Norma. "Relating Life and Literature." *English Notes: A Newsletter of the South Dakota Council of Teachers of English* 25.2 (1979): 6–10.

Winters, Yvor. *Forms of Discovery: Critical and Historical Essays on the Form of the Short Poem in English.* Chicago: Alan Swallow, 1967.

———. "Forms of Discovery: A Preliminary Statement." *Southern Review* ns 3 (1967): 1–12.

———. Letter. *Reporter* 23 Feb. 1967: 8.

———. Letters to N. Scott Momaday. 21 Apr. 1965, 23 July 1968. Momaday personal correspondence file.

Wolfram, Eddie. *History of Collage: An Anthology of Collage, Assemblage and Event Structures.* New York: Macmillan, 1975.

Words and Place: Native Literature from the American Southwest. Ser. of eight videocassettes. Dir. Larry Evers. New York: Clearwater, 1981.

Zachrau, Thekla. "M.[sic] Scott Momaday: Towards Indian Identity." *Dutch Quarterly Review of Anglo-American Letters* 9 (1979): 52–70. Rpt. in *American Indian Culture and Research Journal* 3.1 (1979): 39–56.

Zukav, Gary. *The Dancing Wu Li Masters: An Overview of the New Physics.* New York: Morrow, 1979.

INDEX

Modern Language Association of America
Approaches to Teaching World Literature
Joseph Gibaldi, series editor

Medieval English Drama. Ed. Richard K. Emmerson. 1990.

Melville's Moby-Dick. Ed. Martin Bickman. 1985.

Metaphysical Poets. Ed. Sidney Gottlieb. 1990.

Miller's Death of a Salesman. Ed. Matthew C. Roudané. 1995.

Milton's Paradise Lost. Ed. Galbraith M. Crump. 1986.

Molière's Tartuffe *and Other Plays*. Ed. James F. Gaines and
    Michael S. Koppisch. 1995.

Momaday's The Way to Rainy Mountain. Ed. Kenneth M. Roemer. 1988.

Montaigne's Essays. Ed. Patrick Henry. 1994.

Novels of Toni Morrison. Ed. Nellie Y. McKay and Kathryn Earle. 1997.

Murasaki Shikibu's The Tale of Genji. Ed. Edward Kamens. 1993.

Pope's Poetry. Ed. Wallace Jackson and R. Paul Yoder. 1993.

Shakespeare's King Lear. Ed. Robert H. Ray. 1986.

Shakespeare's The Tempest *and Other Late Romances*. Ed. Maurice Hunt. 1992.

Shelley's Frankenstein. Ed. Stephen C. Behrendt. 1990.

Shelley's Poetry. Ed. Spencer Hall. 1990.

Sir Gawain and the Green Knight. Ed. Miriam Youngerman Miller and
    Jane Chance. 1986.

Spenser's Faerie Queene. Ed. David Lee Miller and Alexander Dunlop. 1994.

Sterne's Tristram Shandy. Ed. Melvyn New. 1989.

Swift's Gulliver's Travels. Ed. Edward J. Rielly. 1988.

Thoreau's Walden *and Other Works*. Ed. Richard J. Schneider. 1996.

Voltaire's Candide. Ed. Renée Waldinger. 1987.

Whitman's Leaves of Grass. Ed. Donald D. Kummings. 1990.

Wordsworth's Poetry. Ed. Spencer Hall, with Jonathan Ramsey. 1986.

Wright's Native Son. Ed. James A. Miller. 1997.